MEXICAN TODAY

MEXICAN
TODAY

New and Rediscovered
Recipes for Contemporary
Kitchens

PATI JINICH

PHOTOGRAPHS BY ELLEN SILVERMAN

A RUX MARTIN BOOK
HOUGHTON MIFFLIN HARCOURT
BOSTON • NEW YORK • 2016

For information about permission to reproduce selections from this
book, write to trade.permissions@hmhco.com or to Permissions,
HOUGHTON MIFFLIN HARCOURT PUBLISHING COMPANY,
3 Park Avenue, 19th floor, New York, New York 10016.

www.hmhco.com

Library of Congress Cataloging-in-Publication Data
Names: Jinich, Pati, author. | Silverman, Ellen, photographer.
Title: Mexican today : new and rediscovered recipes for contemporary
kitchens / Pati Jinich ; photography by Ellen Silverman.
Description: Boston : Houghton Mifflin Harcourt, [2016] | "A Rux Martin
Book."
Identifiers: LCCN 2015042717 (print) | LCCN 2015047487 (ebook) | ISBN
  9780544557246 (paper over board) | ISBN 9780544557253 (e-book) |
ISBN 9780544557253 (ebook)
Subjects: LCSH: Cooking, Mexican. | LCGFT: Cookbooks.
Classification: LCC TX716.M4 J559 2016 (print) | LCC TX716.M4 (ebook) |
DDC 641.5972—dc23
LC record available at http://lccn.loc.gov/2015042717

Book design by JENNIFER K. BEAL DAVIS

Food styling by EUGENE JHO
Prop styling by NIDIA CUEVA
Hair and makeup by ROBIN HAMILTON
Wardrobe by HALEY LIEBERMAN

Printed in China

C&C 10 9 8 7 6 5 4 3 2 1

To my three cookie monsters, for chomping away at everything I put on your plates. No matter what I make, if it tastes good, it will always be dedicated to you.

ACKNOWLEDGMENTS

It has taken me a while to get to where I am, but now I am doing what I was meant to do. I work in a field that I adore with people I love, and with a constant sense of fulfillment. I am very grateful to the many people who have helped me along the way. I am sure these words will probably not suffice and may not cover them all, but I will try my best.

To Rux Martin, the most fun and brilliant editor. I have loved working with you on both my books. Hang on tight and don't go anywhere, because I already know what we should do for the third one!

To Gordon Elliott, for believing in me and my work since the moment we first said hello. It is a sheer delight to work with you, Mark Schneider, and the entire team at Follow Productions. Thank you for teaching me how to take all that I am eager to share and explore to the screen. Dan Connell, I am so grateful for your willingness to always go beyond and especially for all the "walk and talks."

Maria Elena Gutierrez, Robert Sullivan, and Brendan Sloan: Thank you for bringing drive, enthusiasm, and insight to our projects.

To the Mexican Embassy in the U.S., and to Laura Ramirez Rasgado, executive director at the Mexican Cultural Institute, and the entire team. It has been an honor to be the resident chef and cooking instructor for the MCI's culinary program for the past seven years. Thanks to my cooking crew, Julio Torres, Ofelia Torres, Rosa Arroyo, Isabel Solano, Angel Lopez, and Nazario Mendoza, for all the hard work you put into our events and for your warm companionship.

To the Secretariat of Agriculture, Livestock, Rural Development, Fisheries, and Food (SAGARPA); the Agency for Commercialization of Agricultural Products (ASERCA); the National Agricultural Council (CAN); the Secretariat of Tourism (SECTUR); and the Mexico Tourism Board (CPTM): Thank you for helping me share Mexico's cuisine and culture on TV and for all your support.

Thanks to all the Mexican chefs, producers, writers, and friends who have shared their passions with me in the course of my research trips and tapings of my PBS series.

To Martha Rose Shulman: Never did I dream that a writing collaboration could go as smoothly and be as lovely as this one. It has been a privilege to have the opportunity to work with you, to be guided by your patient and kind nature, your wise approach, and your deep knowledge. This book would not be what it is without you, and I am deeply grateful. I hope you will want to work with me on the next book.

To the Houghton Mifflin Harcourt team: To Jessica Sherman, for your hard work on the manuscript, and to copyeditor Judith Sutton, for your deep knowledge of food and for making every recipe clearer. To Jacinta Monniere, for deciphering my handwriting, and for fast and accurate typing. To Jackie Beach, for keeping things running smoothly; to Rachel Newborn, for help on the photo shoot; and to Jennifer Beal Davis, for the splendid book design.

To Ellen Silverman, for giving that photo shoot your absolute all and making the colorful side of my food stand out. To food stylist Eugene Jho, for making my food look so darn pretty, and to prop stylist Nidia Cuevo, for your exquisite taste. To Robin Hamilton, for giving me that lovely updo, and to Haley Lieberman, for helping me look so put together for a change.

To Carrie Bachman: I wanted to hurry up this cookbook largely so we could work together again! Thank you so much for your friendship and hard work.

Thanks to Peter W. Smith for your efforts in paving the way for this book.

To Alvaro Luque, Kevin Hamilton, Ivonne Kisner, and the entire team at Avocados from Mexico. I am so grateful for your support and your appreciation of my work. I have so much fun working with all of you.

My gratitude to Rafael Toro, Joseph Perez, and the entire Goya family for your support, both for the program at the Mexican Cultural Institute and for the PBS series. You have made me feel like part of the Goya family.

To Roberto Romo, Amy Colella, Sara Cook, and the whole team at La Morena. I am looking forward to our continued collaboration.

Thanks to Kristy Noel, for your friendship, for your long hours, and for your thoughtful, dedicated, and outstanding work on everything we do together. Catherine Lafferman: Welcome aboard. I so appreciate your bright and sunny disposition.

Margarita Torres, *la queremos tanto y le estamos tan agradecidos por su cariño, paciencia, y apoyo.*

Thanks to my dear friends Tamara Belt, Debra Eichenbaum, Diana Margolis, Marina Feldman, and Jeanie Milbauer, for being so supportive and enthusiastic about what I do, for sharing the ride with its highs and lows, and for being willing guests on so many episodes!

To my family: Ma, Pa, Kar, Lis, *y* Shar. The older I get, the more I value and reflect on the time we have spent together, our shared meals, lessons learned, and, most of all, our mutual support. Even the bitter times have ended sweetly. I know both my grandmothers would be so happy and proud to know that I turned out to be a good cook, as they were, and that my grandfathers would do their part by wiping their plates clean with a piece of bread.

To my husband's family, especially my in-laws, Carlos and Perla Jinich, who have been so supportive and so proud of me for choosing the path I have taken.

To Daniel: I could not dream of a better man to spend my days with. I can only hope to be the best woman I can possibly be for you.

Recently my oldest son had to find someone who had gone through a radical life change to interview for a school project. He was supposed to find out where they stood: Did they wish they could go back? Were they content? He didn't have to go far, since I switched from policy analysis to chopping onions when he was a young boy. He has been a witness to all my ups and downs in my new endeavors.

As he took out his recorder and asked me in the neutral tone of a journalist to state my name, describe my life change, and say what I would do differently if could, I felt my eyes begin to water. And then I said, "I wouldn't change a thing. I only ask for more days to continue doing what I am doing today, and to see you and your brothers grow old as I do so." Thank you, Alan, for asking that question.

Alan, Sami, and Juju, it is a joy to be your mom. I feel like the luckiest of women. Thank you for being my best travel and work companions, and for joining me with so much support and enthusiasm in all that I do, no matter how silly some parts of it may be.

CONTENTS

INTRODUCTION

THIS IS A BOOK OF RECIPES BORN OUT OF PASSION: passion for my family; passion for my native Mexico and its ancient, modern, and evolving foodways; passion for the changing Mexican cuisine within the United States, my home for the past eighteen years and the birthplace of my children; and passion for delicious, unforgettable, irresistible food.

I am a working Mexican mom with a busy Mexican husband and three Mex-American boys. All of us live fast-paced lives with packed American schedules, but somehow we find the time to sit down together and enjoy our food on a daily basis. That is what we Mexicans do. My intention with this book is to share that food with you, food that reflects the cuisine that I grew up on, and that also reveals the way cultures and foodways have merged and changed both north and south of the border.

In Mexico we have a saying, *"La mejor comida mexicana es la que se come en la calle y en la casa."* (The best Mexican food is the food that we eat on the street and at home.) Even the food that is sold from stands and carts is still largely made at home, with fresh ingredients from scratch, and with *sazón*, the definitively Mexican knack for seasoning that is proudly passed down from generation to generation.

When I delved into the enjoyable task of assembling this collection, I enlisted all of my selves—academic researcher and historian, mom, daughter and granddaughter, Mexican, Mex-American, second-generation Jewish Mexican, television host, teacher, and cook. As I pulled together recipes and tested them in my kitchen, it became clear to me how many threads there are in the colorful tapestry that we call Mexican food. Some of the threads will be familiar; some will surprise you.

Some of my go-to dishes today are adaptations of the food that nurtured me when I was growing up in Mexico City. These foods have a special place in my DC home and in my heart, keeping me linked to my roots and keeping my boys connected as well, giving them a greater sense of who they are and where we come from.

But the memories of my youth encompass much more than traditional Mexican food. Mexico City is a place that hums with old and new possibilities, with recipes passed down through generations by families who have never left, but also with the many new flavors and other traditions that newcomers to this huge metropolis have brought from different regions of Mexico and from different parts of the world. In the pages that follow, alongside the classic tacos and salsas that have been popular forever in taquerías, you will find hot dogs inspired by favorite Mexico City stands, where my sisters and I gorged ourselves at least once a week when we were teenagers; and stir-fries that my grandmother, who came to Mexico from Austria and loved Chinese food, used to make in her trusted wok.

The researcher and adventurous cook in me never stops learning about and discovering new dishes from other cooks in Mexico. Each time I go back, whether on working trips to tape my PBS series or on vacations with my family, the same humbling thing happens: Because I was once a political analyst and historian, I always think I know a state or a region and its cuisine pretty well. But once I get there, I realize that what I knew was only one layer, and that I have overlooked many historical and regional foods, as well as new ways in which cooks are using traditional ingredients and new trends that have developed over the years since I moved to the United States.

And it's not just evolving south of the border. Today Mexican food has a worldwide reach, but it is especially popular throughout the U.S., as the Mexican diaspora spreads far beyond the border states. Long gone are the days when Mexican ingredients were unavailable here, real Mexican food was to be found only in Mexico, and Tex-Mex food was looked down upon by purists. Not only does Tex-Mex food, a regional cuisine in its own right, continue to become more varied and nuanced, but now there is Cal-Mex, Baja Fresh, Chicago-Mex, New York-Mex, Modern Mex, and Fusion Mex. Mexican cuisine has become borderless. As our cooks settle in different regions of the U.S., they are exposed to different food cultures. And so we blend our techniques and the ingredients we love and cannot do without with those that we learn to love. There are so many recipes in this book that illustrate this phenomenon, but probably none better than my family's beloved pizza topped with charred skirt steak that we call Mexican carne asada pizza (page 196).

Regional Mexican cooks working in restaurants outside Mexico are marking this new era of Mexican cooking in America with a special accent. Take a look at who is in the kitchen the next time you go to your favorite sushi place; if you see Mexican cooks, ask for a plate of *chiles toreados* ("Matador Chiles"; page 110) to accompany your sushi, and before you know it, you will have a plate of blistered jalapeños marinated in soy sauce and lime on your table to eat with your sashimi. You will then want that condiment at home, and now you'll have a recipe for it.

The word *fusion* may pop into your head when you look at many of these recipes. Yet fusion is nothing new when it comes to Mexican cuisine. It began when the first conquistadores set foot on Mexican soil with their pigs, cattle, and rice and continued through the Maximilian era, when French cooking was all the rage. Along the way, waves of immigrants from Africa via the Caribbean, the Middle East, and Asia left their mark on Mexican cooking. Many traditional Mexican dishes would have been considered fusion dishes if that had been a concept in the past. Think of crepes with cajeta or even Mexican tortas made on French-derived bolillos. Cuisines need new air to breathe and grow, and Mexican cooking has had plenty of that. It continues to make history as it evolves in our kitchens.

MEXICAN TODAY EVERY DAY

Over the years, I have become more playful in my kitchen, and I encourage you to be so in yours. I apply my inherent Mexican *sazón* to all kinds of food, be it American or Tex-Mex, Japanese or Jewish. In our home and in my classes, we enjoy Chicken Fajita Salad (page 62), Med-Mex Salad (page 45) Macaroni with Chipotle Chicken (page 176), and matzo ball soup with jalapeños (page 34). As you cook your way through these recipes, you'll see how easy it is to put a little bit of Mexico on your plate every day.

Eighteen years ago, when I was a recent arrival living in Dallas, I swore that I would always call Mexican dishes by their proper names. Guacamole would never be "guac" in my home, frijoles would never be "refrieds." Well, a lot has changed since then. Three children, a few moves, and a busy new career later, I am happy to feed my Mex-American family guac and refrieds with their tacos. I have come to appreciate the fact that many of my native dishes are now mainstream American, with mainstream American names. Guac and refrieds are just a beginning; there is so much more that the Mexican people contribute to the American table and way of life, and I see it happening every day.

SOUPS

SOUPS ARE COMFORTING AND SOULFUL, so it's no surprise that they hold such an important place in the regional kitchens of Mexico. The minute I set foot in a new place, I start searching for its signature soup. In any given region, city, or town, there will always be one that is present in every home kitchen and that everybody knows and loves. I know I've hit upon it when I find many variations of the same soup. In Sonora it was cheese soup (page 20), a chowder of sorts made with milk, chiles, tomatoes, potatoes, and cheese that shows off the wealth of good dairy from northern Mexico. Some cooks from Sonora use milk, some use heavy cream, and others use Mexican crema. Some versions include potatoes and green pepper, while others use poblanos (I use both). There are cooks who include tomatoes and those who don't. But all of the versions of Sonoran cheese soup can be defined by what they have in common—a creamy broth with soft cooked vegetables and cheese.

Because today's Mexico is as much about innovation and new inspirations as it is about tradition, I wanted this chapter to reflect soups' diversity—brothy or creamy, chunky or smooth, hot or cold, garnished or plain—that the country has to offer. Need something hearty that will stick to your ribs, the kind of soup my dad loves? Try Bacon and Lentil Soup with Plantains on page 26. Want a perfect dish for both vegetarians and meat eaters—hearty, deeply herbal, and full of vegetables? Serve Green Pozole with Zucchini, Chayote, and Mushrooms (page 29). Looking for something light that takes minutes to blend up? Creamy Watercress Soup with Spiced Fresh Cheese (page 27) is the one for you.

HEARTS OF PALM SOUP WITH SWEET POTATO CROUTONS

SOPA DE PALMITOS CON CRUTONES DE CAMOTE

SERVES 6

PREPARATION TIME: 15 minutes

COOKING TIME: 25 minutes

MAKE AHEAD: The soup, without the sweet potato cubes, can be made up to 4 days ahead, covered, and refrigerated.

¼ cup canola or safflower oil

Kosher or sea salt

½ teaspoon ancho chile powder, chipotle chile powder, or paprika (see page 65) or to taste

Pinch of freshly ground black pepper

1 large sweet potato, peeled and cut into ½-inch dice (about 2 cups)

1 tablespoon unsalted butter

10 scallions (light green and white parts only), thinly sliced (about 1 cup)

2 garlic cloves

2 (14-ounce) cans hearts of palm, drained, rinsed, and sliced

5 cups chicken or vegetable broth, homemade (page 40 or page 41) or store-bought

2 tablespoons chopped chives

This silky, delicate soup is often the most talked-about dish of the evening when I serve it. It's a tribute to Mexico's African heritage. For centuries we Mexicans were taught that our Mestizo heritage was the result of intermarriage between the Spanish and the indigenous people of Mexico. But the African component to our history that dates as far back as the Spanish conquest, a result of several factors, including the slave trade, migration from the Caribbean, and the Africans who came along with the Spanish as conquistadores, was long overlooked. Afro-Mexico is finally getting its due, and even has a name—The Third Root.

1. Preheat the oven to 450 degrees. Line a baking sheet or baking dish with parchment or foil.

2. In a medium bowl, mix together 2 tablespoons of the oil, ½ teaspoon salt, the chile powder or paprika, and pepper. Add the sweet potato and toss until thoroughly coated.

3. Spread the sweet potatoes in a single layer on the baking sheet, taking care not to overcrowd. Roast for 20 to 25 minutes, flipping and turning them halfway through, until golden brown on the outside and soft on the inside. Remove from the heat and set aside.

4. In a large heavy pot, heat the butter and the remaining 2 tablespoons oil over medium-low heat until the butter is melted and bubbling. Stir in the scallions and garlic and cook, stirring occasionally, until completely softened, 12 to 14 minutes.

continued...

5. Raise the heat to medium, add the hearts of palm, and cook, stirring, for a couple of minutes, until heated through. Add the broth and ½ teaspoon salt, raise the heat to medium-high, and bring to a simmer. Simmer for 5 minutes.

6. In batches, pour the soup into a blender and puree until completely smooth, holding down the lid of the blender with a towel to contain the pressure from the hot soup. Pour the soup back into the pot, stir, taste, and adjust the seasonings. Reheat if necessary before serving.

7. Ladle the soup into individual bowls, spoon about ¼ cup sweet potatoes into the middle of each bowl, and sprinkle the chives around the sweet potatoes.

HEARTS OF PALM

These precious vegetables, harvested from the soft inner core of certain types of palm trees, consist of several moist, delicate layers that have a slightly tangy, lemony flavor and a satiny but firm texture that yields to the bite in the most generous way. They are versatile and can be used for far greater things than being left to dry out on a salad bar. Try pureeing them in a soup (page 17) if you have any doubts about how delicious they can be.

Hearts of palm are easy to find in most grocery stores. All you need to do before you use them is drain them thoroughly and give them a quick rinse under cold water to remove any metallic flavor from the can. Let them drain for a few minutes before you slice them and they will shine; then you will understand what an exquisite ingredient they are.

SONORAN CHEESE SOUP

SOPA DE QUESO ESTILO SONORA

SERVES 6 TO 8

PREPARATION TIME: 20 minutes

COOKING TIME: 30 minutes

MAKE AHEAD: The soup can be made up to 4 days ahead, covered, and refrigerated.

3 tablespoons canola or safflower oil

1 to 1¼ pounds potatoes (4 medium), peeled and diced (about 3 cups)

1½ cups chopped white onions

1 cup diced green bell peppers

1 ripe medium tomato, cored and diced

4 poblano chiles (about 1 pound), roasted, peeled, seeded, and cut into strips (see page 21)

¾ teaspoon kosher or sea salt or to taste

4 cups chicken broth, homemade (page 40) or store-bought

2 cups milk

8 ounces white melting cheese, preferably queso Chihuahua, Oaxaca, asadero, mozzarella, or Monterey Jack (see headnote), diced (about 1½ cups loosely packed)

The rich, fertile soil of Sonora, in northern Mexico, makes for happy cows that produce some of the country's best milk and cheese. This mildly spicy soup, a chowder of sorts made with milk, chiles, tomatoes, potatoes, and cheese, shows off that wealth of good dairy. The cheese of choice, queso Chihuahua, is a melting cheese that is a mainstay of the region. But Oaxaca, asadero, mozzarella, or even Monterey Jack can step in as dignified substitutes. Any type of potato will work.

....

1. Heat the oil in a large heavy pot over medium heat. Add the potatoes and onions and cook, stirring often, until the onions are soft and translucent, 4 to 5 minutes. Add the bell pepper, tomato, poblano chiles, and salt and cook until the vegetables are softened, 4 to 5 minutes.

2. Add the broth, bring to a simmer, and cook for 10 minutes, or until the potatoes are tender and the broth has thickened a bit. Taste and adjust the salt. Reduce the heat to medium-low and slowly add the milk, then bring to a gentle simmer.

3. Gradually add the cheese and stir until it is completely melted. Taste again for salt and serve.

PREPARING POBLANOS FOR RELLENOS OR RAJAS

Poblano chiles are rarely used raw in Mexican cooking—they need a bit of coaxing to bring out their best. When roasted, they display their full potential, resulting in an incredibly flavorful ingredient that you can use in many ways. You can prepare them ahead of time and refrigerate, tightly covered, for up to 5 days, or freeze them for up to 6 months.

Here's what you need to do:

1. **Roast:** Preheat the broiler. Line a baking sheet with foil and place the poblanos on it. Place under the broiler, 2 to 3 inches from the heat, and roast for 6 to 8 minutes, flipping them at least once with tongs, until they are blistered and completely charred on the outside. Some people roast the peppers, grill them, or roast them over the flame of a gas burner.

2. **Sweat:** Place the poblanos in a plastic bag or a bowl and seal or cover tightly. Let them sweat for at least 10 minutes, and up to 12 hours.

3. **Peel, rinse, seed, and devein:** Hold the poblanos under a thin stream of cold running water, or put them in a bowl filled with water, and remove the charred skin with your fingers. Make a slit down one side of each pepper and remove the cluster of seeds and veins. Pat dry with paper towels.

4. **Use:** If making stuffed chiles, or chiles rellenos, keep the poblanos as whole as you can and don't remove the stems. For other dishes, remove the stems and slice (for rajas) or chop as directed.

TORTILLA SOUP

SOPA DE TORTILLA

SERVES 6 TO 8

PREPARATION TIME: 15 minutes

COOKING TIME: 25 minutes

MAKE AHEAD: The soup, without the garnishes, can be made up to 4 days ahead, covered, and refrigerated.

1   pound ripe tomatoes

2   garlic cloves, unpeeled

¼   medium white onion

½   canned chipotle chile in adobo sauce, seeded or to taste

1   tablespoon sauce from the canned chipotles in adobo or to taste

½   teaspoon kosher or sea salt or to taste

2   tablespoons canola or safflower oil

6   cups chicken broth, homemade (page 40) or store-bought

2   fresh cilantro sprigs

FOR GARNISH

8   ounces queso fresco, farmer's cheese, or feta, diced or crumbled (1¾ cups loosely packed)

½   cup Mexican crema, crème fraîche, or sour cream

2   ripe Hass avocados, halved, pitted, flesh scooped out and diced

1   cup crumbled chicharrones (optional; see headnote)

Corn Tortilla Strips (page 25)

Beautiful tortilla soups of all kinds are made all over Mexico, so choosing my favorite is almost as difficult as choosing a favorite kid. When I was growing up, my favorite was from Las Mañanitas, a mystical hotel in Cuernavaca, complete with a luxurious swimming pool and flamingoes roaming freely on the grounds. The hotel is an hour's drive from Mexico City, and it was one of the places we always visited as a family to celebrate big birthdays. There the soup was served tableside: The server would bring you a soup bowl, ladle in hot tomato broth, and then return with a tray filled with small pottery bowls that held the garnishes—crispy tortilla strips, chunks of avocado, crumbled cheese, thick crema, and chile crisps. I would add every single option to my soup.

Since I'm a restless cook, I have played around with adding depth of flavor to the broth by roasting some of the ingredients and adding chipotle chiles in adobo sauce. I have kept the magic of serving all of the garnishes separately, so that people can customize their bowls at the table. If you happen to have chicharrones (fried pork rinds) around, break some into small pieces and add as one of the garnishes.

1. Preheat the broiler and line a baking sheet with foil, or heat a comal or skillet over medium heat. Put the tomatoes, garlic cloves, and onion on the baking sheet and place under the broiler, 2 to 3 inches from the heat, or put them on the hot comal. Roast or char for 7 to 10 minutes, flipping them halfway through, until the vegetables are completely charred; the tomato skins should have burst and their juices begun to run, and the tomatoes should be very soft. Remove from the heat.

2. Once they are cool enough to handle, peel the garlic cloves and core and quarter the tomatoes.

3. Place the tomatoes, along with their juices, the garlic cloves, onion, chipotle chile, adobo sauce, and salt in a blender or food processor and puree until smooth.

continued...

4. In a large heavy pot, heat the oil over medium-high heat. When the oil is hot but not smoking, add the tomato puree; it should sizzle loudly and smoke. Cook, stirring occasionally, until the puree thickens and goes from bright red to a darker red, about 8 minutes.

5. Stir in the broth, add the cilantro sprigs, bring to a simmer, and simmer for 10 to 12 minutes. Taste for salt and heat and, if desired, add more adobo sauce. Remove the cilantro.

6. Ladle the soup into individual bowls. Set all the garnishes on the table and let people customize their bowls.

CORN TORTILLA TOSTADAS, CHIPS, or STRIPS

TOSTADAS, TOTOPOS, O TIRITAS

MAKES 10 TOSTADAS OR ABOUT 3 CUPS CHIPS OR STRIPS

PREPARATION TIME: None (for tostadas) to 5 minutes

COOKING TIME: 12 to 20 minutes

MAKE AHEAD: Any of these can be stored in a bag or an airtight container for up to a week.

Canola or safflower oil (unless toasting)

10 corn tortillas (5 to 6 inches in diameter), left whole for tostadas, cut into wedges for chips, or cut into thin strips (about 1 x ½ inch)

½ teaspoon kosher or sea salt or to taste

Yes, store-bought chips and tostadas are fine, but since making them in your kitchen is so easy, ridiculously economical, and miles more delicious, why buy them? You have the choice of frying, baking, or toasting; choose the method you prefer.

1. To fry: In a deep 12-inch skillet, heat ½ inch of oil over medium-high heat until hot but not smoking. The oil is ready when a piece of tortilla dipped in the oil bubbles happily around the edges. Add the tortillas or tortilla pieces in small batches to avoid crowding and fry, turning once, until they are a rich golden brown and nicely crisped. Strips and chips will take 30 to 45 seconds per side; tostadas will take 1½ to 2 minutes per side. Remove with tongs, a slotted spoon, or a spider and transfer to paper towels to drain. Immediately sprinkle with salt so it will stick to the surfaces.

2. To bake: Preheat the oven to 350 degrees. Lightly grease a baking sheet. Place the tortillas or tortilla pieces on the baking sheet. Gently brush or spray the tops with oil and sprinkle with salt. Bake for about 20 minutes, flipping them once halfway through, until golden brown and crispy; the smaller pieces will cook faster.

3. To toast: This method works best for tostadas or chips. You don't need any oil; however, you won't be able to season them with salt as the salt will not stick (which may, in fact, be preferable for some dishes). Heat a comal or large skillet or griddle over low heat until very hot. Working in batches, place the tortillas or tortilla pieces in a single layer on the hot surface and toast for about 12 minutes, flipping and turning them every 2 to 3 minutes, until golden brown and crispy.

BACON AND LENTIL SOUP WITH PLANTAINS

SOPA DE LENTEJAS CON TOCINO Y PLÁTANO MACHO

SERVES 6

PREPARATION TIME: 15 minutes

COOKING TIME: 1 hour

MAKE AHEAD: The soup can be made up to 4 days ahead, covered, and refrigerated. The plantains can be fried up to an hour ahead and kept warm in a low oven.

4 ounces sliced bacon, coarsely chopped

⅓ cup finely chopped white onion

⅓ cup finely chopped peeled carrot

1 garlic clove, minced or pressed

¾ cup finely chopped ripe tomato (seeded if desired)

1 teaspoon kosher or sea salt or to taste

¼ teaspoon freshly ground black pepper

1½ cups brown lentils, rinsed and picked over

½ cup finely chopped fresh cilantro leaves and upper part of stems

8 cups chicken broth, homemade (page 40) or store-bought

2 cups water

Canola or safflower oil, for shallow-frying

2 ripe plantains, peeled and sliced ¼ inch thick on the diagonal

I inherited my taste for contrasting flavors from my dad, who particularly loves sweet and salty combinations. I remember him enjoying this homey, savory lentil soup that my mom used to make. Sometimes she topped the soup with sweet caramelized fried plantain slices, sometimes with cool, tart green banana slices. In this version, I opt for the plantains, which go beautifully with the lentils.

1. Heat a large pot or casserole over medium-high heat. Add the bacon and cook for 4 to 5 minutes, until it has browned and crisped and rendered some of its fat. Take care not to let it burn.

2. Stir in the onion, carrot, and garlic and cook until completely softened and just beginning to brown around the edges, 5 to 6 minutes. Push the vegetables to the sides of the pot, put the tomato in the middle, and cook until they break down and soften completely, about 3 minutes. Stir the tomatoes together with the rest of the vegetables, season with the salt and pepper, and cook for 1 minute.

3. Stir in the lentils, cilantro, broth, and water and bring to a boil. Reduce the heat to low, cover, and simmer for 40 to 45 minutes, until the lentils are completely cooked and soft. Taste for salt and add more if desired.

4. Meanwhile, to prepare the plantains, pour ¼ inch of oil into a medium skillet and heat over medium heat until very hot but not smoking, 2 to 3 minutes. Cover a platter or cooling rack with paper towels. Fry the plantains in batches, without crowding the skillet, turning once, until golden brown, 2 to 3 minutes on the first side and 1 to 2 minutes on the second side. Drain on the paper towels. Transfer to a baking sheet and keep warm in a low oven until ready to serve.

5. Ladle the soup into individual bowls. Pass the plantains at the table so diners can top their soup with as many slices as they want.

MEXICAN COOK'S TIP

For a thicker, creamier soup, remove a cup of the finished soup and puree it in a blender, then stir back into the soup, mixing well.

CREAMY WATERCRESS SOUP WITH SPICED FRESH CHEESE

CREMA DE BERROS CON REQUESÓN

SERVES 6 TO 8

PREPARATION TIME: 15 minutes

COOKING TIME: 30 minutes

MAKE AHEAD: The soup can be made up to 4 days ahead, covered, and refrigerated. The cheese can be seasoned up to 4 days ahead, covered, and refrigerated.

4 tablespoons (½ stick) unsalted butter

1 cup coarsely chopped white onion

2 cups thinly sliced leeks

1 cup thinly sliced celery

1 cup chopped peeled carrots

1 teaspoon kosher or sea salt or to taste

2 tablespoons all-purpose flour

2 cups milk

4 cups chicken broth, homemade (page 40) or store-bought

4 cups watercress leaves and upper part of stems

8 ounces requesón, ricotta, queso fresco, or farmer's cheese

2 tablespoons Mexican crema, crème fraîche, or sour cream

1 jalapeño or serrano chile, finely chopped or to taste

2 tablespoons chopped fresh chives

Freshly ground black pepper

This style of creamy soup is common in the Yucatán Peninsula. At the Hacienda San José near Mérida, the capital of Yucatán, I tasted one that was so delicious I asked the chef to show me how he made it. In exchange, I shared my take on a soft cheese mixture to use as a garnish. The combination is sublime! The soft, moist cheese, seasoned with jalapeño and chives, slowly blends into the watercress soup as you eat it. Your first spoonfuls of hot soup will have distinctive bites of cheese, but by the end, the cheese will have melted into the soup, so it becomes even creamier, its flavors enhanced by the jalapeño and chives.

The version I tasted in Yucatán was made not with watercress but with chaya leaves, which taste like a sort of cross between watercress and baby spinach. Since chaya is practically nowhere to be found in markets north of the border, I developed my version using watercress, which I prefer because of its beautiful color. But feel free to try it with spinach. You could also make the soup with a cilantro base.

1. In a large heavy pot, melt the butter over medium-high heat. Once it foams, add the onion, leeks, celery, and carrots, season with salt to taste, and cook, stirring occasionally, for 10 minutes, or until completely softened but not browned. Sprinkle the flour over the vegetables, stir together, and cook, stirring, for 2 minutes, or until the flour is no longer raw and the mixture smells toasty.

2. Reduce the heat to low, stir in the milk, and bring to a simmer, stirring. Simmer for 5 to 6 minutes, until thick and creamy. Add the broth and watercress, bring to a low simmer, and simmer for 5 minutes. Remove from the heat.

3. Meanwhile, in a medium bowl, mash the cheese and cream with a fork. Add the chile, chives, and salt and pepper to taste. Mix well. Keep covered in the refrigerator until ready to serve.

continued...

4. In batches, puree the soup in a blender until completely smooth; hold a towel tightly over the blender top to prevent hot splashes. (It won't jump quite as much if you let it cool down a little before you puree.) Return to the soup pot and stir. Taste and adjust the seasoning. Reheat gently.

5. Ladle the hot soup into soup bowls. Place a generous dollop of the cheese mixture in the middle of each bowl and serve.

REQUESÓN

I wish there were more of this creamy, moist, soft cheese to be found on this side of the border. With its slight tang and incredibly fresh feel, requesón is both a little sweet and a little salty, much like farmer's cheese. It is perfectly balanced. In texture, it's similar to ricotta, but ricotta is one-dimensional by comparison and a bit sweeter, without requesón's definitive tang. You could also use queso fresco for the garnish in this recipe, but it's a firmer, less creamy cheese. You could use fresh goat cheese as well, though it has a much stronger, more assertive, acidic flavor. But it works well with this soup because it melts like the other cheeses.

GREEN POZOLE WITH ZUCCHINI, CHAYOTE, AND MUSHROOMS

POZOLE VERDE VEGETARIANO

SERVES 8

PREPARATION TIME: 20 minutes

COOKING TIME: 45 minutes

MAKE AHEAD: The pozole, without the garnishes, can be made up to 3 days ahead, covered, and refrigerated.

½ cup pumpkin seeds

1 teaspoon dried oregano, preferably Mexican

1 pound tomatillos (about 6 medium), husked, thoroughly rinsed, and quartered

1 pound poblano chiles (4 or 5), seeded and coarsely chopped

1 cup coarsely chopped white onion

1½ cups coarsely chopped fresh cilantro leaves and upper part of stems

1 garlic clove

1 cup water

3 tablespoons canola or safflower oil

1 teaspoon kosher or sea salt or to taste

8 cups vegetable or chicken broth, homemade (page 41 or 40) or store-bought

3 cups cooked hominy (one 29-ounce can) or cooked dried hominy (see page 31)

1¼ pounds zucchini (about

Green pozole, or hominy stew, is much loved by people from the state of Guerrero, in southwestern Mexico. It is rare to find green pozole made without any meat. My mother, however, prefers it that way. And when you taste the thick, velvety base of toasted pumpkin seeds and oregano combined with poblano chiles and tomatillos, you probably will too. A mix of vegetables—zucchini, chayote, mushrooms—and the cooked hominy play off each other, and nobody will ask where the meat is.

Note: If you taste the pozole before the end of the cooking process, it may taste overly grassy to you. That will change once the vegetables are thoroughly cooked, and then the stew will taste completely fabulous.

....

1. Heat a small skillet or comal over medium heat. Add the pumpkin seeds and toast for 3 to 4 minutes, stirring often, until they begin to brown and pop, like popcorn. Transfer to a bowl.

2. Toast the oregano in the same pan for 8 to 10 seconds, just until it goes from green to brown, stirring constantly and taking care not to burn. Immediately transfer to the bowl with the pumpkin seeds.

3. Place the tomatillos, chiles, onion, cilantro, and garlic in a blender, add the water, and puree until smooth.

4. In a large heavy pot or casserole, heat the oil over medium-high heat until hot but not smoking. Add the green puree. It will sizzle, sear, and smoke, which is what you want! Add the salt and simmer for 10 minutes, stirring occasionally. The sauce will thicken and darken in color and the flavors will intensify.

5. Meanwhile, place the toasted pumpkin seeds and oregano in the blender, along with 3 cups of the broth, and puree until completely smooth.

continued...

3 medium), diced (4 cups)

1¼ pounds chayote squash (about 2), peeled and diced (4 cups)

8 ounces mushrooms, trimmed, cleaned, and diced

FOR GARNISH

2 limes, quartered

Chopped fresh cilantro

Chopped white onion

4 radishes, halved and thinly sliced

6. Stir the pumpkin seed mixture into the simmering green sauce and reduce the heat to medium. Cover partially, as the mixture will splutter, and simmer for 8 minutes. Stir from time to time to prevent it from sticking to the bottom of the pot; it will be thicker and pastier on the bottom.

7. Add the remaining 5 cups broth and bring to a simmer. Add the hominy, cover partially, and simmer for 10 minutes. Stir in the zucchini, chayote, and mushrooms, cover partially, and simmer for another 15 minutes, or until the vegetables are tender and the soup is thick and olive green. Taste and adjust the seasoning.

8. Ladle the pozole into bowls and serve, passing the garnishes on the side.

PUMPKIN SEEDS (PEPITAS)

Pepitas, the seeds of different kinds of pumpkins, are found all over Mexico, from street stands to supermarkets. They're sold unhulled and hulled and eaten raw, toasted, salted, fried, and spiced up as snacks. You will find them in salsas, moles, soups, desserts, drinks and even ice cream, or just sprinkled over dishes to add another layer of flavor and texture. The seeds have been used in Mexican cooking for thousands of years, prized by both the Aztecs and the Mayas, who are thought to be the first people to grind them and use as a base for sauces.

When using them for cooking look for raw, hulled pepitas. But if you are just using them as a garnish you may want to buy hulled pumpkin seeds that are already toasted and salted or spiced. Happily I am seeing both versions in more and more grocery stores in the United States and no longer need to stuff them into my suitcase when I come back from Mexico as I used to do.

CHAYOTE

Chayote is a firm, pear-shaped squash. Its flavor is subtle and mild, much like other firm summer squash like pattypan, with a hint of sweetness, but its texture is crispier. The light, clean-tasting vegetable can be cooked in many ways. We use it in soups, as a warm vegetable side or a stuffed vegetable, and in salads. Although there are different varieties of chayotes and also different names (xuxu, choco, vegetable pear, mirliton, and christophene), the ones you see most often in the U.S., and the ones I use in my recipes, are the pale green, smooth-skinned chayotes. Choose chayotes that are rock-hard with no wrinkles. They will keep for a couple of weeks in the refrigerator.

COOKING HOMINY

To cook hominy, throw 1 cup dried hominy—also called giant white corn, *maíz mote pelado*, or *cacahuacintle*—into a pot, cover it by at least 4 inches of water, add 3 or 4 garlic cloves, bring to a simmer, and let it simmer, partially covered, for 4 to 5 hours, until it blooms, opening up into a shape similar to popcorn. The kernels should not be disheveled, though. Once you see that the hominy has opened or has started to open, you are almost there. Don't forget about it; if the pot seems to be drying out, add another cup of two of hot water (it's important that it be hot).

GREEN POZOLE WITH ZUCCHINI,
CHAYOTE, AND MUSHROOMS

MATZO BALLS WITH MUSHROOMS AND JALAPEÑOS IN BROTH

BOLAS DE MATZÁ CON HONGOS Y CHILES

SERVES 6 TO 8

PREPARATION TIME: 15 minutes

COOKING TIME: 30 minutes

MAKE AHEAD: The soup can be made up to 3 days ahead, covered, and refrigerated.

1 cup matzo ball mix (or two 2-ounce packages)

2 tablespoons finely chopped flat-leaf parsley

¼ teaspoon freshly grated nutmeg

Kosher or sea salt

4 large eggs

8 tablespoons canola or safflower oil

2 tablespoons toasted sesame oil

2 tablespoons sparkling water

½ cup finely chopped white onion

1 garlic clove, finely chopped

2 jalapeño chiles, finely chopped (seeded if desired) or to taste

8 ounces white and/or baby bella (cremini) mushrooms, trimmed, cleaned, and thinly sliced

8 cups chicken broth, homemade (page 40) or store-bought

This is a Mexican rendition of matzo ball soup, with jalapeños sweated along with mushrooms, adding subtle heat to the broth. The mushroom base is easy to make. It's a wonderful way to dress up chicken soup for the holidays or for entertaining. My maternal grandmother used to season her matzo balls with nutmeg and a bit of parsley. I add a splash of toasted sesame oil too. Her secret ingredient for making them fluffy was a dash of sparkling water. She used mushrooms of all sorts in the soup, but she was moderate in her use of chiles. In honor of my late grandfather, who was obsessed with chiles, I add a lot more to this soup than she would have.

....

1. In a large bowl, combine the matzo ball mix, parsley, nutmeg, and ¾ teaspoon salt. In another small bowl, lightly beat the eggs with 6 tablespoons of the canola oil and the sesame oil. Fold the beaten eggs into the matzo ball mixture with a rubber spatula. Add the sparkling water and mix until well combined. Cover and refrigerate for at least 30 minutes.

2. Heat the remaining 2 tablespoons oil in a large pot over medium heat. Add the onion, garlic, and chiles and cook, stirring, for 4 to 5 minutes, until they have softened a bit. Stir in the mushrooms and ¾ teaspoon salt, cover, and steam the mushrooms for 6 to 8 minutes. Remove the lid and cook uncovered until the liquid in the pot evaporates. Add the chicken broth and bring to a simmer. Taste and adjust the seasonings.

3. Meanwhile, when ready to cook the matzo balls, bring about 3 quarts salted water to a rolling boil in a large pot over high heat. Reduce the heat to medium and keep at a steady simmer. With wet hands, shape the matzo ball mix into 1- to 1½-inch balls and gently drop them into the water. Reduce the heat to low, cover, and simmer for 25 to 30 minutes, until the matzo balls are completely cooked and have puffed up. Remove with a slotted spoon and transfer to the soup. Serve.

BLACK BEAN SOUP WITH MASA, MINT, AND QUESO FRESCO DUMPLINGS

SOPA DE FRÍJOL NEGRO CON CHOCHOYOTES, MENTA, Y QUESO FRESCO

SERVES 6

PREPARATION TIME: 10 minutes

COOKING TIME: 1 hour

MAKE AHEAD: The soup can be made up to 4 days ahead, covered, and refrigerated.

¼ cup canola or safflower oil

½ cup chopped white onion

1   garlic clove

2   chiles de árbol, stemmed and coarsely chopped (seeded if desired)

8   ounces ripe tomatoes (about 2 medium), cored and chopped

Kosher or sea salt

3   cups Basic Black Beans (page 244), with ½ cup of their cooking broth

8   cups chicken or vegetable broth, homemade (page 40 or 41) or store-bought

1   cup corn masa flour, such as Maseca (preferably masa mix for tamales, but masa for tortillas will also work)

¾ cup water

4   ounces queso fresco, farmer's cheese, or ricotta, crumbled (about ½ cup loosely packed)

2   tablespoons finely chopped fresh mint

Mexican crema, for garnish (optional)

Sublime in its simplicity, this soup is Mexican country food at its finest. It is made from the most basic ingredients in the Mexican diet: beans, chiles, and corn masa. But the devil is in the details. The beans are black beans—inky, rich, intense—seasoned with golden-brown onion, garlic, and spicy, toasty chiles de árbol and pureed into a silky potage. What makes this luxurious is the enrichment—soft masa and queso fresco dumplings that cook in the simmering soup.

Of the many preparations made with corn masa, *chochoyotes*, or little masa dumplings, are among the most fun. And they are so cute! The ones in this soup are particularly special, as the masa mix is combined with queso fresco and spiked with fresh mint, which makes them shine. As the dumplings finish cooking, a thin film of masa melts into the silky black bean puree, infusing it with a refreshing hint of mint, so that you taste the herb not only when you bite into the dumplings, but also with each spoonful of the soup.

1. Heat 2 tablespoons of the oil in a large heavy pot or casserole over medium-high heat. Add the onion and cook for 5 to 6 minutes, until it has completely softened, the edges are golden brown, and there is a toasted, sweet aroma wafting from the pot. Add the garlic and chiles and cook, stirring, for 1 minute, or until the garlic is fragrant and has colored and the chiles have softened a bit and intensified to a darker and more burnt red. Stir in the tomatoes and ½ teaspoon salt and cook, stirring, for 5 minutes, or until the tomatoes have cooked down to a soft, thick paste.

2. Add the beans with their broth and 4 cups of the chicken or vegetable broth. Bring to a boil, then reduce the heat to medium, cover partially, and simmer for about 10 minutes. The beans should be completely soft and the broth thick and soupy.

3. Meanwhile, prepare the masa for the dumplings: In a medium bowl, combine the corn masa flour with the water and ¼ teaspoon salt. Knead together with your hands. The dough will be very coarse and seem dry.

Add the remaining 2 tablespoons oil, the cheese, and mint and mix together until the dough is very soft and homogenous, about 1 minute.

4. Working in batches, puree the soup in a blender until completely smooth. Cover the blender lid with a towel to avoid splashes. Pour back into the pot and stir in the remaining 4 cups broth. Bring to a simmer over medium heat, then reduce the heat to low.

5. To form the dumplings: For each one, scoop up enough masa to make a 1-inch ball, roll it between your hands (moisten your hands if the dough sticks), and gently drop into the soup. Once all the masa balls have been shaped and added to the soup, partially cover the pot and let the soup simmer gently for about 20 minutes, until the dumplings are cooked through. They will thicken the soup as they simmer. Taste the soup for salt and add more if necessary.

6. Serve hot, garnishing each bowl with a spoonful of crema, if desired.

VARIATION: This soup will be much more delicious if you use home-cooked black beans, but if you are in a time crunch, feel free to use canned. Two 15-ounce cans plus an extra ½ cup chicken or vegetable broth or water can stand in for homemade.

MEXICAN COOK'S TIP

If you are lucky enough to live next to a tortillería or store that sells fresh corn masa already mixed up, go for it! You will need about 12 ounces. Just mix it with the queso fresco, oil, mint, and salt. If you can't get hold of fresh masa, rest assured that the dumplings will still be excellent. Look for masa harina for tamales. Masa harina for tortillas is finer than the flour for tamales, but it will work.

CUSTOMIZING THE HEAT OF YOUR CHILES

Chiles are an essential ingredient in Mexican cuisine. They vary in both flavor and heat, and while the heat can sometimes be a wild card, there is a way to take a measure of control. All hot peppers contain a compound called capsaicin, which is mainly contained in the ribs and the seeds. Remove the seeds, and you lose some heat; remove the seeds, the ribs or veins, and the placenta (the fleshy pocket that is attached to the inner part of the stem), and you douse the flames. Remember, you can always add more heat, but once the chiles are in the dish, the heat can't be taken away.

CHIPOTLE MISO SOUP WITH NOPALES

SOPA DE MISO ENCHIPOTLADA CON NOPALITOS

SERVES 8

PREPARATION TIME: 15 minutes

COOKING TIME: 20 minutes

MAKE AHEAD: The soup can be made up to 2 days ahead, covered, and refrigerated.

Kosher or sea salt

1 pound nopales (cactus paddles), cleaned and diced (see page 39)

2 tablespoons dried wakame seaweed

2 cups boiling water

2½ quarts water

1 tablespoon plus 1 teaspoon granulated dashi mix (boni-to soup stock)

½ cup (4 ounces) red miso paste

2 to 4 tablespoons sauce from canned chipotle chiles in adobo (to taste)

8 ounces soft tofu, diced

4 scallions (white and light green parts only), thinly sliced, for garnish

This soup brings together distinctive foods from two very different gastronomic worlds—subtly smoky Japanese dashi broth, bold red miso paste, and mild tofu on the one hand and spicy-smoky chipotles and tangy nopalitos on the other. It may strike you as strange to combine Japanese and Mexican ingredients, but such fusion dishes have existed since the first large Japanese migration into Mexico at the beginning of the twentieth century. It was mostly men who arrived, looking for land and work. They brought their culture and their cuisine, but not their women, so many married Mexican women, and they developed a taste for Mexican flavors. You see expressions of this in the Matador Chiles (page 110) that are served along with soy sauce and wasabi in the wildly popular Japanese restaurants throughout Mexico City.

1. Fill a medium saucepan with water and bring to a boil. Salt the water generously and add the diced nopales. Bring back to a boil, reduce the heat to medium, and simmer for 8 to 10 minutes, until the nopales are thoroughly cooked but still crisp-tender. Drain in a strainer and immediately rinse the cactus of any gelatinous residue with cold water. Set aside.

2. Meanwhile, place the wakame in a medium bowl and cover with the 2 cups boiling water. Leave to rehydrate for 10 to 15 minutes.

3. Drain the wakame, rinse well under cold water, and drain again. Coarsely chop and set aside.

4. In a large pot, bring the 2½ quarts water to a boil, then reduce the heat to a medium simmer. Stir in the dashi and simmer for 5 minutes, or until well dissolved.

5. In a medium bowl, combine the miso and adobo sauce with 1 cup of the dashi broth. Stir well until completely dissolved. Pour back into the pot and mix until well combined. Add the nopales, wakame, and tofu, stir together gently, and bring to a low simmer. Simmer for 5 minutes.

6. Serve hot, garnishing each bowl with sliced scallions.

NOPALES

Cactus paddles (nopales) have been a crucial food since pre-Hispanic times, eaten at meals from breakfast to dinner and anywhere in between. The most common is the prickly pear cactus. Its fleshy paddles are used as a vegetable in salads, soups, egg dishes, stews, all sorts of appetizers, and smoothies and juices. They are nutritious, filling, delicious, and versatile. Lately I've been seeing nopales in supermarkets, Latin markets, and farmers' markets already cleaned and even diced, as they are sold all over Mexico.

Working with Fresh Nopales

Nopales have shiny green skin that is covered with tiny, almost transparent thorns that happen to be quite vicious when you try to remove them from the little bumps they grow out of (if the paddles aren't harvested, those bumps grow into *tunas*, or prickly pear fruits). This may be one reason why the vegetable hasn't spread like wildfire. The other is that many people don't know how to cook nopales, and when they try, they don't know how to deal with the gelatinous, viscous liquid the cactus paddles exude as they cook.

Cleaning

Choose paddles that are bright green and tender but not limp. The smaller the paddle, the more tender it will be (though large ones are delicious too). If it's your first time, I advise you to use latex gloves. Rinse the paddles under cold water, being careful about the thorns, which can be almost invisible. If you avoid the bumps, you'll avoid the thorns. Using a vegetable peeler or small sharp knife, peel away the bumps and thorns, the way you would peel asparagus. You may want to lean the nopales against a cutting board while you do this. Try to keep as much of the outer dark green skin on as possible, focusing on the bumps. Rinse again after peeling. Lay each paddle flat on a cutting board and trim about ¼ inch all the way around the edges of it, then cut away about ½ inch of the thick base. Slice or dice as instructed, or keep whole if the paddles will be grilled, roasted, or used as a base. I usually cut them into little squares or rectangles, as I use them mostly for salads and soups.

Cooking

There are many ways to cook nopales and many old wives' tales about how to deal with the gelatinous liquid they will exude, such as adding tomatillo husks, scallion tops, baking soda, or even a copper coin to the cooking water. I simply boil them in salted water until crisp-tender, then give them a thorough rinse after I drain them. This is a good way to prepare them if I'm adding them to soups or stews. If I'm using them for salads or sides, my favorite way to cook them is to sear them in a skillet in a small amount of oil for a few minutes, cover the pan and cook until they have released all of their liquid, and then finally cook them uncovered until the liquid cooks off. This method adds a nice seared flavor to the cactus, and you don't have to spend a lot of time draining and rinsing.

CHICKEN BROTH AND SHREDDED COOKED CHICKEN

CALDO DE POLLO Y POLLITO DESHEBRADO

MAKES ABOUT 8 CUPS BROTH AND 6 CUPS SHREDDED CHICKEN

PREPARATION TIME: 5 minutes

COOKING TIME: 50 minutes

MAKE AHEAD: The chicken broth can be kept in the refrigerator for up to 4 days or frozen for up to 6 months. The cooked chicken keeps in the refrigerator for up to 3 days.

1 whole chicken, cut into pieces, or about 3 pounds mixed chicken pieces (with skin and bones)

3 carrots, peeled and cut into large chunks

1 white onion, halved

3 celery stalks, cut into large chunks

1 garlic clove

6 black peppercorns

5 or 6 flat-leaf parsley sprigs

½ teaspoon dried marjoram

½ teaspoon dried thyme

2 bay leaves

1 tablespoon kosher or sea salt or to taste

3½ quarts water

I usually opt for chicken broth for my soups, because I have found vegetable broths to be a bit mild for my appetite and richer-tasting preferences.

Combine these ingredients in a large pot and simmer for 50 minutes, and you will have two invaluable resources for your cooking week. The broth can be used for soups, pastas, rice dishes, and stews, and the shredded chicken for multiple antojitos (small plates), salads, sandwiches, soups, stews, and casseroles. No commercial chicken broth will
compare with homemade, and it is so easy to make!

1. Place all of the ingredients in a large pot and bring to a boil. Reduce the heat to medium-low, skim off any foam, and simmer, partially covered, for 50 minutes to an hour. Turn off the heat and let cool.

2. Remove the chicken pieces and place in a bowl. Strain the broth into a container and refrigerate, or freeze in smaller containers.

3. Remove the skin and bones from the chicken and shred or cut the meat into chunks for further use. Place in a bowl, cover, and refrigerate.

MEXICAN COOK'S TIP

To keep refrigerated chicken moist and flavorful, douse it with chicken broth.

VEGETABLE BROTH

CALDO DE VERDURAS

MAKES 8 CUPS

PREPARATION TIME: 10 minutes

COOKING TIME: 1 hour and
5 minutes

MAKE AHEAD: The broth will keep,
refrigerated, for a day and can be
frozen for up to 2 months.

2   ripe medium tomatoes

1   large onion, quartered

1   head garlic, cut horizontally
    in half

2   tablespoons canola or
    safflower oil

2   large carrots, peeled and
    cut into large dice

4   celery stalks (from the
    center of the bunch), cut
    into thick slices

1   leek (white and light green
    parts only), cut lengthwise
    in half and then into thick
    slices, cleaned, and drained

8   ounces turnips, peeled and
    quartered

1   teaspoon kosher or sea salt
    or to taste

Stems from ½ to 1 pound
    mushrooms

1   bay leaf

5   cilantro sprigs

5   parsley sprigs

½ to 1 teaspoon dried thyme

½ to 1 teaspoon dried
    marjoram

12 black peppercorns

2½ quarts water

Many soups in this chapter make great vegetarian dinners with this vegetable broth substituted for chicken broth. For this broth, I have beefed up the flavor, so to speak, by roasting the onion, garlic, and tomatoes first and adding lots of meaty-tasting mushroom stems. I save the caps for soups and salads.

· ·

1. Preheat the broiler. Line a baking sheet or dish with foil. Put the tomatoes, onion, and garlic on the baking sheet, place 2 to 3 inches from the heat, and broil for 4 to 5 minutes. Flip the vegetables over and broil for another 4 to 5 minutes, until charred. Remove from the heat.

2. When they are cool enough to handle, coarsely chop the tomatoes.

3. Heat the oil in a large pot over medium heat. Add the carrots, celery, and leek and cook, stirring, for 6 to 8 minutes, until they begin to soften. Add the charred vegetables and cook, stirring often, for 3 minutes. Add the remaining ingredients and bring to a boil. Reduce the heat, cover partially, and simmer for 50 minutes. Season with salt to taste if necessary.

4. Strain the broth through a fine strainer (or a medium strainer lined with cheesecloth). Use right away, refrigerate, or freeze in smaller containers.

CHAPTER 2

SALADS

THE ARRAY OF SALADS THAT CAN BE MADE using Mexican ingredients

has not been fully explored outside of Mexico. This may be a "lost in translation" issue. Although the word *ensalada* usually refers to dishes that have lettuce in them, this doesn't account for the infinite number of other Mexican dishes that can be categorized as salads. Salpicón (page 60), for instance, is Mexico's version of a Niçoise salad. The Morelia-style gazpacho on page 64 is really a fruit salad with some savory elements, but we call it a fruit gazpacho.

My years in the U.S. have given me enough distance from my beloved country to allow me to plunge headlong into new flavors, culinary concepts, and ingredients. It's irresistible to take a Mexican idea or flavor and work it into a salad that could be a main dish or a side, a snack, or an appetizer that is so pretty it can be served in cocktail glasses at a gala. I have married Mediterranean ingredients with Mexican (as has been done for centuries) in a combination of chickpeas, feta, avocados, sun-dried tomatoes, and a spicy pesto (page 45). I have turned the traditional Mexican potato and roasted poblano pepper strips (rajas) you usually find in taco and quesadilla fillings into a warm potato salad with wilted yet still crunchy red onions dressed in a warm vinaigrette (page 54). Even quinoa got the Mexican treatment, tossed with jalapeño, zucchini, and cucumber in a lime–orange juice dressing (page 56).

When I want to make a meal out of a salad, I often use vegetables as a tangy bed for shredded flank steak. Or join me at one of my favorite Mexican beach stands as we cook shrimp with garlic, add a little orange zest for fun and flavor, and set the shrimp atop a crunchy lime-dressed mix of fennel and avocado (page 58).

MED-MEX SALAD WITH CHICKPEAS, AVOCADOS, AND SUN-DRIED TOMATOES

ENSALADA MEDITERRANEA DE GARBANZO, AGUACATE, Y TOMATES DESHIDRATADOS

SERVES 6

PREPARATION TIME: 15 minutes

MAKE AHEAD: The salad can be made up to 12 hours in advance, covered, and refrigerated. Add the feta cheese just before serving.

½ cup chopped red onion

1 garlic clove, minced or pressed

1 to 2 jalapeño chiles, finely chopped (seeded if desired)

½ cup chopped fresh mint

½ cup chopped fresh basil

¼ cup freshly squeezed lemon juice

3 tablespoons extra-virgin olive oil

¾ teaspoon kosher or sea salt or to taste

¼ teaspoon freshly ground black pepper

1 (15.5-ounce) can chickpeas, rinsed and drained

3 baby cucumbers, cut into ½-inch dice (about 3 cups)

¼ cup chopped sun-dried tomatoes packed in oil

¼ cup chopped pitted kalamata olives

2 ripe Hass avocados, halved, pitted, flesh scooped out and diced

¼ cup crumbled feta cheese or queso fresco or to taste

Pita chips, tortilla chips, or pita bread (optional)

Mexican cuisine has always embraced foreign ingredients and cooking techniques. This salad is a case in point. It brings together foods that the world is grateful to Mexico for (avocados, chiles, tomatoes) with much-loved ingredients from the Mediterranean (sun-dried tomatoes, olives, feta, olive oil, basil, chickpeas). In their company, jalapeño chiles couldn't be happier! The vinaigrette is a tangy pesto of basil and mint mashed together with lemon juice and olive oil.

This salad is incredibly versatile. It can be a lunch, and it can also act as a delicious sidekick to a grilled entrée. I have served it as an appetizer with tortilla or pita chips, as if it were a super-chunky guacamole, and when I am lucky enough to have leftovers, I spoon them into a pita for one of the tastiest sandwiches ever.

1. Place the onion, garlic, jalapeños, mint, and basil in a molcajete or small bowl and grind to a coarse paste with a pestle or fork. Add the lemon juice, oil, salt, and pepper and work into the pesto. Set aside.

2. In a large bowl, combine the chickpeas, cucumbers, sun-dried tomatoes, olives, and avocados. Toss well with the pesto. Sprinkle the cheese over the top. Serve with pita chips, tortilla chips, or pita bread, if you like.

ARTICHOKE HEART, MUSHROOM, AND AVOCADO SALAD WITH LIME VINAIGRETTE

ENSALADA DE CORAZONES DE ALCACHOFA, CHAMPIÑONES, Y AGUACATE CON VINAGRETA DE PARMESANO Y LIMÓN

SERVES 4 TO 6

PREPARATION TIME: 20 minutes

COOKING TIME: 3 minutes

MAKE AHEAD: The vinaigrette can be made up to 3 days in advance, covered, and refrigerated.

2   chiles de árbol or ½ teaspoon red pepper flakes or to taste

⅔ cup finely grated Parmigiano-Reggiano, ricotta salata, or queso añejo (see page 47)

¼ cup plus 1 tablespoon extra-virgin olive oil

1   garlic clove, minced or pressed

1   teaspoon Dijon mustard

¼ cup plus 2 tablespoons freshly squeezed lime juice

2   teaspoons finely chopped capers

1   teaspoon kosher or sea salt or to taste

¼ teaspoon freshly ground black pepper

8   ounces white button or baby bella (cremini) mushrooms, trimmed and thinly sliced

In this salad, sassy, smoky chiles and creamy avocados embrace mushrooms, artichokes, and capers, ingredients that I grew up viewing as exotic and special. For the dressing, Mexican limes combine with Mediterranean olive oil, and the salad is enriched with salty cheese that can come from either Mexico (queso añejo) or Italy (Parmigiano-Reggiano or ricotta salata). I toss the ingredients together in the dressing in two stages so that the chunks of avocado stay intact. You could also slice the mushrooms, artichoke hearts, and avocados very thin and arrange them carpaccio style in a pinwheel on a platter, then top with the dressing.

....

1. If using chiles de árbol, heat a small skillet over medium heat. When the skillet is hot, add the chiles and toast until they are fragrant and deeply browned but not burned, about 1 minute per side. Remove from the heat, remove the stems, and finely chop.

2. In a small bowl, combine the cheese, oil, garlic, mustard, lime juice, capers, chiles de árbol or red pepper flakes, salt, and pepper. Mix well with a fork or whisk.

3. Combine the mushrooms and artichoke hearts in a salad bowl. Add half the vinaigrette and toss well. Add the avocado with the remaining vinaigrette and gently toss until completely coated. Garnish with the parsley, if using, and serve.

PARMIGIANO-REGGIANO, RICOTTA SALATA, AND QUESO AÑEJO

These three cheeses could be cousins; all three are dry, assertive, and salty, perfect for grating or shaving onto salads or pasta.

Queso añejo translates as "aged cheese." It used to be made only from goat's milk, but it is now also being made from cow's milk. It's semihard and a bit sharper, drier, and more crumbly than Parmigiano-Reggiano and ricotta salata, with a flavor that is less complex. Añejo is used in a multitude of antojitos. Until recently it was not easy to find in the United States, but now it is becoming increasingly available. Of these three cheeses, it is the most affordable.

Ricotta salata and Parmigiano-Reggiano are Italian cheeses. Ricotta salata is made from sheep's milk and Parmigiano-Reggiano from cow's milk. Proper Parmigiano-Reggiano comes from the Parma region of Italy, made with the milk of cows that graze on fresh grass and hay. It's drier than ricotta salata and has a nuttier taste. All three cheeses will work in this salad.

1 (14-ounce) can artichoke hearts, drained, rinsed under cold water, thoroughly drained, patted dry, and cut lengthwise into thin slices

2 ripe Hass avocados, halved, pitted, flesh scooped out and cut into bite-size chunks

1 to 2 tablespoons finely chopped fresh flat-leaf parsley, for garnish (optional)

AVOCADO, ROASTED ASPARAGUS, AND CHERRY TOMATO SALAD

ENSALADA DE AGUACATE, ESPÁRRAGOS, Y JITOMATITOS ROSTIZADOS

SERVES 6

PREPARATION TIME: 15 minutes

COOKING TIME: 20 minutes

MAKE AHEAD: This salad is best tossed just before eating, but the ingredients can be prepared a few hours ahead and kept at room temperature.

1 pound asparagus

2 tablespoons chopped fresh basil or 2 teaspoons dried

2 tablespoons chopped fresh mint or 2 teaspoons dried

2 tablespoons chopped fresh sage or 2 teaspoons dried

¼ cup plus 2 tablespoons extra-virgin olive oil

Kosher or sea salt

1 teaspoon freshly ground black pepper or to taste

¼ cup thinly sliced shallots

1 pound cherry tomatoes

Grated zest of 1 lime

2 tablespoons freshly squeezed lime juice

1 teaspoon Dijon mustard

2 large eggs, hard-boiled, cut in half, yolks separated from whites, and whites finely chopped

2 large ripe Hass avocados, halved, pitted, flesh scooped out and cut into large bite-size pieces

This combination of creamy, crunchy, and juicy vegetables holds the number-one slot on my list of favorite salads. First you toss cherry tomatoes and asparagus in an aromatic olive oil and herb marinade, then you roast them until the asparagus is lightly charred but still has some crunch and the tomatoes are soft. Their juices seep onto the baking sheet, where they thicken slightly and mix with the marinade and herbs. Then all those flavorful juices and herbs are swirled into a luxurious dressing that envelops big chunks of ripe avocado, which are topped with the roasted tomatoes and asparagus.

1. Preheat the oven to 425 degrees.

2. Trim away the dry hard ends of the asparagus (about 1 inch from the bottom). Using a vegetable peeler, peel each asparagus stalk, beginning 1½ to 2 inches below the tips and peeling all the way down to the bottom.

3. In a large bowl, combine the basil, mint, and sage with ¼ cup of the olive oil, 1½ teaspoons salt, the pepper, and shallots. Beat with a whisk or fork until well mixed.

4. Set a rimmed 18-x-13-inch baking sheet on the countertop. Add the cherry tomatoes to the marinade, toss well and, with a slotted spoon, arrange on half of the baking sheet. Place the asparagus on the other half. Pour the remaining marinade over the asparagus and toss until thoroughly coated. Spread out in a single layer.

5. Roast the vegetables for 12 to 13 minutes, until the asparagus is crisp-tender. Remove the asparagus and set on a cutting board to cool. Return the tomatoes to the oven for another 5 to 6 minutes, until they have burst, deflated, and begun to char. Remove from the oven and let cool.

6. Using a slotted spoon, gently transfer the tomatoes to a bowl. Pour all the juices from the baking sheet into a blender.

7. Once the asparagus has cooled, cut away 1 inch from the bottom of each stem and add the ends to the blender. Cut the rest of the asparagus into 1½-inch pieces and set aside.

8. Add the lime zest and juice to the blender, along with the remaining 2 tablespoons oil, the mustard, ½ teaspoon salt, and the egg yolks. Puree until completely smooth.

9. Place the avocado chunks in a large serving bowl, pour on the vinaigrette and gently toss until the avocado is thoroughly coated. Arrange the asparagus on top. Spoon the roasted tomatoes over the asparagus, garnish with the chopped egg whites, and serve.

MEXICAN COOK'S TIP

Grooming Your Asparagus

After you rinse asparagus stalks, cut away about 1 inch from the lower part of the stems. That part tends to be tough, dry, and not so tasty. Using a vegetable peeler, remove the thin skin, peeling from just underneath the tips of the asparagus all the way to the bottom. Peeling makes asparagus silky on the outside, tender, and bright.

MEXICAN COOK'S TIP

Egg-Yolk Boost

My mom taught me the trick of using a hard-boiled egg yolk (or two) to thicken a salad dressing. Not only does it give it a creamy and thicker consistency (without using cream), but it also gives it more body. I use the chopped whites to decorate the salad.

AVOCADO, ROASTED
ASPARAGUS, AND CHERRY
TOMATO SALAD

GREEN BEAN AND CHERRY TOMATO SALAD WITH BLUE CHEESE DRESSING AND CRISPY SHALLOTS

ENSALADA DE EJOTES Y JITOMATITOS CON QUESO AZUL Y ECHALOTES CRUJIENTES

SERVES 6

PREPARATION TIME: 15 minutes

COOKING TIME: 20 minutes

MAKE AHEAD: The dressing can be made up to 5 days in advance, covered, and refrigerated. The crispy shallots and croutons can be made up to 12 hours ahead of time; keep covered at room temperature.

2 cups diced (¾ inch) baguette

3 large shallots, halved lengthwise and thinly sliced (about 1½ cups)

3 tablespoons olive oil

¼ teaspoon kosher or sea salt or to taste

Pinch of freshly ground black pepper

8 ounces green beans, trimmed (see Note)

2 ounces Roquefort or Gorgonzola cheese, crumbled (about ½ cup)

½ cup Mexican crema, crème fraîche, or sour cream

½ cup whole milk

¼ cup coarsely chopped fresh dill leaves and upper part of stems, or 1 tablespoon dried

I bathe this mix of cherry tomatoes, green beans, and red leaf lettuce, topped with sweet, crispy roasted shallots and crunchy croutons in a tart and creamy blue cheese dressing laced with dill.

Most of the time my guiding principle for salads is that they should be lightly coated with their dressing, not drenched. But not here: This salad, and especially the croutons, love being soaked. The salad makes a great light lunch or dinner, as well as a phenomenal starter or side.

Note: Although I usually make this salad with thin French green beans—haricots verts—you can use any fresh green beans. Just make sure you don't overcook them. They should remain crisp.

. . . .

1. Preheat the oven to 350 degrees.

2. Place the diced baguette and shallots on a baking sheet, drizzle with the oil, sprinkle with the salt and pepper, and toss to coat. Spread out in an even layer. Bake for 20 to 22 minutes, flipping the croutons and shallots over using tongs or a spoon halfway through, until they are crisp and browned. Remove from the heat and set aside.

3. Fill a large saucepan with salted water and bring to a boil over medium-high heat. Add the green beans and boil for 3 to 4 minutes, until crisp-tender. Drain in a colander and rinse with cold water. Drain well.

4. Combine the cheese, cream, milk, dill, vinegar, and lime juice in a blender and puree until completely smooth. Taste for salt and add if desired (I find that the blue cheese and Mexican crema contribute enough salt, but if you are using crème fraîche or sour cream, you will probably need to add salt).

5. In a salad bowl, combine the lettuce, green beans, and tomatoes. Add the dressing and toss well. Sprinkle with the croutons and shallots and serve.

VARIATIONS

- If you want something a little more substantial, add a quartered hard-boiled egg to each serving.

- If you are famished, lay a grilled chicken breast or piece of grilled skirt steak on top of each serving for a hearty meal.

2 tablespoons white wine vinegar

2 tablespoons freshly squeezed lime juice

2 heads red leaf lettuce, washed and torn into bite-size pieces

2 cups cherry or grape tomatoes, halved if desired

POTATO AND POBLANO RAJAS SALAD

ENSALADA DE PAPITAS CON RAJAS

SERVES 6

PREPARATION TIME: 10 minutes

COOKING TIME: 30 minutes

MAKE AHEAD: The salad can be made 2 days ahead of time, covered, and refrigerated. Bring to room temperature and toss well again before serving.

Kosher or sea salt

2　pounds baby red potatoes

½ cup extra-virgin olive oil

2　tablespoons toasted sesame oil

1　medium red onion, halved lengthwise and thinly sliced (1½ cups)

3　poblano chiles (about 1 pound), roasted, peeled, and cut into strips (see page 21)

1　teaspoon dried tarragon

¼ teaspoon ground allspice

½ teaspoon kosher or sea salt or to taste

¼ cup sesame seeds

3　tablespoons white wine vinegar

1　tablespoon unseasoned rice vinegar

Roasted, peeled, and sliced poblanos (rajas) mixed with potatoes has always been a popular combination in Mexico, whipped up as a tasty filling for all sorts of antojitos—tacos, enchiladas, crepes. I love this combination so much that I decided to use it in a dish where it could shine on its own. And what better idea than a new take on a potato salad? I toss the still-warm potatoes and rajas in a warm, bold vinaigrette, along with lightly browned red onions that finish cooking in the dressing and sesame seeds. The potatoes absorb the dressing as they cool. When I first perfected the recipe, there was none left for my family to try—I'd eaten the whole salad myself!

1. Bring a large pot of salted water to a rolling boil over medium-high heat. Add the potatoes and cook for about 20 minutes, until they are tender but not falling apart. You should be able to insert the tip of a sharp knife all the way through without resistance. Drain.

2. Once the potatoes are cool enough to handle, cut them in half.

3. In a large deep skillet, heat the olive oil over medium heat. Add the sesame oil, then carefully add the onion and cook, stirring once in a while, until it is completely softened and the edges have begun to brown slightly, about 8 minutes. Stir in the poblanos, then add the tarragon, allspice, salt, and sesame seeds and cook, stirring, for 2 minutes, or until the ingredients are nicely blended. Stir in the white wine vinegar and rice vinegar and cook for another minute. Remove from the heat.

4. Place the potatoes in a large bowl. Add the poblano mixture, scraping every last bit out of the pan with a rubber spatula. Gently toss together. Serve warm, at room temperature (my preference), or cold.

CRUNCHY QUINOA SALAD

ENSALADA CRUJIENTE DE QUINOA

SERVES 6

PREPARATION TIME: 15 minutes

COOKING TIME: 10 minutes

MAKE AHEAD: The vinaigrette can be made up to 1 day in advance, covered, and refrigerated. The salad, once mixed, will be lovely the next day as well.

1½ cups quinoa, cooked al dente (see page 57) and drained (about 4 cups cooked)

3 celery stalks, finely chopped (about ¾ cup)

1 medium cucumber, cut into ¼- to ½-inch dice (about 2 cups)

1 medium zucchini, cut into ¼- to ½-inch dice (about 2 cups)

1 jalapeño chile, finely chopped (seeded if desired) or to taste

3 tablespoons finely chopped red onion

½ cup freshly squeezed orange juice

¼ cup freshly squeezed lime juice

2 tablespoons peanut oil

2 tablespoons toasted sesame oil

1 teaspoon kosher or sea salt or to taste

Freshly ground black pepper

Seeds from 1 pomegranate

Chopped fresh cilantro or chives, for garnish (optional)

A salad is a great home for quinoa, especially when the super-healthy grain is cooked al dente, as it is here. I combine it with finely chopped celery, diced cucumber and raw zucchini, red onion, and just enough jalapeño to allow the salad to flirt with heat, then I toss the mixture with a nutty dressing made with flavorful peanut and sesame oils mixed with orange juice and lime juice. I also throw in some pomegranate seeds to make everything sparkle. If you've never tasted raw zucchini, you're in for a nice surprise; I love the way it absorbs the bright, flavorful dressing. You can serve this salad on its own as a starter or as a side dish.

. . . .

1. In a large bowl, combine the quinoa, celery, cucumber, zucchini, jalapeño, and onion and toss together.

2. In a small bowl, whisk together the orange juice, lime juice, peanut oil, and sesame oil. Season with the salt and pepper to taste and whisk again. Pour over the quinoa mixture, add the pomegranate seeds, and toss together. Let the salad sit for at least 15 minutes before serving so that the quinoa can absorb the dressing.

3. Garnish the salad with cilantro or chives, if using, and serve, or arrange the salad on individual plates and garnish with the herbs.

MAKE MY QUINOA CRUNCHY, PLEASE

All the hype about quinoa is true. It is an incredibly nutritious grain. Native to the Andes, it is making the rounds globally—so much so that in Mexico some adventurous cooks are starting to make tortillas with it!

Quinoa is best when the grains are still intact and crunchy. It is dreadful when it is overcooked, which is easily done. The problem lies in the cooking instructions on the packaging, which direct the cook to simmer the quinoa for too long (usually 20 minutes), resulting in a bowlful of mush.

To cook it properly, use 2 parts liquid to 1 part quinoa. Once the water or broth comes to a boil, add the quinoa and salt to taste, stir once, reduce the heat to very low, cover, and set your timer for 8 minutes. At that point, remove a spoonful and check to see if the little coils on the surface of the grains are beginning to uncoil. If they are starting to release, even barely, but the centers of the grains still look raw (they will be darker than the outside of the grain, like al dente pasta), the quinoa is ready. If not, it may need just another minute or two, but no more! Remove it from the heat, drain it in a strainer, and rinse it with a little cold water. Then drain completely.

GARLIC SHRIMP WITH FENNEL, ORANGE, AND AVOCADO SALAD

ENSALADA DE CAMARONES AL AJILLO, HINOJO, NARANJA, Y AGUACATE

SERVES 4

PREPARATION TIME: 20 minutes

COOKING TIME: 5 minutes

MAKE AHEAD: The vinaigrette can be made up to 5 days ahead, covered, and refrigerated.

1 orange

¼ cup plus 2 tablespoons freshly squeezed orange juice

3 tablespoons freshly squeezed lime juice

6 tablespoons extra-virgin olive oil

Kosher or sea salt and freshly ground black pepper

2 ripe Hass avocados, halved, pitted, flesh scooped out and cut into bite-size chunks

1 medium fennel bulb, trimmed, halved, cored, and thinly sliced (2 cups), a few sprigs reserved for garnish if desired

5 garlic cloves, thinly sliced

2 chiles de árbol, stemmed, seeded, and thinly sliced, or more to taste

1½ pounds medium shrimp, shells and tails removed

Normally garlic is used in very judicious amounts in Mexican kitchens. The exception is dishes whose names contain *al ajillo*, "with garlic." *Camarones al ajillo*, or garlic shrimp, is one of the signature dishes of Mexico. Other fish and seafood—just about the entire seafood kingdom, in fact—can be prepared *al ajillo*, but garlic shrimp is the most widely known, popular throughout coastal Mexico on both the Pacific and Gulf sides of the country. It is usually served with rice as a main dish, hot from the skillet, the shrimp browned on the outside but still moist on the inside, with lots of chewy charred garlic and a half lime to squeeze on top. If you're lucky to hit the right *palapa* (beach hut) restaurant, a green salad with avocado is served on the side.

In this version, the garlic shrimp share equal billing with a citrus-dressed fennel-avocado salad. The two are gently tossed and then topped with orange sections. You can serve the salad appetizer-style in small cups or elegant martini glasses, or in larger portions as a main dish.

1. Zest the orange on a fine grater and measure out 1 teaspoon. Slice off the top and bottom. Cut the orange into suprêmes by standing it upright on a cutting board and cutting away the peel and pith, slicing down the curve of the fruit. Then, holding the peeled orange over a bowl, slide a paring knife between the membranes and the orange flesh to free each segment. Set aside.

2. In a medium bowl, combine the orange juice, lime juice, 2 tablespoons of the oil, ¼ teaspoon salt, and pepper to taste. Mix well. Add the avocado and fennel and toss until coated with the dressing.

3. Heat 2 tablespoons of the oil in a large heavy skillet over medium-high heat until hot but not smoking. Add half the garlic and cook, stirring constantly for 20 to 30 seconds, until fragrant and beginning to brown. Add half the chiles and cook, stirring constantly, for 20 to 30 seconds,

until they begin to crisp. Add half the shrimp, taking care to avoid crowding the pan, and season with salt, pepper, and half the orange zest; the shrimp should start to sear right away. Cook for a minute per side, or until lightly browned. Transfer the contents of the pan to a bowl and repeat with the remaining oil, garlic, chiles, shrimp, and orange zest. Transfer the second batch of shrimp to the bowl with the first batch.

4. Add the shrimp to the salad and gently toss together. Taste for salt and add more if desired. Top with the orange suprêmes and reserved fennel sprigs, if using.

MEXICAN COOK'S TIP

Work in batches when you cook the shrimp to avoid crowding the pan, or the shrimp and garlic won't brown properly. Crowding will create steam, which would keep the garlic and shrimp from searing as they should.

SHREDDED BEEF AND VEGETABLE SALAD

SALPICÓN DE CARNE

SERVES 4 TO 6

PREPARATION TIME: 25 minutes

COOKING TIME: 1 hour

MAKE AHEAD: The vinaigrette can be made up to 1 week ahead, covered, and refrigerated. The salad, without the lettuce and avocado, can be prepared a day ahead, covered, and refrigerated.

2   pounds flank steak, cut into 2-inch pieces

½ white onion

7   garlic cloves

2   bay leaves

Kosher or sea salt

¾ cup white wine vinegar

¾ cup extra-virgin olive oil

¾ cup canola or safflower oil

½ teaspoon freshly ground black pepper

1   teaspoon packed brown sugar

½ cup thinly sliced red onion

1   pound baby red potatoes, rinsed

3   medium carrots (about 8 ounces), peeled and sliced about ¼ inch thick on the diagonal (2 cups)

8   ounces green beans, trimmed and cut in half on the diagonal

1   cup fresh or thawed frozen peas

4   radishes, trimmed, halved, and sliced into half-moons

This salad makes a fabulous meal. Think of it as a Mexican version of a French Niçoise or a Thai beef salad. With its sweet/acidic/savory vinaigrette and spicy condiments, it actually has more in common with the Thai salad. *Salpicón* comes from the verb *salpicar*, which means to "splatter" or splash, because what you see on the platter or plate is such a mix, or splattering, of ingredients. In the Yucátan Peninsula, salpicón is made with venison; on the coast, fish rules; in central Mexico, where I grew up, beef is tops. You can eat this salad as-is or opt to serve some warm corn tortillas on the side and cobble together some salpicón tacos.

1. Place the meat in a large heavy pot and add the white onion, 5 of the garlic cloves, the bay leaves, and 1 tablespoon salt. Cover by at least 1 inch with water and bring to a boil over high heat. Reduce to the lowest possible heat, cover, and cook for 1 hour, or until the meat is so soft that it shreds easily when pulled apart with a fork.

2. Meanwhile, combine the vinegar, oils, the remaining 2 garlic cloves, 1 tablespoon salt, pepper, and sugar in a blender and puree until completely smooth. Pour into a jar, add the red onion, and shake well; set the vinaigrette aside.

3. Bring a medium saucepan of salted water to a boil. Add the potatoes, then reduce the heat to medium and, keeping the water at a steady, gentle boil, cook just until they are tender all the way through, about 20 minutes. Remove the potatoes with a slotted spoon and place in a bowl. (Keep the water in the saucepan at a gentle boil.) As soon as the potatoes are cool enough to handle, cut them in half, return them to the bowl, and toss with ½ cup of the vinaigrette so they will absorb the dressing while still warm.

4. Add the carrots to the boiling water and cook until barely cooked, less than 1 minute. Remove with the slotted spoon and place in another bowl. Add the green beans to the boiling water and cook until crisp-tender, about 3 minutes, then remove with the slotted spoon and add to the

carrots. Add the peas to the boiling water and cook for 20 to 30 seconds, until barely cooked through; remove with the slotted spoon and add to the green beans and carrots. Add the radishes to the bowl, along with ½ cup of the vinaigrette, and toss together.

5. When the meat is done, drain it and discard the cooking liquid. Once the meat is cool enough to handle, shred it and place in a bowl.

6. Shake the vinaigrette again and add ½ cup to the meat, along with the macerated red onions, and toss together.

7. When ready to serve, place the lettuce in a salad bowl. Shake the vinaigrette again and toss the lettuce well with about ¼ cup of it. Arrange the dressed potatoes and vegetables on top, then the meat. Taste for salt and add more if desired. Garnish with the avocado, cilantro, and pickled jalapeños. Serve, with tortillas if you like.

1 head romaine lettuce, sliced crosswise into 1-inch-wide strips

FOR GARNISH

1 ripe Hass avocado, halved, pitted, flesh scooped out and sliced

2 tablespoons chopped fresh cilantro

Sliced store-bought pickled jalapeños (I use at least 1 whole chile per person)

Corn tortillas, warmed (optional)

CHICKEN FAJITA SALAD

ENSALADA DE FAJITA DE POLLO

SERVES 4 TO 6

PREPARATION TIME: 20 minutes

COOKING TIME: 25 minutes

MAKE AHEAD: The chicken can be marinated for up to 12 hours, covered, and refrigerated. The vinaigrette can be made up to 5 days ahead, covered, and refrigerated.

2 pounds skinless, boneless chicken breasts

½ teaspoon ground cumin

1 teaspoon ancho or chipotle chile powder (see page 65)

¼ cup plus 2 tablespoons olive oil

¼ cup freshly squeezed lime juice

2 garlic cloves, minced or pressed

¼ cup sauce from canned chipotles in adobo

Kosher or sea salt and freshly ground black pepper

½ red onion, slivered or thinly sliced (about 1 cup)

1 red bell pepper, cored, seeded, and cut into thin strips (about 2 cups)

1 yellow bell pepper, cored, seeded, and cut into thin strips (about 2 cups)

½ cup freshly squeezed orange juice

2 teaspoons unseasoned rice vinegar

Fajitas are one of those bicultural, cross-border, identity-confused dishes like nachos, wraps, and chimichangas. Did they originate north or south of the border? Was the first person to make fajitas a Mexican, a Mexican American, or an American making "Mexican" food? Purists claim that fajitas are an American invention that has nothing to do with Mexico. Yet many Mexicans who live across the border in the United States assert that fajitas are in fact authentic Mexican food, that they were made by their grandmother or their closest *tía* (aunt).

Wherever their origins, fajitas can now be found in Mexico as well (but without the sour cream and shredded cheddar, for sure). Their appeal is universal. This is my very Mex take on the Tex-Mex classic. Instead of wrapping the fajita mixture in tortillas, I serve it as a salad and sprinkle crispy tortilla strips on top. Once you make this salad, you will see why I call it a fajita fiesta. It has so many delicious elements, you may have trouble deciding which part you want to eat first.

. . . .

1. Place the chicken in a container or baking dish. In a medium bowl, combine the cumin, chile powder, 2 tablespoons of the oil, the lime juice, garlic, 2 tablespoons of the adobo sauce, ½ teaspoon salt, and pepper to taste. Whisk together well and pour over the chicken. Turn the chicken over a few times to ensure that it is entirely covered. Let marinate for at least 30 minutes, or for up to 12 hours (if for more than 30 minutes, cover and refrigerate).

2. Heat 1 tablespoon of the oil in a large skillet over medium-high heat. Remove the chicken from the marinade, reserving the marinade, and sear for 3 to 4 minutes, until browned and lightly charred. Reduce the heat to medium, flip the chicken breasts over, and pour 1 cup of the reserved marinade over them. Cover and cook for 12 to 15 minutes, until the chicken is cooked through but still moist and tender. Transfer to a cutting board. If there are any juices left in the pan, spoon them on top of the chicken. Cover loosely with foil and let rest for at least 5 minutes, then slice the chicken into ½- to ¾-inch-wide strips.

3. Clean and dry the skillet, set it over medium-high heat, and add 1 tablespoon of the oil. When the oil is hot, add the onion and bell peppers, season with a bit of salt, and cook, stirring often, for 3 to 4 minutes, until lightly browned and slightly softened. Remove from the heat.

4. In a large salad bowl, combine the remaining 2 tablespoons oil, the orange juice, rice vinegar, white vinegar, and the remaining 2 tablespoons adobo sauce. Season with ¼ teaspoon salt and pepper to taste and whisk well; taste for salt and add more if desired. Add the lettuce, beans, and tomato and toss to coat. Top the salad with the grilled chicken, onion, and peppers and garnish with the avocado, scallions, queso fresco, and tortilla strips.

VARIATION: You can also grill the chicken and vegetables, either on an outdoor grill or in a grill pan. Brush the grill or pan with oil and grill the chicken (discard the marinade) over medium-high heat for about 5 minutes per side. Grill the peppers and onion in a grilling basket until softened and lightly charred.

2 teaspoons distilled white vinegar

1 head romaine lettuce, thinly sliced

1½ cups Basic Black Beans (page 244) or 1 (14-ounce) can black beans, drained and rinsed

1 ripe tomato, seeded and diced

1 large ripe Hass avocado, halved, pitted, flesh scooped out and diced

3 scallions (white and light green parts only), thinly sliced

¾ cup crumbled queso fresco

1½ cups corn tortilla strips, homemade (page 25) or store-bought, for garnish

RICE VINEGAR

Unseasoned (or natural) rice vinegar is one of the ingredients I gravitate toward when I make vinaigrettes. I use it because its sweet, mildly fruity flavor is the closest substitute for the homemade fruit vinegars of the Mexican countryside. These fruit-based vinegars, usually made by fermenting pineapple (or other fruits)—rinds, fruit, and pulp—in lightly sweetened water, have a mild acidity and a mellow sweetness. But they are not sold in stores. Don't confuse unseasoned rice vinegar with seasoned rice vinegar, which is salted and sweetened and used for flavoring sushi rice. If you cannot find unseasoned rice vinegar, substitute apple cider vinegar.

MORELIA-STYLE SAVORY FRUIT SALAD

GAZPACHO MORELIANO

PREPARATION TIME: 20 minutes

MAKE AHEAD: The gazpacho can be made a few hours ahead, covered, and refrigerated.

- 2 cups peeled, diced ripe mangoes (2 Champagne mangoes)
- 2 cups peeled, cored, and diced pineapple
- 2 cups peeled, diced jicama (1 small to medium)
- ¼ cup plus 2 tablespoons finely chopped white onion
- ¾ cup finely crumbled Cotija, queso fresco, or mild feta cheese
- 3 cups freshly squeezed orange juice
- ¼ cup plus 2 tablespoons freshly squeezed lime juice
- Kosher or sea salt
- Chile piquín or Mexican chile powder

Gazpacho moreliano (also spelled "gaspacho") is a very popular dish from Morelia, the capital of the central Mexican state of Michoacán. There is feverish debate about who invented the dish, and should you find yourself in the *zócalo* (the main plaza), you will see many a beautiful courtyard restaurant and stand claiming to be the home of the "Original Gazpacho." I am quite certain that the person who invented this fruit salad is a man by the name of El Güero, but the problem is that there are now a number of descendants of the original El Güero in the *zócalo*, and they all boast having the "original" recipe. I always go to the same Güero, and this recipe is based on his.

Despite the name, this is not a chilled soup in the style of Spain; the name seems to have come from the fact that, like Spanish gazpacho, it is made with raw ingredients, including onion—the only ingredient it has in common with Old World gazpacho. It is decidedly a salad like no other, a fruit salad with a savory side, and quite addictive. You can serve it in individual cups or in a large bowl.

Note: Traditional gazpacho Moreliano is made with mango, pineapple, and jicama, but other fruits and vegetables may also be used.

Place one third of the mangoes, pineapple, and jicama in a large bowl. Add one third of the onion and one third of the queso, followed by one third each of the orange and lime juices. Season with salt and chile to taste. Repeat with two more layers. Finish with a sprinkle of salt and chile powder to taste. Serve chilled or at room temperature.

MEXICAN COOK'S TIPS

- This dish is so good you may want to go ahead and dice the entire pineapple, to have more handy for a second round.
- I like to use Champagne mangoes, the type they use in Michoacán. Called *mango manila* in most regions of Mexico, these mangoes are meaty, soft, and very sweet. If you can't find them, Kent mangoes are also great. But any mango, as long as it's ripe and sweet, will do.

GROUND DRIED CHILES

Dried chiles, just like fresh chiles, have different flavors and personalities. It's good to know these flavors and characteristics to better understand their impact on the dishes they are used in. Usually if a specific dried chile powder is called for in a recipe, there is a reason, but that doesn't mean you can't substitute one chile powder for another if you find that you only have one type on hand. Explore and get to know dried chiles, and play around with them in different dishes so that you can decide what you prefer to use, and also what you can get away with when your choices are limited.

These are the chiles you are most likely to find ground in the U.S.

- Chipotle chiles (smoke-dried jalapeños) are smoky, rustic, and spicy.

- Ancho chiles (dried poblanos) are mildly spicy and bittersweet, leaning more toward the sweet, with overtones of prunes and chocolate.
- Pasilla chiles are beautifully bitter, dark, and rich.
- Guajillos are mild, peppy, and happy, always a crowd-pleaser.
- Chiles de árbol are spicy and intense, with a toasted flavor.
- Piquín chiles, tiny and pebble-shaped, dry to a deep burnt red and make a spicy, feisty, chile powder that is a favorite for sprinkling on fresh fruits and vegetables, street-cart style, with freshly squeezed lime juice and salt.

TORTAS, SANDWICHES, HAMBURGERS, AND HOT DOGS

WHEN YOU THINK OF MEXICAN FOOD, *tortas*—sandwiches—may not immediately come to mind, but they are huge in Mexico, right up there with tacos and enchiladas. On our way to family weekends in the country, my dad would always stop to pick up all sorts of deli meats, Mexican cheeses, pickled chiles, ripe avocados, and fresh bread. Then we'd be impatient to arrive, because we knew what was coming. There was no need to tell him what we wanted in our tortas—he knew exactly what each of us liked, and we trusted him. To pay my dad back for all those great sandwiches, I came up with a torta especially for him (see page 70), filled with a sweet and savory combination of refried beans, plantains, and adobo-marinated chicken.

Tortas are not the only type of sandwich that we love in Mexico. Our street food also includes hamburgers and hot dogs. You didn't know? We adore them. In absolutely every *zócalo* ("downtown square") in every city, you will find among the taco stands at least one hot dog stand, and a hamburger stand as well. As teenagers, my sisters and I had such a weakness for bacon-wrapped hot dogs topped with onions, pickled jalapeños, tomatoes, and a special salsa (page 91) from a Mexico City stand that my father had to put his foot down and limit our visits to once a week, once he figured out why we were not hungry for my mother's dinners.

Newer types of sandwiches are also showing up in Mexico. We've developed a great fondness for the crusty, spongy Italian ciabatta, which we call *chapata*, both the bread and the sandwiches we make with it, and that inspired me to come up with a vegetarian chapata filled with grilled eggplant, zucchini, and poblanos doused with a cilantro vinaigrette and topped with queso fresco (page 78).

I can never resist playing with new ideas, or rather Mexicanizing old ones. Looking for something different for brunch? How about an open-faced gravlax sandwich (page 84) with a Mexican twist, the salmon cured with tequila instead of aquavit and seasoned with cilantro in place of dill? Need a knockout slider for your next cocktail party? Check out the barbacoa sliders on page 87. How about a burger made with chipotle-spiked pork and chorizo instead of beef (page 89)? Top it with the creamy avocado sauce, and you may never think about ketchup again.

Beyond the flavors and ingredients in these tortas and sandwiches, you will find them to be utterly Mexican in character because they are accommodating to no end. Serve them for lunch or for dinner, for snacks, or even for breakfast.

MEXICAN SANDWICH BREADS

Bolillos and teleras are right up there with tortillas when it comes to daily staples in the Mexican diet. Just as it is hard to find a small village, town, or city without its own tortillería, it is almost impossible to find one without a *panadería* (bakery).

A *panadería* begins its shifts long before the rooster has had its chance to crow at 3:00 or 4:00 in the morning; the mariachis haven't even finished their singing for the night. Its main products are bolillos and teleras, both descendants of the French baguette. Few things are as delicious a few minutes after they have been taken out of a smoldering-hot brick oven.

Like baguettes, bolillos and teleras are very crunchy and golden on the outside, but they are different in a few ways. They are rolls rather than long thin breads, ranging from 5 to 6 inches in length, and chubbier, either round or oval. Bolillos and teleras have a thinner crust and more soft bread inside than in baguettes. That bready interior is called *migajón*, and it is usually removed before assembling tortas (but most people don't discard it, they munch on it right after they remove it). Cooks also use *migajón* for bread crumbs or stuffings, or as an ingredient in *albóndigas*—meatballs—or meat loaf.

The difference between bolillos and teleras is just the shape. A telera is a bit flatter and

rounder than a bolillo and has two vertical lines running down its top, dividing the bread into thirds, which helps you cut it into pieces when you attempt to eat it. A bolillo has a fold down the middle and two knots at each end, which are tighter than the ends of a telera. I have found that the roll that I call a bolillo is called a Portuguese bun in many Latin grocery stores in the DC area.

To keep your Mexican bread (as the rolls are also called in some stores) fresh, store the rolls well sealed in a paper bag inside a closed plastic bag. If you know you are not going to eat all of the rolls within a couple of days, freeze them just as you would bagels.

Bolillos and teleras are used for so many things! They are cut and placed in a bread basket in restaurants and homes; they are dunked in coffee, hot chocolate, or atoles (masa based beverages) in the mornings; and, of course, they are used to make an infinite number of tortas. They are incredibly delicious spread with refried beans with cheese melted on top (*molletes*)— and make great bread crumbs and croutons. Can't find bolillos or teleras (or Portuguese buns)? You can substitute French rolls, baguettes cut into shorter lengths, or petite baguettes.

CRAZY TORTAS WITH CHICKEN, REFRIED BEANS, AND PLANTAINS

TORTAS LOCAS DE POLLO, FRIJOLES REFRITOS, Y PLÁTANO MACHO

MAKES 6 TORTAS

PREPARATION TIME: 15 minutes

COOKING TIME: 25 minutes

MAKE AHEAD: The chicken can be marinated for up to 2 days, covered and refrigerated.

- 6 boneless, skinless chicken thighs (about 1½ pounds)
- 2 teaspoons distilled white vinegar
- 2 tablespoons canola or safflower oil, plus additional for frying the plantains
- ¼ teaspoon ground cumin
- ¼ teaspoon ground canela (Ceylon cinnamon; see page 264)
- ¼ teaspoon ground allspice
- ¾ teaspoon kosher or sea salt or to taste
- ¼ teaspoon freshly ground black pepper
- 4 whole cloves, stems removed and discarded, tops crushed
- 2 very ripe plantains, peeled and sliced on the diagonal
- 1½ cups refried beans, homemade (page 247) or store-bought
- 6 bolillos, teleras, Portuguese rolls, or small baguettes or 2 or 3 baguettes, cut into 4- to 6-inch lengths, split in half

I make these tortas for my father to satisfy his taste for sweet and savory pairings. One of his favorite combinations is caramelized plantains with earthy mashed refried beans. I add chicken marinated in a light, flavorful adobo and baked until lightly browned but still moist, then tuck everything into a crunchy torta. Its flavors and textures will transport you to the Mexican Gulf Coast. No need to book a flight.

1. Place the chicken in a baking dish, making sure there is space between the thighs.

2. In a small bowl, combine the vinegar, oil, cumin, cinnamon, allspice, salt, pepper, and cloves and stir with a fork or whisk until thoroughly mixed. Pour over the chicken, and turn the chicken over a few times to make sure that each piece is well coated. You can marinate the chicken for up to 2 days in the refrigerator, or cook it immediately. Refrigerate if not cooking within 30 minutes.

3. Preheat the oven to 425 degrees.

4. If the chicken thighs have flattened out, tuck in the sides so that they look as if they were still on the bone. Roast for 25 minutes. Raise the oven temperature to 500 degrees and roast for another 5 minutes, or until the chicken has browned on the top and bottom and the meat is thoroughly cooked. Allow the meat to rest for a few minutes before you slice it.

5. Once they are cool enough to handle, slice each thigh across the grain into ½-inch-thick slices.

6. Heat about ½ inch of oil in a large skillet over medium to medium-high heat. Test the heat by adding a plantain slice; active bubbles should form around it at once, but there should not be any crazy foaming. Fry the plantain slices, in batches if necessary to avoid crowding the pan, until golden brown, lightly caramelized, and crisp on the outside,

2 to 3 minutes per side (fried ripe plantains will always be soft and mushy on the inside). Remove and drain on paper towels.

7. Heat the refried beans in a small skillet over medium heat.

8. If the bread rolls are not fresh, toast lightly. Spread 2 to 3 tablespoons refried beans on the bottom half of each roll, top with some sliced chicken, and finish with 4 or 5 plantain slices. Cover with the top halves of the rolls and cut in half.

HOW I PACK MY SANDWICHES

I love making food to go, whether it's something that my boys will need in eight hours or for a three-hour train ride that I will be taking later in the day. Whether a sandwich is cold or hot, I like to wrap it tightly in plastic wrap (if hot, right away). I then wrap a paper towel around a cold sandwich and into a paper bag it goes; the paper towel will double as a napkin. If the sandwich is hot, after wrapping tightly in plastic, I then wrap it tightly in aluminum foil to help keep it warm. The paper towel goes into the bag with the sandwich, folded and tucked beside it.

DIJON STEAK AND SWISS CHEESE TORTAS WITH MATADOR CHILES

TORTAS DE CARNE A LA MOSTAZA CON QUESO SUIZO Y CHILES TOREADOS

MAKES 6 TORTAS

PREPARATION TIME: 10 minutes

COOKING TIME: 20 minutes

MAKE AHEAD: The meat can be marinated for up to 24 hours, covered and refrigerated.

¼ cup olive oil

¼ cup soy sauce

3 tablespoons Dijon mustard

4 garlic cloves, pressed or minced

¼ teaspoon freshly ground black pepper or to taste

2 pounds flank steak

6 bolillos, teleras, Portuguese rolls, or small baguettes or 2 or 3 baguettes cut into 4- to 6-inch lengths, split in half

6 thick slices Swiss or Muenster cheese

Matador Chiles (page 110)

Who doesn't love a great steak sandwich? This hearty version is one of my boys' favorites. Simple to make, it packs a punch with the Dijon and garlic marinade, the strong cheese that melts into the bread, and the spicy, bright, salty, extra-hot, lime-soaked *chiles toreados* and their marinade.

1. In a small bowl, whisk together the oil, soy sauce, mustard, garlic, and pepper. Place the steak in a large baking dish and pour the marinade over it. Turn a few times to make sure that the meat is completely coated. Marinate for at least 30 minutes, and up to 24 hours. If marinating for more than 30 minutes, cover and refrigerate.

2. Preheat the broiler.

3. Place the baking dish with the meat under the broiler, 3 to 4 inches from the heat, and broil for 5 to 7 minutes per side, depending on how cooked you want it. For medium-rare, 5 minutes per side; for just over medium, the way I like it, 6 minutes on the first side and 7 minutes on the other. (Alternatively, you can grill the meat over medium-high heat on an outdoor grill or a grill pan for 5 to 6 minutes per side, depending on how well done you like it; I go for 6 minutes per side.) Transfer the meat to a cutting board, cover loosely with foil, and let rest for 5 minutes.

4. Thinly slice the meat against the grain.

5. Preheat the oven to 350 degrees. Place the split rolls on a baking sheet, cut side up, and place a slice of cheese on each bottom half. Bake until the bread crisps and the cheese melts, about 5 minutes.

6. Top the cheese with the meat and let diners spoon on as much of the Matador Chiles, along with their sauce and onions, as they want (or do it for them if you know their tastes). Cover the sandwiches with the top halves of the rolls and serve, with more Matador Chiles on the side.

POTATO AND CHORIZO TORTAS WITH QUICK PICKLED ONIONS

TORTAS DE PAPAS CON CHORIZO CON CEBOLLITAS ENCURTIDAS

MAKES 6 TO 8 TORTAS

PREPARATION TIME: 20 minutes

COOKING TIME: 20 minutes

MAKE AHEAD: The onion can be refrigerated, covered, for up to 5 days. The potato-chorizo mix can be prepared up to 3 days ahead, covered, and refrigerated; reheat gently before using. The tortas can be assembled up to 10 hours ahead and wrapped tightly.

1 cup very thinly sliced red onion, plus ½ cup chopped onion

2 tablespoons freshly squeezed lime juice

Kosher or sea salt

1 tablespoon olive oil

1 pound Red Bliss potatoes, rinsed and diced

8 ounces uncooked Mexican chorizo, casings removed and coarsely chopped

1 tablespoon canola or safflower oil if needed

6 to 8 bolillos, teleras, Portuguese rolls, or small baguettes or 3 or 4 baguettes cut into 4- to 6-inch lengths, split

1 or 2 ripe Hass avocados, halved, pitted, flesh scooped out and sliced

One of my favorite Mexican fillings, whether for tacos, quesadillas, enchiladas, tortas, or *antojitos* is *papas con chorizo,* a hearty mix of tender cooked potatoes and rich, highly seasoned Mexican chorizo, cooked until crisp and seasoned with softened onions or scallions. All this sandwich needs to complete it are a few slices of avocado and some crunchy, pungent pickled onions. You could also use the Pickled Onions and Cabbage on page 119.

1. Place the sliced onion in a bowl and cover with very cold water (add a few ice cubes if your water is not very cold). Leave for 10 to 15 minutes.

2. Drain the onions in a sieve. Add the lime juice and ½ teaspoon salt to the same bowl and stir. Stir in the olive oil, mixing well. Add the drained onion and toss to coat well, then let sit for 10 to 15 minutes. It may seem like there is very little vinaigrette for the onion, but after a few minutes, the onion will begin to wilt into the lime-oil mix (though it won't lose its crunch). If you won't use the onion within 30 minutes, cover and refrigerate. Taste for salt before using.

3. Fill a medium saucepan with salted water and bring to a boil over high heat. Add the potatoes, reduce the heat to medium, and simmer for 10 to 12 minutes, until tender. Drain.

4. Place the chorizo in a large skillet over medium-high heat. As the chorizo starts to cook, use a wooden spoon or spatula to crumble it into smaller pieces. Once it begins to brown and crisp, after 3 to 4 minutes, add the chopped onion and stir to combine; if the chorizo you are using is on the lean side and there is no fat in the pan, move it to the edges of the pan and add the canola or safflower oil to the middle of the pan, then add the onion. Cook, stirring often, until the onion is tender and the chorizo has browned and the edges are crisp, 3 to 4 minutes.

continued...

5. Add the potatoes and 1 teaspoon salt, and mash the potatoes into the chorizo mixture with a potato masher or the back of a wooden spoon. Then cook and mash together for about 1 minute, until well combined. Remove from the heat, taste, and add more salt, if desired.

6. Scoop about ½ cup of the potato and chorizo mix onto the bottom half of each roll. Add 2 or 3 slices of avocado and finish with some pickled onion. Top with the other half of the rolls.

TAMING ONIONS

Raw onion is delicious and pungent, but sometimes it can be a bit too much. To remove some of the edge, after you slice or chop it, put it in a bowl and cover with very cold water. If necessary, chill the water with ice cubes. Let the onion sit for 10 to 15 minutes, then drain well. This will mellow the onion, without masking its flavor or diminishing its crunch, so that it can mingle with other ingredients in a more eater-friendly way.

MEXICAN CHORIZO

Mexican chorizo typically comes in deep-burnt-red links of heavily seasoned and spiced fresh ground pork. It requires cooking before it can be eaten (unlike Spanish chorizo, which is dried and smoke-cured, and can be sliced and eaten without further cooking). When cooked, it becomes crispy. Most Mexican chorizo contains dried chiles and a mix of spices that may include oregano, cumin, thyme, marjoram, bay leaf, cinnamon, coriander seeds, allspice, paprika, achiote (see page 113), and/or cloves. There is usually garlic, sometimes onion, and always vinegar, which makes the meat flake as it browns and gives it a welcome hint of acidity.

You find vastly different flavors and characteristics in chorizo throughout Latin America. Mexican chorizo is the spiciest and most robust, with its complex layering of flavors. Salvadoran chorizo has a good depth of flavor but isn't as hot as the Mexican product. Honduran and Guatemalan chorizos tend to be even more sedate. Colombian is the saltiest, and Argentineans add wine and a heavy dose of garlic to the mix, which lets the flavor of the meat shine. By and large, Latin American chorizos made in their countries of origin tend to be fattier than those made and sold in the United States. These days you can find chorizo made with chicken, turkey, and beef in addition to pork; there are even vegan chorizos!

If you can't find a Latin chorizo, you can substitute any other raw seasoned sausage, such as Italian. If you want to get closer to the Mexican flavor, go for the spicy Italian.

STEAK AND GUACAMOLE TORTAS

PEPITOS

MAKES 6 TORTAS

PREPARATION TIME: 15 minutes

COOKING TIME: 20 minutes

MAKE AHEAD: These are best eaten hot.

- 1 (2-pound) flank steak
- 2 tablespoons freshly squeezed lime juice
- 2 tablespoons canola or safflower oil
- 3 garlic cloves, pressed or minced
- 1 teaspoon kosher or sea salt or to taste
- ¼ teaspoon freshly ground black pepper or to taste
- 6 bolillos, teleras, Portuguese rolls, or small baguettes or 2 baguettes, cut into 4- to 6-inch lengths, split
- 1 cup refried beans, homemade (page 247) or store-bought
- 6 ounces Oaxaca, asadero, Monterey Jack, mozzarella, or Muenster, grated (about 1½ cups)
- 1 recipe My Go-To Guacamole (page 115)

How did this scrumptious steak, guacamole, and grilled cheese sandwich on bread slathered with refried beans get its name? I wish I could tell you that a famous man whose nickname was Pepito invented it, but there is no record of that. What I do know is that these sandwiches, like the name Pepito, are very popular throughout Mexico.

You find them all over the country in coffee shops and at casual restaurant chains. Many times they come in pairs or trios, made on smaller rolls, which explains the name (Pepito is a diminutive of Pepe). Whenever we prepare Pepitos at home, we make them assembly-line style. First I slather the rolls with refried beans, top them with grated cheese, and bake them until the cheese melts and the rolls crisp, then I set them out next to the thinly sliced flank steak and guacamole. The boys add as much meat and guacamole as they can fit on top of their rolls, and dinner is ready.

1. Place the flank steak in a baking dish. In a small bowl, whisk together the lime juice, oil, garlic, salt, and pepper. Pour over the meat and turn the meat over a few times to coat. Make sure that the meat is thoroughly coated.

2. Preheat the broiler. Place the baking dish with the meat under the broiler, 3 to 4 inches from the heat, and broil the steak for 5 to 7 minutes per side, depending on how cooked you want it: For medium-rare, cook for 5 minutes per side; for just over medium, the way I like it, 6 minutes on the first side and 7 minutes on the other. (Alternatively, you can grill the steak over medium-high heat on an outdoor grill or a grill pan for 5 to 6 minutes per side, depending on how well done you like it; I go for 6 minutes per side.) Transfer the meat to a cutting board, cover loosely with foil, and let rest for 5 minutes.

3. Thinly slice the steak against the grain.

continued...

4. Preheat the oven to 350 degrees. Place the split rolls on a baking sheet. Spread about 3 tablespoons refried beans on each bottom half and top with 3 to 4 tablespoons cheese. Bake until the bread crisps and the cheese melts, about 5 minutes.

5. Top each bottom roll with a generous amount of meat and then 3 to 4 tablespoons of guacamole. Close the sandwiches and eat while hot.

CHOPPED EGG AND AVOCADO SANDWICHES

SANDWICHES DE AGUACATE CON HUEVO

MAKES 4 SANDWICHES

PREPARATION TIME: 15 minutes

COOKING TIME: 10 minutes

MAKE AHEAD: The egg salad can be made up to 1 day ahead, covered, and refrigerated.

3 hard-boiled eggs, chopped

3 tablespoons finely chopped red onion

2 tablespoons finely chopped parsley

2 teaspoons chopped fresh dill or ½ teaspoon dried dill

½ teaspoon Dijon mustard

2 teaspoons mayonnaise or to taste

2 teaspoons sauce from canned chipotles in adobo or to taste

1 large ripe Hass avocado, halved, pitted, flesh scooped out and diced

Kosher or sea salt and freshly ground black pepper

8 slices brioche, challah, or soft bread of your choice, lightly toasted

4 thick slices Oaxaca, Monterey Jack, or Muenster cheese

Sliced and seeded tomatoes (optional)

My paternal grandmother used to make chopped egg salad and a seasoned avocado mash, with slices of fluffy soft white bread on the side, as appetizers for family gatherings. We would always layer them both on our bread slices, so one day she decided to mix them together into one big salad with her own blend of spices. It was an instant family hit. I've played around with my grandmother's spice mix, and instead of serving it as a dainty appetizer, I make sandwiches filled with generous scoops of the robust egg and avocado salad and topped with cheese. The cheese is a caprice that I couldn't help adding, and I love how it tastes, but the egg and avocado salad makes a great sandwich without it.

1. In a medium bowl, mix together the eggs, onion, parsley, dill, mustard, mayonnaise, and chipotle sauce. Add the avocado, season with salt and pepper to taste, and gently mash and mix everything together.

2. Scoop a generous amount of the egg and avocado salad onto 4 of the toasted bread slices and spread evenly. Top with slices of cheese and tomatoes, if using, cover with the remaining slices of bread, and serve.

GRILLED EGGPLANT, ZUCCHINI, AND POBLANO CIABATTAS WITH QUESO FRESCO

CHAPATA DE VERDURAS AL CILANTRO CON QUESO FRESCO

MAKES 6 SANDWICHES

PREPARATION TIME: 15 minutes

COOKING TIME: 20 to 30 minutes

MAKE AHEAD: The vinaigrette can be made up to 5 days ahead, covered, and refrigerated.

1½ pounds zucchini (about 2 large), trimmed and sliced lengthwise about ¼ inch thick

1½ pounds eggplant (about 1 large), trimmed and sliced lengthwise about ¼ inch thick

¼ cup olive oil, plus more for cooking the vegetables

Kosher or sea salt and freshly ground black pepper

1 cup tightly packed fresh cilantro leaves and upper stems, coarsely chopped

¼ cup canola or safflower oil

¼ cup red wine vinegar

2 garlic cloves

½ teaspoon packed dark brown sugar

1 pound poblano chiles (3 or 4) roasted, peeled, seeded, and sliced into strips (see page 21)

6 ciabatta, sourdough, or other crusty rolls

1½ cups crumbled queso fresco, mild feta, or farmer's cheese (6 ounces)

This vegetarian sandwich has a lot of personality. When I was a young teen in Mexico City, the cool torta to have was a chapata made on Italian ciabatta bread. I don't know how ciabatta found a fast ticket to Mexico, but once it arrived, it spread like wildfire in the city. The slightly sour, hard-crusted rolls are perfect for this mix of roasted vegetables bathed in a slightly acidic cilantro vinaigrette, as the spongy interior of the bread soaks up the flavorful dressing but the sandwiches don't become soggy, because of the hard crust. The slightly salty queso fresco that tops the vegetables balances all the flavors.

1. Brush the zucchini and eggplant slices with olive oil. Season with ½ teaspoon salt, or to taste, and pepper to taste.

2. If grilling, prepare a medium fire in an outdoor grill, heat to medium, and brush the grates with olive oil. Or heat a grill pan over medium-high heat and brush with oil. Grill the zucchini and eggplant slices for 15 to 20 minutes, flipping halfway through, until fully cooked, tender, and a bit charred on the outside. Allow to cool slightly.

3. Alternatively, if roasting in the oven, preheat the oven to 450 degrees, with the racks in the lower and upper thirds. Brush two baking sheets with olive oil and place the eggplant slices on one and the zucchini on the other; do not crowd the pans (you may have to do this in batches). Roast, switching the pans from top to bottom and front to back halfway through, for 25 to 30 minutes, until the vegetables are completely cooked, tender, and slightly charred or starting to brown. The eggplant may take 3 to 5 minutes longer than the zucchini, as you want it to be soft and thoroughly cooked. Allow the vegetables to cool for a few minutes.

4. In a blender, combine the cilantro, remaining ¼ cup olive oil, canola or safflower oil, vinegar, garlic, brown sugar, and 1 teaspoon salt and puree until smooth. Pour the vinaigrette into a large bowl. Add the eggplant and zucchini and the poblano strips and gently toss together.

Let the vegetables sit for at least 5 minutes and up to 30 minutes before assembling the ciabattas.

5. Split the rolls in half and toast them lightly. Place a generous amount of the dressed vegetables on the bottom halves and top each with ¼ cup of cheese. Put the top halves of the ciabatta rolls on top, press together, and serve.

SHRIMP, MANGO, AND AVOCADO ROLLS

ROLLOS DE CAMARONES AL AJILLO, MANGO, Y AGUACATE

MAKES 6 ROLLS

PREPARATION TIME: 20 minutes

COOKING TIME: 15 minutes

MAKE AHEAD: These should be served right away.

12 bacon slices

¼ cup finely chopped shallot

2 garlic cloves, finely chopped

1 tablespoon plus 1 teaspoon sherry vinegar

½ teaspoon honey

½ teaspoon Dijon mustard

Kosher or sea salt and freshly ground black pepper

2 large ripe Hass avocados, halved, pitted, flesh scooped out and diced

2 large ripe Champagne or Kent mangoes, peeled, sliced off the pits, and diced

1 tablespoon olive oil

1 tablespoon unsalted butter

1½ pounds fresh or thawed frozen medium shrimp, shells and tails removed

6 hot dog buns or soft rolls

If I ever open a restaurant, this will be one of the top items on my menu—a shrimp roll on a soft bun, with bacon, sweet-tart chunks of mango, and creamy bites of avocado tossed in a thick, smoky vinaigrette made with a judicious amount of garlic and shallot fried in the rendered bacon fat. The combination of mango and avocado has to be one of the best-kept secrets in the culinary world.

1. Heat a large skillet over medium heat. Add the bacon and cook for 3 to 4 minutes per side, until browned and crisp. Transfer the bacon to a paper towel–lined plate, leaving the fat in the skillet, and set aside.

2. Return the pan with the fat to medium heat, add the shallot and garlic and cook for about 2 minutes, until fragrant, tender, and just beginning to brown. Scrape the garlic and shallot into a medium heatproof bowl, along with the fat. Don't wash the pan; just set it aside.

3. To prepare the vinaigrette: Add the vinegar, honey, mustard, ½ teaspoon salt, and pepper to taste to the bowl with the garlic and shallot. Whisk or mix with a fork until well emulsified. Add the avocados and mangoes, gently toss together, and set aside.

4. Heat the oil and butter over high heat in the skillet you used for the bacon until the oil is hot but not smoking and the butter has begun to foam. Add the shrimp, without crowding the pan (cook them in two batches if necessary). Season with ½ teaspoon salt and pepper to taste, and cook, flipping them over once, until seared and browned, no more than 2 minutes. Transfer to a bowl.

5. Open the buns or rolls, trying not to separate the tops from the bottoms, and arrange a layer of cooked shrimp on the bottom of each one. Top the shrimp with the avocado and mango mix and crown each with a couple of slices of bacon. Close the sandwiches and serve.

CHIPOTLE SALMON, BACON, AND AVOCADO SANDWICHES

SANDWICHES DE SALMON, TOCINO, Y AGUACATE

MAKES 6 SANDWICHES

PREPARATION TIME: 20 minutes

COOKING TIME: 20 minutes

MAKE AHEAD: The salmon can be marinated for up to 12 hours, covered and refrigerated. The vinaigrette can be made up to 2 days ahead, mixed with the red onion but not the baby lettuces, covered, and refrigerated.

¼ cup freshly squeezed lime juice

¼ cup plus 1 tablespoon extra-virgin olive oil, plus more for the baking dish

¼ teaspoon Dijon mustard

½ teaspoon agave syrup, maple syrup, or honey

Kosher or sea salt and freshly ground black pepper

¼ cup slivered or thinly sliced red onion

3 tablespoons sauce from canned chipotles in adobo

3 garlic cloves, minced or pressed

½ teaspoon ground cumin

3 (8-ounce) salmon fillets

12 bacon slices

3 cups baby greens

12 slices multigrain or whole wheat sandwich bread

2 ripe Hass avocados, halved, pitted, flesh scooped out and sliced

I have three kids with very different tastes, so when I make something that all three devour and ask me to make again, I know that I have a winning recipe. This is one, a dinner sandwich with salmon marinated in a not too spicy chipotle sauce, quickly baked until tender and moist, and topped with wilted greens and crisp onion dressed in a flavorful agave syrup, lime, and Dijon vinaigrette. There's also bacon (no wonder my kids like it so much!), crisp and smoky, and creamy, ripe avocado slices that balance out all the strong flavors. The sandwich makes a filling meal, but if you have room for a side, try Sami's Smashed Potatoes (page 249).

1. Preheat the oven to 400 degrees.

2. To make the vinaigrette: In a medium bowl, whisk together 2 tablespoons of the lime juice, 3 tablespoons of the oil, the mustard, agave syrup, ¼ teaspoon salt, and ¼ teaspoon pepper. Add the onion, toss together, and let sit for at least 5 minutes. (You can do this a couple of days ahead, cover, and refrigerate.)

3. To make the marinade: In a medium bowl, whisk together the remaining 2 tablespoons lime juice, the remaining 2 tablespoons oil, the adobo sauce, garlic, cumin, ¼ teaspoon salt, and ¼ teaspoon pepper.

4. Brush a baking dish with oil. Place the salmon skin side down in the dish and pour the marinade over it, spreading it evenly over the fish. Bake for 12 to 15 minutes, depending on the thickness of the fish, until the salmon is cooked through yet still very moist. Remove from the oven and cut each fillet into 2 equal pieces.

5. Heat a large skillet or grill pan over medium heat. Add the bacon and cook for 3 to 4 minutes per side, until crisp and browned. Transfer to a plate lined with a paper towel. When cool enough to handle, break each slice in half.

6. When ready to make the sandwiches, whisk or stir the vinaigrette until well mixed and emulsified. Add the baby greens and toss well. Taste for salt and add more if desired.

7. Toast the bread. Place a piece of salmon on 6 of the slices, breaking the fish up a little, and top with 2 pieces of bacon, some dressed baby greens, and 2 or 3 avocado slices. Top with the other slices of bread and serve.

OPEN-FACED MEXICAN GRAVLAX SANDWICHES

SANDWICHES ABIERTOS CON GRAVLAX ESTILO MEXICANO

MAKES 8 OPEN-FACED SANDWICHES

PREPARATION TIME: 15 minutes plus 2 days marinating time

MAKE AHEAD: The gravlax needs to be started at least 2 days ahead. It will keep, covered, in the refrigerator for up to 2 weeks. The avocado crema can be made up to 12 hours ahead, covered, and refrigerated.

FOR THE GRAVLAX

2 teaspoons chipotle chile powder (see page 65)

1 teaspoon ground cumin

3 tablespoons kosher or sea salt

3 tablespoons packed dark brown sugar or grated piloncillo (see page 86)

1 tablespoon freshly ground black pepper

1½ cups fresh cilantro leaves and upper part of stems, finely chopped

Grated zest of 1 lime

1 (1-pound) skin-on fresh salmon fillet, any pin bones removed

2 tablespoons silver tequila

FOR THE AVOCADO CREMA

1 cup Mexican crema, crème fraîche, or sour cream

I serve these open-faced sandwiches as a light dinner or for brunch, usually with a potato salad (page 54) or cilantro potatoes (page 250) on the side and a fruit salad (page 64) to start or end the meal. You could also make the sandwiches on smaller pieces of bread for appetizer bites.

All you need to make the gravlax is very fresh salmon fillet, some seasonings, a couple of baking dishes, and 2 days for the salmon to cure. No cooking required!

I've put a Mexican spin on this Scandinavian dish, substituting intense silver tequila for the traditional aquavit and a mix of cilantro, cumin, ground chipotle chile, sea salt, and dark brown sugar for the traditional cure of sugar, salt, and dill. The tangy, slightly salty puree of Mexican crema and avocado, seasoned with lime, is the perfect sauce.

. . . .

1. To make the gravlax: Combine the chipotle powder, cumin, salt, brown sugar or piloncillo, pepper, cilantro, and lime zest in a small bowl. Lay the salmon skin side up in a large glass or ceramic baking dish. Using a sharp knife, make 10 to 12 slashes, about 1 inch long, in the skin, just deep enough to reach the flesh. Rub one third of the salt mixture over the skin and into the slashes. Flip the fish over, spoon the tequila over the fish, and rub in the rest of the salt mixture. Place a large sheet of plastic wrap directly on the surface of the fish. Place a slightly smaller baking dish on top of the fish and weight it down with heavy cans; use as many as will fit in the top baking dish.

2. Refrigerate the salmon for at least 2 days, basting it with the juices in the baking dish each night and re-covering and weighting again.

3. To make the crema: Combine the cream, avocado, lime zest and juice, and salt and pepper to taste in a blender and puree until smooth. Transfer to a bowl, cover, and refrigerate until ready to serve.

continued...

1 ripe Hass avocado, halved, pitted, flesh scooped out and finely chopped

¼ teaspoon grated lime zest

2 tablespoons freshly squeezed lime juice

Kosher or sea salt and freshly ground black pepper

8 slices black bread, rye, pumpernickel, or other dark bread of your choice, toasted

4 to 6 scallions (white and light green parts only), thinly sliced, for garnish (optional)

4. To serve: Thinly slice the salmon, cutting it on the diagonal (take care not to cut through the skin). Arrange the slices on a cold platter. Serve with the avocado crema, toasts, and scallions, if you like, and have diners assemble their own open-faced sandwich. Or assemble the sandwiches yourself and serve.

PILONCILLO

Piloncillo is cane sugar in its most unrefined form. The freshly pressed cane juice is poured into molds and left to dry and solidify. Piloncillo typically comes in blocks, either cone-shaped, square, or round. Brown sugar can be substituted; however, piloncillo is more rustic, with a slightly acidic tang, similar to agave syrup, and a dark amber color. When I taste it, I think of foods I've eaten in small villages or pueblos, far away from big cities. It adds an extra *no se qué,* that "I don't know what," that makes a dish stand out.

The easiest way to use piloncillo is to grate it on the large holes of a grater; the small holes are too troublesome, as it is rather hard. You can also dissolve it by placing it in a small saucepan with a couple of tablespoons of water, covering, and heating over low heat. It also dissolves when added to hot liquids.

BARBACOA SLIDERS

BOCADOS DE BARBACOA

MAKES 24 SLIDERS

PREPARATION TIME: 10 minutes

COOKING TIME: 2½ to 3 hours

MAKE AHEAD: The meat can be marinated for up to 48 hours, covered and refrigerated.

4 pounds beef round roast or brisket, cut into 4-inch chunks

1 recipe Barbacoa Adobo (page 111)

1 pound banana leaves, or aluminum foil

1 (12-ounce) bottle light beer

24 small slider buns (brioche or challah buns are especially good with this)

Drunken Prune Salsa with Pasillas and Orange (page 105)

Pickled Onions and Cabbage (page 119) and/or store-bought pickled jalapeños (optional)

Barbacoa, which resembles American barbecue in name only, is one of those iconic Mexican foods that many people have heard of but few outside of Mexico have tried. In Mexico, the meat, wrapped tightly in banana leaves (see page 88), is cooked for many hours in an underground clay-sealed brick-walled pit over smoldering rocks set over burning wood, then steamed and slowly cooked overnight.

Of course that is not what I do when I make barbacoa at home, but my meat, infused with a rustic, smoky flavor and a tropical fragrance, is still juicy and falling-off-the-bone tender. The key here is the amazing barbacoa adobo marinade, an intense sauce made with dried chiles, cider vinegar, and spices that you marinate the meat in before slow-roasting it in foil packets or banana leaves in the oven.

This barbacoa is inspired by the beef barbacoa typical of the central Mexican state of Michoacán. In other parts of Mexico, lamb or goat are more traditional. Tuck it into brioche or soft buns along with store-bought pickled jalapeños and/or pickled cabbage and red onion, and to make them stellar, add a spoonful of drunken salsa. The sliders are gorgeous on a party-table spread, and they can also serve as hearty appetizers. Or use regular-size buns for a meal that will serve eight. You can also feel free to use the meat for tacos, or serve it with white rice (page 241).

1. Place the beef in a large bowl and cover it with the adobo marinade. Marinate for at least 30 minutes or for up to 48 hours. If marinating for longer than 30 minutes, cover and place in the refrigerator.

2. Preheat the oven to 350 degrees.

3. Wrap the individual meat chunks in pieces of banana leaf or aluminum foil, as you would wrap burritos or tamales, making sure to include a generous amount of marinade in each packet.

4. Place the packets in a large heavy ovenproof Dutch oven or casserole, pour in the beer, and cover with a tight-fitting lid. (Alternatively, you

continued...

can use a roasting pan and seal it with aluminum foil.) Roast for about 3 hours, until the meat is succulent and comes apart when pulled with a fork. Remove from the oven and let rest for 10 to 15 minutes before opening the packets. Shred with forks or with your fingers.

5. Serve the barbacoa on the slider buns, with the salsa, pickled onions and cabbage, and pickled jalapeños, if desired.

BANANA LEAVES

I recommend that you seek out banana leaves for your bar-bacoa. They infuse the meat with a grassy, intensely aromatic, tropical flavor. These long, beautiful deep-green leaves were difficult to find when I first moved to the United States, but now you see them in many supermarkets and Latin and ethnic grocery stores, usually in the frozen vegetable section. They are used in Mexican cooking to wrap and cook many kinds of foods, including tamales, meats, fish, and poultry. They are malleable and sturdy, and cooking in them both concentrates the flavors of the wrapped foods and infuses the foods with their own flavor.

PORK AND CHORIZO BURGERS WITH AVOCADO CREMA

HAMBURGUESAS DE CERDO Y CHORIZO CON CREMA DE AGUACATE

MAKES 8 BURGERS

PREPARATION TIME: 20 minutes

COOKING TIME: 15 minutes

MAKE AHEAD: The meat can be seasoned and mixed up to 1 day ahead, covered, and refrigerated.

2 pounds lean ground pork

1 pound uncooked Mexican chorizo, casings removed, finely chopped

3 tablespoons finely chopped white onion

1 tablespoon sauce from canned chipotles in adobo or to taste

1 teaspoon dried oregano, preferably Mexican

Kosher or sea salt

¼ teaspoon freshly ground black pepper

2 ripe Hass avocados, halved, pitted, flesh scooped out and cut into chunks

¼ cup mayonnaise

¼ cup freshly squeezed lime juice

3 tablespoons coarsely chopped fresh chives

Canola or safflower oil for the grill or skillet

8 slices asadero, Monterey Jack, Muenster, or Chihuahua cheese (optional)

8 large brioche or hamburger buns, split

It was my friend Tamara's birthday party. Her husband, Sean, an American who speaks and acts like a Mexico City native (as a native myself, I would know), had made different types of hamburgers for the dinner for the forty-plus guests. When he saw me walk in, he gave me a plate of chipotle-pork sliders topped with a layer of melted cheese and said, "You are going to like these." I didn't even try the other sliders. All I wanted were these.

Later that weekend I made them, adding onion, oregano, and plenty of chorizo to the meat mix. I served them on brioche buns (you could also use hamburger rolls) with a thick avocado spread embellished with chives.

Although pork, chorizo, and chipotle are heavenly together, spicy Italian sausage will do, or, if you don't eat pork, you can mix ground turkey with turkey chorizo. If you want the burgers really spicy, chop up a couple of chipotle chiles in adobo and add them to the mix.

1. In a large bowl, mix the pork with the chorizo, onion, adobo sauce, oregano, 1 teaspoon salt, and the pepper until well combined. Moisten your hands and form the meat into 8 patties, about ¾ inch thick. Place them on a baking sheet or platter.

2. Prepare a medium-hot fire in an outdoor grill, or heat a grill pan or large heavy skillet over medium heat.

3. In a medium bowl, mash the avocados with a fork until smooth. Stir in the mayonnaise, lime juice, chives, and ½ teaspoon salt. Blend well and set aside.

4. Once the grill, grill pan, or skillet is hot, brush lightly with oil (the chorizo in the burgers will quickly release its seasoned fat). Place the patties on the grill or pan and cook for 5 minutes. Flip the patties and,

continued...

if adding cheese, place a slice on each patty. Cook for another 3 to 4 minutes for medium, or 5 to 6 minutes for medium-well.

5. Meanwhile, a couple of minutes before the burgers are ready, place the split buns on the cooler part of the grill (or in a 325-degree oven or toaster oven) and let them warm up for just a minute, until they barely begin to toast.

6. Place a patty on the bottom half of each bun, spoon on a generous amount of avocado crema, and top with the other half of the bun. Eat the burgers while hot!

MEXICAN CHEESES

Panela: In Mexico, this cheese is often used by cooks who want low-fat or healthier options. That doesn't mean it isn't irresistible! It is moist and fresh, mild, and very mellow, but its texture is very firm and it can be cut into thick slices, broken into smaller pieces easily, or grated for *antojos* (snacks). Panela is used in sandwiches, tortas, and quesadillas, and it's fabulous for grilling because it doesn't melt or string with the heat; instead, it develops a lovely crust. One of my favorite ways to use panela is to grill it and cover it with salsa verde. Unfortunately, I have found no good substitute for panela in the United States.

Melting Cheeses

I use these cheeses for both tortas that require melting cheeses and tortas that do not. Their flavors are different, but they are usually interchangeable in recipes.

- **Asadero:** A creamy, slightly buttery, very good melting cheese. Asadero is popular for quesadillas, dips, and *queso derretido*, or melted cheese. It's also used for sandwiches and tortas. Monterey Jack is a good stand-in.
- **Oaxaca:** This tastes very similar to mozzarella, though it is a bit more salty when fresh and it has a slightly different shape. Though they are both "rope" cheeses, mozzarella is pulled into a ball, while Oaxaca is wound into a tight knot. It tends to be stringier and pulls apart into much thinner strings than mozzarella. It has a mellow flavor and is easy to shred.
- **Mexican Manchego:** A multipurpose cheese that has a stronger flavor and richer mouthfeel than asadero and Oaxaca. It sometimes has tiny holes throughout. It is a phenomenal melting cheese, and it melts fast. It can also be grated. It is hard to find in the U.S.
- **Chihuahua:** This is a strong cheese like Mexican Manchego, but it is less nutty tasting. It is a good melting cheese and can also be grated. Muenster is a good substitute.

MEXICAN DREAMBOAT HOT DOGS

HOT DOGS DEL GALÁN

MAKES 6 TO 8 HOT DOGS

PREPARATION TIME: 15 minutes

COOKING TIME: 15 minutes

MAKE AHEAD: These should be served right away.

6 to 8 bacon slices

6 to 8 turkey hot dogs

2 tablespoons canola or safflower oil

1 white onion, chopped

1 tomato, seeded and chopped

¼ cup chopped store-bought pickled jalapeños or to taste

1 cup ketchup

¼ cup yellow mustard

6 to 8 hot dog buns

6 to 8 thick slices cheddar cheese

Some aficionados complain about Mexican food being Americanized in the United States, but it also works in reverse, and I have never been one to complain about it. Especially when it comes to the incredible hot dogs my three older sisters and I used to eat at the El Galán hot dog stand in Mexico City. As soon as my oldest sister could drive, we would stop at this stand on our way back from school every day to eat one, or why not two, or even three hot dogs *con todo* ("with all the trimmings").

El Galán, a dreamboat (*el galán* means a "very handsome man"—a hunk), would drizzle some oil on his hot *plancha* (griddle) and throw on some chopped white onions, store-bought pickled jalapeños, and tomatoes. Then, as they sizzled, he'd squirt on some yellow mustard and ketchup with a secret sweet ingredient (we later found out that it was orange soda!) and mix everything up. Onto that delicious mess, he threw a slice of cheddar and once it melted, he piled everything onto a soft bun and topped it with a steaming hot dog. If you wanted your hot dog *extra especial*, a couple of crispy bacon slices would also show up at the party.

1. On a cutting board, roll one slice of bacon around each hot dog. Place the tip of the hot dog over one end of the bacon slice, then roll the sausage around and around on the diagonal so that the bacon wraps around it and covers it entirely. If you get to the end of the hot dog and there is still some bacon left, roll back in the other direction until the whole strip of bacon is rolled around the hot dog.

2. Heat a large skillet over medium heat. Add the bacon-wrapped hot dogs and cook, turning every 2 to 3 minutes, until crisped and browned on all sides. Remove from the heat.

3. To make the *salsa especial*, heat the oil in a medium skillet over medium heat. Add the onion and cook, stirring occasionally, until it is tender and the edges are beginning to brown, 5 to 6 minutes. Stir in the tomato and

continued...

HOT DOGS WITH CHICHARRÓN, AVOCADO, AND QUESO FRESCO (left); MEXICAN DREAMBOAT HOT DOGS (right)

cook for another minute or so, until the tomato has softened a bit. Stir in the jalapeños, ketchup, and mustard and cook just until heated through, about 1 minute. Remove from the heat.

4. Preheat the oven or a toaster oven to 350 degrees.

5. Open the buns but try not to separate the tops from the bottoms. Top the bottom or both halves (to taste) with cheese (break up the cheese if desired) and place on a baking sheet. Bake for 2 to 3 minutes, until the cheese has melted and the buns are lightly toasted.

6. Place a bacon-wrapped hot dog on the bottom half of each bun and top with a generous amount of *salsa especial*. Cover with the top halves and serve right away.

HOT DOGS WITH CHICHARRÓN, AVOCADO, AND QUESO FRESCO

HOT DOGS DEL MERCADO

MAKES 6 TO 8 HOT DOGS

PREPARATION TIME: 15 Minutes

COOKING TIME: 15 Minutes

MAKE AHEAD:

6 to 8 turkey hot dogs, boiled, grilled, or fried

1 tablespoon safflower or canola oil, more if used for cooking the hot dogs

6 to 8 scallions, trimmed, white and light green parts thinly sliced (about ½ cup)

1 fresh jalapeño or serrano chile, finely chopped (with or without seeds), or more to taste

½ cup corn kernels (either fresh or thawed frozen)

¾ teaspoon kosher or sea salt or to taste

2 tablespoons freshly squeezed lime juice

2 to 3 tablespoons brine from pickled jalapeños

1 large ripe Hass avocado, halved, pitted, meat scooped out and finely diced (at least 1 cup)

2 to 3 ounces chicharrón, coarsely chopped into ½-inch pieces

Mayonnaise for spreading on the hot dog buns

6 to 8 hot dog buns

½ cup crumbled queso fresco

These hot dogs are topped with a pico de gallo of sorts made with ripe avocado, lightly sautéed scallions, fresh chiles, and *chicharrón*— fried pork rind. The chicharrón is crispy when you take your first bite, but it slowly soaks up the lime juice and jalapeño brine and, as it loses its crunch, it becomes infused with the tangy/briny/spicy flavor. I truly can't decide which I like the best, the first bite or the last.

1. Cook the hot dogs and keep warm.

2. Heat the oil in large skillet over medium heat. Once hot, add the scallions, jalapeño, corn, and ¼ teaspoon of the salt, and cook for about 1 minute, stirring frequently, just until the vegetables have seared and softened slightly. Transfer to a bowl. Add the lime juice, jalapeño brine, avocado, and remaining ½ teaspoon salt to the bowl and mix everything together.

3. Just before assembling the hot dogs, add the chicharrón pieces to the bowl and toss well.

4. Open up the hot dog buns but try to keep them intact and heat in the oven or toaster oven. Spread mayonnaise on the bottom half of each bun, place the hot dogs on top and spoon on a generous amount of the avocado, corn, and chicharrón mix. Top with crumbled queso fresco and serve.

CHICHARRÓN

Chicharrón is fried pork rind and it's incredibly popular in Mexico. Large food companies have even begun to create vegetarian versions of this treat, and in some Latin and international markets, you can find both. Chicharrón is crunchy, porous, and salty. As they absorb the sauces that accompany them, they become saturated and chewy.

CHAPTER 4

SPREADS, GUACAMOLES, SALSAS, ADOBOS, AND GARNISHES

SALSA IS SO IMPORTANT TO THE MEXICAN WAY OF LIFE that we

actually have the verb for it: *salsear*. The literal definition of *salsear* is to add salsa to something, to make it mouthwatering. But the word has taken on a broader meaning—that you are making something better, adding an extra layer of life, of seasoning, of joy.

I try to keep an arsenal of spreads, salsas, dips, and drizzles on hand in my refrigerator, where they keep well for days if not weeks. On a lazy weekend morning, I will start the salsa even before I've put the coffee on. By the time my boys are ready for breakfast, the salsa is ready too, and a dish like huevos rancheros casserole (page 181) can be our Sunday morning feast.

Not all salsas are spicy, even though by definition all salsas contain at least one type of chile (if not, it is not *digna*, or worthy, of calling itself a salsa). But not all chiles are hot. Many fresh and dried varieties of chiles have little or no heat: Their essence is more vegetal than spicy. Take, for example, the ancho chiles in the Barbacoa Adobo on page 111. These have a sweet, meaty essence with a hint of chocolate; they contribute substance and great depth of flavor to the sauces, but not a lot of heat.

Much more than a condiment, salsas are often the foundation of a dish. Salsa verde bathes *enchiladas suizas* (page 161), is the base for the shredded meat and potato stew on page 206, and is an essential element in the tamal casserole on page 183. Yet the same salsa can be used more simply, to drizzle onto tacos or quesadillas or over your sunnyside-up eggs in the morning.

Our salsas come in many different forms—mashed and pureed, raw and cooked; some are made with simmered vegetables, some with toasted and charred vegetables, and others with both. Some salsas call for dried toasted chiles, others use fresh. Sometimes raw and cooked ingredients are combined. There are the quick, chunky, and raw salsas known as *picos*, and the pasty, cooked-down ones like the *salsa macha* on page 108. The adobos,

CHILES

Chiles are a symbol of the Mexican identity. We use the language of chiles all the time in conversation, in our humor, in double entendres, and in metaphors, especially when referring to anything masculine, yet I find many chiles to be feminine and sensuous.

A BIT OF HISTORY

They originated in Mexico. We know from archaeological records that they were grown and used in Mexico since pre-Hispanic times, and that they were cultivated even before corn and tomatoes. They were so prized that they were used as tribute to rulers. The Spanish took them back to the Old World, and via the Spanish trade routes they spread to Asia, where they were adopted eagerly and where new varieties were cultivated.

STRENGTH IN NUMBERS

Both fresh and dried chiles go by different names in different regions (for example, the jalapeño is known in various parts of Mexico as cuaresmeño, jarocho, rayado, or alegría gordo), which can be complicated, especially when it comes to taking the measure of the number of different chiles cultivated in Mexico. But we know that Mexico grows more chiles than any other country in the world and has the largest variety: over twenty species that are used fresh, and over twenty varieties used dried. They range in heat from spicy to sweet.

WHAT THEY DO

Of course chiles contribute heat to dishes, but they are not just spicy. They also add color, flavor, and texture. I refer to them as vegetables with a whole lot of character. They are used as vegetables rather than seasonings in dishes like poblano rajas (see page 21) and the chiles rellenos on page 234.

which are typically used as a marinade, turn into a sauce as well by the time the dish is cooked.

In addition to salsas, you will find in this chapter some of the other accompaniments—pickles and drizzles, guacamoles and cremas—that make Mexican food pop and complete a dish. Want your fish tacos to be completely authentic? Balance out the fried fish and salsa with the tangy, Creamy Slaw on page 118. Here is also where you'll find the pickled onions and cabbage that accompany the Fast-Track Chicken Pibil (page 214), as well as so many other condiments; like my Go-To Guacamole (page 115). All of these recipes will make a splash at just about any meal, and many can be used interchangeably.

QUICK SALSA VERDE

SALSA VERDE RÁPIDA

MAKES ABOUT 2 CUPS

PREPARATION TIME: 10 minutes

COOKING TIME: 15 minutes

MAKE AHEAD: The salsa can be made up to 4 days ahead, covered, and refrigerated.

2 pounds tomatillos, husks removed and thoroughly rinsed

2 jalapeño or serrano chiles

2 garlic cloves

½ cup coarsely chopped fresh cilantro leaves and upper part of stems

¼ cup coarsely chopped white onion

¾ teaspoon kosher or sea salt or to taste

Salsa verde is one of the basic items always found in a Mexican restaurant or home, because once you have it, you can't live without it! It is used as the base for multiple dishes, such as Tamal Casserole with Chicken and Salsa Verde (page 183). Just spooning it over sunny-side-up eggs makes a perfect light meal of *huevos con salsa verde*. Good and easy to make, it's a great garnish or topping for tacos, quesadillas, and many antojitos.

1. Combine the tomatillos, chiles, and garlic in a medium saucepan, cover generously with water, and bring to a simmer over medium heat. Cook for 10 to 12 minutes, until the tomatillos go from pale to olive green and are thoroughly tender but not falling apart. Drain.

2. Transfer the tomatillos and garlic to a blender. Remove the stems of the chiles and set 1 chile aside. Add the other to the blender, along with the cilantro, onion, and salt, and puree until smooth. Taste for salt and adjust if desired. If you want more heat, add some or all of the remaining chile and blend together. Serve.

VARIATION: To give this salsa a different spin, rather than using fresh chiles, swap in a toasted dried chile de árbol or two. The chile de árbol will give the salsa a slightly smoky and woody taste, as well as a dash of color.

RED SALSA

SALSA ROJA

MAKES ABOUT 4 CUPS

PREPARATION TIME: 3 minutes

COOKING TIME: 25 minutes

MAKE AHEAD: The salsa can be made up to 5 days ahead, covered, and refrigerated.

2   pounds ripe tomatoes

2   garlic cloves

2   serrano or jalapeño chiles

2   tablespoons coarsely chopped white onion

¾   teaspoon kosher or sea salt or to taste

2   tablespoons canola or safflower oil

1   cup chicken or vegetable broth, homemade (page 40 or 41) or store-bought

I use this mouthwatering all-around salsa as a base or a drizzle for everything from chips and antojitos to tacos, enchiladas, and stews. First you puree the ingredients, then you sear the puree in hot oil and simmer it. The longer you cook it, the richer it will be. Once you make it, you'll see why it's silly to buy bottled salsa.

1. Place the tomatoes, garlic, and chiles in a medium saucepan, cover with water, and bring to a boil over medium-high heat. Reduce the heat to medium and simmer for 10 to 12 minutes, until the tomatoes are very soft. Drain.

2. Transfer the tomatoes, garlic, and 1 of the chiles (stem it first) to a blender. Add the onion and salt and puree until completely smooth. Taste and blend in some or all of the other chile (stemmed) if more heat is desired.

3. Heat the oil in a medium saucepan over medium heat until a spoonful of the tomato puree sizzles immediately when added. Add all of the tomato puree, being careful as it will splutter. Stir well and cover partially. Simmer for about 5 minutes, stirring occasionally. Add the broth, stir, and cook for another 6 to 8 minutes, until the salsa has thickened slightly. Taste—it should be well seasoned; adjust the salt if necessary. Serve warm, at room temperature, or cold.

FRESH TOMATILLO-AVOCADO SALSA VERDE

SALSA VERDE CRUDA CON AGUACATE

MAKES ABOUT 2 CUPS

PREPARATION TIME: 10 minutes

MAKE AHEAD: The salsa can be made up to 3 days ahead, covered, and refrigerated.

1 pound tomatillos, husks removed, thoroughly rinsed, and halved

1 ripe Hass avocado, halved, pitted, and flesh scooped out

2 tablespoons coarsely chopped white onion

¼ cup coarsely chopped fresh cilantro leaves and upper part of stems

1 jalapeño or serrano chile or to taste

¾ teaspoon kosher or sea salt or to taste

People who are unfamiliar with this type of salsa, standard fare in some of my favorite Mexico City taquerías, may be perplexed when they taste it for the first time. Is it a salsa or a guacamole? Well, it is a hybrid: part tangy salsa and part smooth guacamole. The tartness of the raw tomatillos makes for a fresh, crisp salsa that brightens the creamy, buttery avocado. Usually it's citrus that brings the tang to guacamole, but this time citrus takes a back seat, and the brilliant punch comes from the tomatillos.

Combine the tomatillos, avocado, onion, cilantro, chile, and salt in a blender or food processor and puree until smooth. Taste and adjust the salt. Serve.

MEXICAN COOK'S TIP

When shopping for tomatillos, make sure that they are firm and bright green. Don't be afraid to check under the husks for any bruising, extremely pale color, or wrinkles. If they feel sticky and have any dirt stuck to the flesh, that is completely normal; it happens because of the waxy skin of the tomatillo and the humidity that results from being covered by the husk. Any dirt and stickiness will come right off when you give them a good rinse.

JULIO'S SALSA TAQUERA

SALSA TAQUERA DE JULIO

MAKES ABOUT 4 CUPS

PREPARATION TIME: 10 minutes

COOKING TIME: 15 minutes

MAKE AHEAD: The salsa can be made up to 5 days ahead, covered, and refrigerated.

6 dried guajillo chiles, stemmed and seeded

2 dried chiles de árbol, stemmed and seeded

2 dried chipotle chiles, stemmed and seeded

1 pound ripe Roma tomatoes (about 4 medium)

12 ounces tomatillos (about 4 medium), husks removed and thoroughly rinsed

2 garlic cloves

1 jalapeño chile, seeded and sliced

2 tablespoons coarsely chopped white onion

1 teaspoon kosher or sea salt or to taste

This salsa comes from the expert hands of Julio Torres, a former taquería cook I've been lucky to have as part of my cooking team at the Mexican Cultural Institute in Washington, DC. It took years for Julio to entrust me with his special salsa recipe. Whenever I asked him to teach me how to make it, there was always a step that for one reason or another I "happened" to miss. He finally gave me the whole recipe, and he is happy to know that I am sharing it with you. The salsa may look like it has a random mix of ingredients, but they are all there for a purpose, which is to bring together the flavors of many different taquería salsas into one. This saves time in the end, as we Mexicans have a hard time making up our minds as to which salsa to add, so we tend to mix different salsas in our tacos. Don't be misled by the wide variety of chiles called for; the salsa is not very spicy.

1. Heat a comal or skillet over medium heat. Toast the dried chiles, flipping them often, until their color darkens and they smell toasty—you may feel like coughing a bit because of the fumes. Take care not to burn them.

2. Transfer the toasted chiles to a large saucepan. Add the tomatoes, tomatillos, garlic, and jalapeño and cover with water. Bring to a boil, reduce the heat to medium, and simmer for 10 to 12 minutes, until the tomatoes and tomatillos are soft, the tomatillos have gone from a bright green to olive, and the dried chiles are rehydrated and soft.

3. Drain and transfer to a blender. Add the onion and salt and puree until smooth. Taste for salt and add more if desired.

THE BEAUTY OF DRIED CHILES

Dried chiles sometimes go by different names than their fresh counterparts. Chipotles, for example, are smoke-dried jalapeños, and anchos are dried poblanos. Once dried, the chiles take on a completely new identity. This is partly because chiles harvested for drying are allowed to fully ripen before being picked, whereas fresh chiles are usually harvested while still green. Then the drying process concentrates and transforms their flavor. Some chiles, such as guajillos, anchos, and pasillas, are simply dried in the sun, usually on straw mats, for days and days. Other chiles, such as chipotles, are both dried and smoked.

Dried chiles are fabulous ingredients to have in your kitchen toolbox. They are inexpensive and keep forever (if stored in a closed container or bag in a dark dry area), and they are also nutritious (packed with vitamins!). They help speed up your metabolism, and they stimulate the appetite.

SHOPPING FOR AND USING DRIED CHILES

Dried chiles are in a sense put to sleep by the dehydrating process, so when they are used in cooking they require waking up. This is done by briefly toasting or frying the chiles, often followed by simmering, pickling, or macerating them. These are the easy steps that most recipes require.

- **Purchasing:** Look for chiles with their stems still attached. Although dried chiles can hold onto their concentrated flavor for a very long time, if the stems are gone, it is likely that they were removed before the drying process, so some of their flavor has been lost. If you buy them with stems, they will also be more attractive, as they will hold their shape much better if the stems are left on until the last minute.
- **Stemming and seeding:** Make a slit down the side of the chile with a knife or a pair of scissors. Break off the stem, then remove the seeds and pull out any visible membranes. Some dishes, such as certain mole and pipián sauces, do use the seeds, but the recipes will let you know. To remove the capsaicin (chile heat) from your hands, wash them thoroughly after you've stemmed and seeded the chiles.
- **Toasting:** Many recipes call for toasting the chiles after stemming and seeding them. Toasting kick-starts the release of their flavors. To toast dried chiles, heat a comal or skillet over medium heat until thoroughly hot but not smoking. This requires a minimum of a few minutes so the surface will be evenly heated. You don't want to use high heat, or you will risk burning the chiles. Turn on your exhaust fan and/or open a window. Once you set the chiles on the hot surface, flip them often so they will toast and not burn, for about 2 minutes. The chile skins will blister and toast, and the flesh will become opaque. You can toast them until quite dark as long as you keep flipping them from side to side. The toasting chiles will send up fumes that make you cough a bit (or a lot). But the fumes are a good sign—it means that the chiles are ready to pack a punch when you add them to your dish.
- **Frying:** Sometimes chiles are fried rather than toasted, as in my recipe for Salsa Macha (page 108). Frying has the same effect as toasting—it awakens the chiles and transforms them into a flavorful component in any dish.
- **Simmering or macerating:** The toasted or fried chiles are often simmered in water, broth, or the stew or soup where they end up. This plumps up the chiles and revives them even more, bringing out their full potential. And sometimes dried chiles, rather than being simmered, are simply pickled or macerated.

RUSTIC RANCHERO SALSA

SALSA RANCHERA RÚSTICA

MAKES ABOUT 3 CUPS

PREPARATION TIME: 10 minutes

COOKING TIME: 25 minutes

MAKE AHEAD: The salsa can be made up to 5 days ahead, covered, and refrigerated.

2 pounds ripe tomatoes (left whole) or 1 (28-ounce) can fire-roasted tomatoes, drained (reserving juice) and chopped

3 tablespoons canola or safflower oil

½ cup chopped white onion

2 garlic cloves, finely chopped

1 or 2 jalapeño or serrano chiles, finely chopped (seeded if desired) or to taste

1 cup chicken broth, homemade (page 40) or store-bought

¾ teaspoon kosher or sea salt or to taste

Chunky, rustic, and delicious, this is the salsa that starts off the weekend in our home. We use it for the baked huevos rancheros casserole on page 181, or simply to spoon over—or under—sunny-side-up eggs. But no matter how big a batch I make, it never lasts for long.

1. If using fresh tomatoes, preheat the broiler. Line a baking sheet with foil and place the tomatoes on the foil. Broil for 4 to 5 minutes, until charred on the first side. Flip over and roast for another 4 to 5 minutes, until the tomatoes are completely charred, soft, and juicy. Remove from the heat. Once the tomatoes are cool enough to handle, core and chop, without discarding the skin, juices, or seeds.

2. In a large skillet or saucepan, heat the oil over medium heat. Add the onion and cook, stirring often, for about 5 minutes, until it is completely tender and the edges are beginning to brown. Add the garlic and cook for 1 minute, or until fragrant and starting to color. Stir in the chiles and cook for another minute, or until beginning to soften.

3. Add the tomatoes, with all of their seeds and juices, and cook, stirring often, for 6 to 8 minutes, until they have cooked down into a chunky puree. Stir in the broth and salt, bring to a simmer, and simmer for another 6 to 8 minutes, or until thick and chunky. Remove from the heat. Serve warm, at room temperature, or cold.

DRUNKEN PRUNE SALSA WITH PASILLAS AND ORANGE

SALSA BORRACHA DE PASILLA, CIRUELA, Y NARANJA

MAKES ABOUT 3 CUPS

PREPARATION TIME: 10 minutes

COOKING TIME: 20 minutes

MAKE AHEAD: The salsa can be made up to 5 days ahead, covered, and refrigerated.

6 to 8 dried pasilla chiles, stemmed and seeded

2 garlic cloves, unpeeled

1 cup boiling water

1 cup beer, preferably a lager or pale ale

1 cup freshly squeezed orange juice

1½ cups pitted prunes

1 teaspoon kosher or sea salt

Luxurious, thick, citrusy, welcomingly sweet—everybody will remember this salsa after they've tasted it. It's a popular accompaniment to rich, gamy meats that can stand up to the salsa without being outshone by it. It is also a stunner served with shrimp or pork chops. There are many versions of *salsa borracha*; my take is particularly fruity and rich, with the unusual addition of prunes, which contribute great depth of flavor.

1. Heat a comal or large skillet over medium heat. Add the chiles and toast, flipping them from side to side often and being careful not to burn them, until the skin is toasted and blistered and you can smell their fragrance (and feel the fumes), about 2 minutes. Transfer to a medium saucepan.

2. Toast or roast the garlic cloves for 8 to 10 minutes, either on the hot comal or skillet or under the broiler, until toasted and charred in spots and soft inside, 4 to 5 minutes per side. Remove from the heat and, once cool enough to handle, remove the skin.

3. Pour the boiling water, beer, and orange juice into the saucepan with the chiles. Add the prunes and bring to a simmer over medium heat. Simmer for 10 minutes, until the chiles and prunes are soft and plump.

4. Transfer the chiles, prunes, and cooking liquid to a blender. Add the garlic and salt. Puree until smooth. Transfer to a bowl and serve.

BARBACOA ADOBO
(PAGE 111)

RED SALSA
(PAGE 100)

QUICK SALSA VERDE
(PAGE 99)

DRUNKEN PRUNE SALSA
WITH PASILLAS AND ORANGE
(PAGE 105)

PICKLED ONIONS
(PAGE 121)

MEXICAN CREMA

CHIPOTLE, PEANUT,
AND SESAME SEED SALSA
(PAGE 108)

MY GO-TO GUACAMOLE
(PAGE 117)

CHIPOTLE, PEANUT, AND SESAME SEED SALSA

SALSA MACHA

MAKES ABOUT 3 CUPS

PREPARATION TIME: 10 minutes

COOKING TIME: 3 minutes

MAKE AHEAD: The salsa will keep, covered, in the refrigerator for up to 6 months.

1½ cups olive oil

½ cup unsalted raw peanuts

4 garlic cloves

2 tablespoons sesame seeds

2 ounces (1½ to 2 cups) dried chipotle chiles (see page 109), stemmed and seeded

1 tablespoon packed brown sugar or to taste

1 teaspoon kosher or sea salt or to taste

3 tablespoons distilled white vinegar

The name of this salsa is a funny one: *Macha* is the feminine form of *macho*. So you could call this a macho female salsa. *Macha* can also mean "brave." Call it what you may, this salsa, which originated in the state of Veracruz, on the Gulf of Mexico, has a very strong personality and many uses. It is made by sautéing just a few ingredients—dried chipotle chiles, garlic, peanuts, and sesame seeds—in a generous amount of olive oil, then blending the mixture with a splash of vinegar and a sprinkle of sugar and salt. You end up with a mix that, unlike a typical salsa, is a very wet and textured paste. It will keep for months in the refrigerator, getting better and better as time goes by. Since this salsa has a substantial amount of olive oil, the chile paste will sink to the bottom if it stands for a while. You can choose to stir it up and serve the salsa as a paste, or you can use a bit of the flavored oil for multiple purposes, such as drizzling over fish, shrimp, potatoes, pizza, toast, cooked vegetables, or even an omelet!

Note: Other nuts, such as almonds, pecans, walnuts, hazelnuts, or pine nuts, can be substituted for the peanuts.

1. In a large skillet, heat the oil over medium heat until hot but not smoking. Add the peanuts and garlic cloves and cook, stirring, for 30 seconds, or just until they begin to color. Be on the lookout, as peanuts can be deceiving and not really reveal how brown they are getting until it is too late. Add the sesame seeds and chiles and cook, stirring, for 1 minute, or until the chiles are lightly toasted.

2. Transfer the contents of the pan, including all of the oil, to a food processor or blender. Add the sugar, salt, and vinegar and process until smooth. Pour into a container, let cool, and refrigerate if you are not using the salsa that day.

MEXICAN COOK'S TIP

Chipotles

Don't confuse the chipotles in adobo sauce that come in a can with dried chipotles from a bag. Chipotles in adobo sauce are dried chiles that have been rehydrated and marinated in a highly seasoned pickling adobo; they are very soft and have the added flavors of the sauce. Dried chipotles are somewhat leathery and hard. Their flavor is the pure flavor of smoked dried jalapeños. When buying dried chipotles, you may have a choice between chipotles *moritas* or *mecos*. If so, go for *moritas*, which are smaller than *mecos*, with a prune-like color. They are more flavorful, flirty, and perfumed than the tobacco-colored or lighter brown *mecos*. Most brands don't specify the type of chipotles, but even if you get *mecos*, any type of dried chipotle is better than none, and both types will work in my recipes.

MATADOR CHILES

CHILES TOREADOS

MAKES 1¼ CUPS

PREPARATION TIME: 5 minutes

COOKING TIME: 10 minutes

MAKE AHEAD: The toreados can be made up to 3 days ahead, covered, and refrigerated.

4   jalapeño or serrano chiles

3   tablespoons canola or safflower oil

1   cup thinly sliced or chopped white onion

¼   cup plus 2 tablespoons freshly squeezed lime juice

¼   cup soy sauce

Chiles toreados are jalapeño or serrano chiles that have been rolled against a work surface. The quick massage helps release their oils from the veins and seeds inside, which store the most flavor and heat. *Torear* means to compete in a bullfight, which gives you an indication of how fierce the result can be.

Interestingly, they are common in sushi restaurants, steak houses, and taquerías specializing in meat grilled on big *planchas*, or griddles. They are charred in oil, then bathed in a mix of freshly squeezed lime juice and soy sauce, with some slivered or chopped white onion tossed in as well. The lime juice and soy cause them to lose some of their heat, so even though they sound like something to shy away from, I would give them a 4 out of 10 in spiciness.

1. Roll the chiles back and forth a few times under your palm on your kitchen counter.

2. Heat the oil in a medium skillet over medium heat. Add the chiles and cook, flipping them over every 2 minutes, until deeply browned on all sides, 5 to 6 minutes. Transfer the chiles and oil to a heatproof bowl.

3. Once the chiles are cool enough to handle, remove them from the bowl, remove the stems, and chop; discard the seeds, if desired, though I never do. Return the chopped chiles to the bowl with the oil and stir in the onion, lime juice, and soy sauce until well combined. Let sit for at least 10 minutes and serve.

BARBACOA ADOBO

ADOBO PARA BARBACOA

MAKES ABOUT 2½ CUPS

PREPARATION TIME: 15 minutes

COOKING TIME: 25 minutes

MAKE AHEAD: The adobo can be made up to 7 days ahead, covered, and refrigerated.

- 8 guajillo chiles, stemmed and seeded
- 8 ancho chiles, stemmed and seeded
- ⅓ cup apple cider vinegar
- 1 medium ripe tomato, cut into quarters
- ½ cup coarsely chopped white onion
- 3 garlic cloves
- 1 tablespoon dried oregano, preferably Mexican
- ½ teaspoon ground canela (Ceylon cinnamon; see page 264)
- ½ teaspoon ground allspice
- ½ teaspoon freshly ground black pepper
- 5 whole cloves, stems removed
- 2½ teaspoons kosher or sea salt or to taste
- 3 tablespoons canola or safflower oil

This is a serious adobo, much stronger, darker, deeper, and more severe than the Achiote Adobo on page 112. This adobo is traditionally used for slow-cooked lamb and goat barbacoa, but in some states in central Mexico, such as Michoacán, it is also used for barbacoa made with beef (page 87).

1. Heat a comal or a large skillet over medium heat. Add the chiles and toast, flipping them often, until they are colored, a bit fragrant, and well toasted but not burned, about 2 minutes. Transfer the chiles to a medium saucepan, cover with water, and bring to a simmer over medium heat. Simmer for about 15 minutes, until the chiles have rehydrated and softened.

2. With a pair of tongs or a slotted spoon, transfer the chiles to a blender. Add 2 cups of their cooking water (discard the remaining liquid), the vinegar, tomato, onion, garlic, oregano, cinnamon, allspice, pepper, cloves, and salt and puree until completely smooth.

3. Rinse out and dry the saucepan. Add the oil and heat over medium heat for 1 to 2 minutes, until hot but not smoking. The blended marinade mixture should sizzle and splutter when you add a drop of it to the pan. Add the pureed marinade, being careful to avoid splutters, as the sauce is sure to splash! Stir once, cover partially, and cook for 10 to 12 minutes, stirring occasionally, until the color darkens and the mixture thickens to a wet, paste-like consistency. Remove from the heat.

ACHIOTE ADOBO

ADOBO DE ACHIOTE

MAKES ABOUT 2 CUPS

PREPARATION TIME: 10 minutes

COOKING TIME: 15 minutes

MAKE AHEAD: The adobo can be made up to 5 days ahead, covered, and refrigerated. Mix well before using.

2 dried guajillo chiles, stemmed and seeded

3 garlic cloves

½ cup coarsely chopped onion

2 tablespoons chopped achiote paste (the one that comes in a bar, not a jar; see opposite)

⅓ cup freshly squeezed orange juice

⅓ cup freshly squeezed lime juice

⅓ cup distilled white vinegar

1 teaspoon freshly ground black pepper

½ teaspoon ground cumin

½ teaspoon ground canela (Ceylon cinnamon; see page 264)

½ teaspoon ground allspice

1 teaspoon dried oregano

1 teaspoon packed dark brown sugar

1 teaspoon kosher or sea salt or to taste

What defines this happy, bright sauce, or any adobo, is the presence of at least one kind of chile, a mix of spices, and vinegar. I have a few adobos in my repertoire, but I think this one is the most stellar. The secret to its beauty lies in the addition of achiote paste, a Yucatecan staple made with charred garlic and onion, toasted herbs, spices, and pungent brick-red annatto seeds that add a strong saffron-like flavor and a yellow-orange color. Traditionally the paste is diluted with bitter orange juice, but since that is hard to come by in the United States, I have come up with a great alternative: orange juice, lime juice, and vinegar. My Tacos al Pastor (page 138) win accolades because of this adobo. Try it with seafood or chicken too.

1. Heat a comal or small skillet over medium heat. Add the chiles and toast, flipping them often from side to side, until they are colored, a bit fragrant, and well toasted but not burned, about 2 minutes. Transfer the chiles to a small saucepan, cover with water, and bring to a simmer over medium heat. Simmer for 12 to 15 minutes, until plumped and rehydrated.

2. Transfer the chiles, along with ½ cup of their cooking liquid, to a blender. Add the remaining ingredients and puree until smooth.

HAVE YOU FOUND THE RIGHT ACHIOTE PASTE?

Achiote paste is one of the main seasonings of the Yucatán Peninsula. It has a strong, warm red brick–like color; a grainy and moist clay-like texture; and a robust, pungent, and deeply complex flavor. Although it is mainly known for its use in pibil-style dishes (see page 214), it is also used to enrich other foods, such as some versions of Tacos al Pastor (page 138) and in achiote adobos like this one.

The paste is made with achiote, or annatto seeds; charred garlic and onion; toasted herbs and spices such as oregano, cloves, cumin, black peppercorns, allspice, and coriander seeds; salt; and citrus or vinegar. You can find excellent freshly made achiote paste in the markets in the Yucatán, sold in little bags, which is how most Mexican cooks buy it—very few go to the trouble of making

their own. Happily, I am finding an increasing number of high-quality commercial achiote pastes in Mexican markets in the U.S. and online.

But don't use just any achiote paste—you need to get your hands on a good one. There are two ways of knowing that you've found the right candidate: One, the paste should come in the form of a bar or brick, not as a wet paste in a jar (those pastes tend to be disastrous). Two, if it comes from the Yucatán, there is no doubt you've found a good one. The paste keeps for months in the cupboard; after you open the package, put it in a plastic bag and seal tightly or wrap tightly in plastic so it will not dry out. Use good achiote paste in your achiote adobo, and the foods you marinate in it will have an unforgettable flavor.

MY GO-TO GUACAMOLE

MI GUACAMOLE DE CAJÓN

MAKES ABOUT 1½ CUPS

PREPARATION TIME: 10 minutes

MAKE AHEAD: The guacamole can be made up to 12 hours ahead, covered, and refrigerated.

4 or 5 scallions (white and light green parts only), thinly sliced (3 to 4 tablespoons)

1 jalapeño or serrano chile, finely chopped (seeded if desired) or to taste

3 tablespoons coarsely chopped fresh cilantro leaves and upper part of stems or to taste

2 tablespoons freshly squeezed lime juice or to taste

¾ teaspoon kosher or sea salt or to taste

3 large ripe Hass avocados, halved, pitted, flesh scooped out and coarsely mashed or diced

The world is split into two groups: those who think guacamole should include tomatoes, and those who don't. I am of the latter camp. I do use tomatoes in special guacamoles that also call for other ingredients such as corn (see page 117), but otherwise I feel that tomatoes water down the guacamole experience. I don't skimp on the lime juice, though, because I find the acidity welcome. I also use scallions rather than onions, as they have a subtler taste and texture and don't interfere with the smooth gentle avocado.

I call it Guacamole de Cajón after the Mexican expression *de cajon* for things we keep in our top drawer and return to again and again (*cajón* means "drawer").

. . . .

Place the scallions, chile, cilantro, lime juice, and salt in a medium bowl and mix well, mashing gently with a fork or spoon. Add the avocado and gently mash with a fork to incorporate. Taste for salt and serve.

VARIATION: To this standard guacamole base, you can add other ingredients, either sweet and tart (mango, pineapple, or pomegranate), or savory, such as chicharrón (fried pork rind). You can also crumble queso fresco over the top before serving.

THE PERFECT AVOCADO

- **Choose the one I love:** Go for the Mexican Hass. Mexico is where the avocado tree originated, and the Hass grows mostly in the central Mexican state of Michoacán, in mineral- and nutrient-rich volcanic soil, with a generous amount of rainfall throughout the year and varying temperatures (cold at nighttime and hot in the daytime, which the avocado tree absolutely adores). Although there are more than a dozen different Mexican avocados, the Hass has the most meat, the creamiest and richest texture, and a mild and nutty taste that accommodates so many companions. You never find strings in the Hass the way you do in some other varieties, such as El Fuerte, and, unlike some avocados from other countries, the Mexican Hass is never watery and its flavor never astringent. Mexican Hass flowers not twice, but four times a year, which means that there is a continuous source of fresh avocados year-round.

- **Choose wisely:** A ripe avocado has pebbly almost entirely black skin, feels heavy for its size, and gives slightly in your hand.

- **Treat them well:** Place your avocados in a bowl. If they are ripe and you are not going to eat them for a day or two, place them in the refrigerator, where they will keep for 3 to 4 days more. If you cut one open and don't finish it, either rub or squeeze some lime or lemon juice on the cut flesh and cover tightly with plastic wrap, or omit the citrus and simply wrap in plastic. Either way, you can keep it in the refrigerator for 2 to 3 days. Then remove the plastic wrap and slice off the exposed part of the avocado flesh that may have gone a bit brown.

RUSTIC CORN GUACAMOLE

GUACAMOLE RÚSTICO CON ELOTE

SERVES 6

PREPARATION TIME: 10 minutes

COOKING TIME: 10 minutes

MAKE AHEAD: The guacamole can be made up to 12 hours ahead, covered, and refrigerated.

2   garlic cloves, unpeeled

1   jalapeño or serrano chile (seeded if desired), or more to taste

¾ cup fresh or thawed frozen corn kernels

1   tablespoon freshly squeezed lime juice

¾ teaspoon kosher or sea salt or to taste

2   large ripe Hass avocados, halved, pitted, flesh scooped out and coarsely mashed or diced

¾ cup cherry or grape tomatoes, halved if desired

The flavors of this guacamole remind me of the countryside in central Mexico, where I grew up. Roasted garlic and chiles give it great depth, while the corn contributes a sweet crunch, and the cherry tomatoes add a juicy splash that cuts through the creamy guacamole. Serve it with chips or use it to top quesadillas. It is also fantastic spooned inside my Lime-Rubbed Chicken Tacos (page 134), the dish that inspired this recipe.

1. Preheat the broiler or heat a comal or skillet over medium heat. If using the broiler, line a small baking sheet or baking dish with aluminum foil. Put the garlic and chile on the foil and place under the broiler 2 to 3 inches from the heat, or place them on the hot comal or skillet. Roast until charred on one side, 4 to 5 minutes. Flip over and roast for another 4 to 5 minutes, or until both the garlic skin and the chile are completely charred; the chile should appear wilted and the garlic cloves should be very soft. Remove from the heat.

2. Once the garlic and chile are cool enough to handle, peel the garlic cloves and finely chop them with the chile, or mash them together in a molcajete or with a mortar and pestle.

3. Fill a small saucepan with water and bring to a boil over medium-high heat. Add the corn kernels and cook for 30 seconds. Drain.

4. In a medium bowl or in a molcajete, combine the jalapeño, garlic, lime juice, and salt and mix and mash together with a spoon or fork. Add the avocado and gently mash to incorporate. Add the corn and tomatoes and gently stir together. Taste for salt and serve.

CREAMY SLAW

ENSALADA CREMOSITA DE COL

MAKES ABOUT 3 CUPS

PREPARATION TIME: 12 minutes

MAKE AHEAD: The slaw can be made up to 3 days ahead, covered, and refrigerated. Mix well before using.

½ cup Mexican crema, crème fraîche, or sour cream

½ cup mayonnaise

3 tablespoons freshly squeezed lime juice

¼ teaspoon sugar

Kosher or sea salt and freshly ground black pepper

2 cups shredded green cabbage

1 cup shredded red cabbage

This crunchy, fresh-tasting slaw is just what the battered fish in my Cal-Mex Fish Tacos (page 127) needs to jump off the plate. The slaw can also be served as a side or tucked into other tacos and sandwiches.

. . . .

Combine the cream, mayonnaise, lime juice, sugar, and salt and pepper to taste in a large bowl and mix well. Add the cabbage and toss with the dressing. Taste and adjust the salt. Serve.

PICKLED ONIONS and CABBAGE

CEBOLLA MORADA Y COL EN ESCABECHE

**MAKES A GENEROUS
4 CUPS**

PREPARATION TIME: 10 minutes, plus 30 minutes resting time

COOKING TIME: 3 to 4 minutes

MAKE AHEAD: The pickles can be made up to 3 days ahead, covered, and refrigerated.

1 large red onion, halved lengthwise and thinly sliced (about 2 cups)

¼ cup extra-virgin olive oil

2 jalapeño chiles or to taste

¼ cup freshly squeezed grapefruit juice

¼ cup freshly squeezed orange juice

¼ cup freshly squeezed lime juice

¼ cup unseasoned rice vinegar

1¼ teaspoons kosher or sea salt or to taste

¼ teaspoon freshly ground black pepper

3 cups finely shredded green cabbage (about 12 ounces)

Pickled onions and vegetables (cabbage, known as *repollo* in the Yucatán and *col* in the rest of Mexico, or other crunchy veggies such as carrots, cauliflower, jicama) are a typical condiment on the Yucatán Peninsula, where you will always find a bowl of them in the center of your restaurant table. My mix of pickled cabbage and red onion seasoned with seared jalapeños sits in a brine made with citrus juice, rice vinegar, and extra-virgin olive oil. It is a match made in heaven for my Fast-Track Chicken Pibil (page 214), and it is also extraordinary served with Barbacoa Sliders (page 87), or used as an additional garnish for Tacos al Pastor (page 138).

Don't be alarmed by the chiles—they remain whole, so the heat they share with the other vegetables is mild. If you want more heat, you have the option of biting into them, which is what we do at home.

. . . .

1. Place the onion in a small bowl, cover with cold water, and let sit for 10 to 15 minutes; drain well.

2. In a small skillet, heat the oil over medium-low heat. Add the jalapeños and cook, turning a few times, for about 2 minutes, or until lightly browned on all sides. Remove from the heat and let cool slightly.

3. In a large bowl, combine the grapefruit, orange, and lime juices with the vinegar, salt, and pepper. Add the oil from the skillet and whisk to combine well. Toss in the onion and cabbage and mix well. Add the jalapeños and toss. Let the mix pickle at room temperature for 20 minutes to 1 hour, then cover and refrigerate.

TACOS AND TOSTADAS

THE BEST TACO I HAVE EVER EATEN

THE BEST TACO I HAVE EVER EATEN was in an avocado orchard in the Hass avocado capital of the world, Uruapan, in the central Mexican state of Michoacán. During their lunch break, the growers and farmworkers sat down at a picnic table in a shaded area and slit open a few of the avocados that were ripening in baskets nearby. The wife of one of the farmworkers appeared with a bundle of hot freshly made corn tortillas. We tucked thick, creamy slices of avocado into the hot tortillas and sprinkled them with the coarse salt that was in a little bowl on the table. Just as I was about to take my first bite, I noticed a little bucket with some gorgeous dark amber–colored honey. I was told that it was avocado-tree honey, which was too rare to sell and very luscious. I drizzled a little bit onto my salted avocado slices, closed up the warm tortilla, took a bite, and fell in love.

I can't think of a more emblematic Mexican dish than the taco, and so it is no surprise to me that all over the U.S. we have embraced them and created "taco nights." What could be more satisfying and fun than a whole meal conveniently sitting on a tortilla, the most delicious of edible wraps? Silverware optional! There are fillings and salsas to fit every occasion and no mood a taco can't tackle. You're hungry and low on cash? A *taco de nada* ("with nothing"), sprinkled with coarse salt or warmed with a schmear of butter (a favorite with kids) will hold you off until dinner. Tacos al Pastor (page 138) are said to help repair broken hearts, while tacos de canasta (page 130) will combat the blues.

Even in my own house, where I serve warm corn tortillas with just about every meal, we've embraced the concept of a weekly taco night. It encompasses everything that people associate with the festive side of Mexican eating. The theme acts as a magnet for my kids' friends, who love to come over and join in the party atmosphere, filling their tortillas with whatever fillings they like, customizing the tacos as they choose their salsas and toppings.

Hand in hand with tacos go tostadas. The difference between the two is the tortilla base, which is crispy and flat for tostadas, either deep-fried or toasted. Our favorite traditional tostada (page 140) consists of a tostada spread with a thin layer of refried beans and topped with shredded chicken, tomato, lettuce, and ripe avocado, with salsa and crema drizzled on top. But I am equally in love with my Asian-inspired Tuna Tataki Tostadas (page 141), with their topping of seared sesame-encrusted tuna, avocado, and Sriracha sauce. This tostada is definitely an example of today's evolving Mexican cuisine.

BRICKLAYER TACOS

TACOS DE ALBAÑIL

SERVES 6

PREPARATION TIME: 10 minutes

COOKING TIME: 25 minutes

MAKE AHEAD: Don't make these ahead! That said, if you have leftovers, reheat them for great next-day quesadillas.

1 pound ripe tomatoes or 1 (14-ounce) can fire-roasted tomatoes

8 ounces sliced bacon, cut crosswise into ¼-inch-wide strips

2 pounds boneless beef sirloin or tenderloin, cut into 1-inch pieces

Kosher salt or sea salt and freshly ground black pepper

1 large or 2 medium onions, cut lengthwise in half and then into thin slivers (about 2 cups)

2 garlic cloves, chopped

2 jalapeño chiles, thinly sliced (seeded if desired) or to taste

12 flour or corn tortillas, warmed (see page 126)

Fresh Tomatillo-Avocado Salsa Verde (page 101)

When you see the word *albañil*, or "bricklayer," in its name, grab a napkin. "Bricklayer," in culinary lingo, means a meat-based dish sauced with a combination of onion, jalapeños, and tomatoes that can be easily tucked into tortillas for a fast meal. The tacos are so named because they were an easy, filling hot lunch served at construction sites; a woman would come by with a comal, tortillas, and a stew, and the workers would come and fill their own tortillas. I like the name because it shows the humble, hardworking side of Mexicans. Even if you have only a few minutes to eat on the job, your meal must be delicious.

In this recipe, bacon is first crisped in a heavy skillet. Then the beef is cooked in the smoky bacon fat (no need to add any other oil), and a chunky sauce is made in the same pan with tomatoes, onions, and jalapeños. I build on the sauce's natural smokiness by roasting the tomatoes first, which also adds extra sweetness and depth. Salsa verde cruda makes a bright, fresh contrast to the rich, smoky filling.

1. If using fresh tomatoes, preheat the broiler. (You can also roast the tomatoes on a hot comal or in a skillet, but a broiler is quicker.) Line a baking sheet or baking dish with foil. Put the tomatoes on the foil and place under the broiler, 2 to 3 inches from the heat. Broil for 4 to 5 minutes, then flip over. Broil for another 4 to 5 minutes, until the skin is charred and the tomatoes are completely soft. Remove from the heat.

2. Once the tomatoes are cool enough to handle, coarsely chop them. Transfer the tomatoes, with their juices and seeds, to a bowl. Or if using fire-roasted tomatoes, drain them, reserving the juices, and coarsely chop, then transfer the tomatoes to a bowl along with the juices.

3. Heat a 12-inch deep skillet over medium-high heat. Add the bacon and cook for 4 to 5 minutes, until it starts to crisp and lightly brown. Add the meat and season with salt and pepper to taste. Sear the meat, in batches if necessary, for about 4 minutes, turning once.

continued...

4. Add the onions, garlic, and chiles to the pan and cook, stirring, for 3 to 4 minutes, until softened. Add the tomatoes and their juices and simmer, stirring occasionally, for 4 to 5 minutes more. Taste and adjust the seasonings. Turn off the heat.

5. Serve with the warm tortillas and salsa.

HEATING TORTILLAS FOR TACOS

I heat as many tortillas at a time as will fit in my skillet or comal. I don't heat them in a stack, either in the oven, microwave, or above steaming water, because this method can cause the tortillas to moisten and stick together. Also, you don't get that wonderful toasty flavor that you get by heating them in a comal or skillet, and the tortillas aren't as malleable.

Heat a wide skillet or comal over medium-low heat for at least 3 minutes. The surface of the pan or comal must be hot before you add the tortillas or they will stick and crack when you attempt to turn them. Once the pan is hot, place as many tortillas as will fit in a single layer in the skillet or comal and heat for about 1 to 2 minutes per side, until completely malleable and lightly browned in spots. If they puff a little when they are heating it's a great sign—it means that they are heating both inside and out. But they will still taste delicious if they don't puff. As you take the tortillas off the heat, place them in a tortilla warmer or wrap them in a clean kitchen towel or cloth napkin to keep them warm.

CAL-MEX FISH TACOS WITH CREAMY SLAW

TACOS DE PESCADO CON ENSALADA DE COL CREMOSITA

SERVES 6

PREPARATION TIME: 15 minutes

COOKING TIME: 25 minutes

MAKE AHEAD: The fish sticks can be made a couple of hours ahead and kept warm in a very low oven or warmer, or under a heating lamp. Leave uncovered, or the puffy coating will deflate. If you have any leftover fish sticks, they can be reheated the next day in a medium-low oven.

FOR THE BATTER

2 large egg whites

1 cup all-purpose flour

1 teaspoon kosher or sea salt or to taste

⅛ teaspoon ground cumin

1 cup Mexican beer, preferably a light beer (but anything short of a very dark, bitter beer will work)

FOR THE FISH TACOS

Canola oil or safflower for shallow-frying

1 pound mild, firm white fish fillets, such as tilapia, cod, haddock, or halibut, cut into 1-x-4-inch strips

Kosher or sea salt and freshly ground black pepper

Flour, for dusting

12 corn or flour tortillas, warmed (see page 126)

Creamy Slaw (see page 118)

Chipotle, Peanut, and Sesame Seed Salsa (page 108)

It's hard to pin down where the fever for fish tacos started, since the delicious battered fish is a signature dish on both sides of the border. I can spot the Mexican version immediately. It has a fluffier and puffier batter, because of the way the batter is made. The flour mixture is mixed into the whipped egg whites rather than the other way around. Also, in Mexico, the tacos are served on corn tortillas rather than flour, and the slaw is creamier and tangier. The crunchy slaw makes a light, refreshing partner for the fried battered fish, which gets a flavor kick from the bold salsa macha.

1. To make the batter: In the bowl of a stand mixer or in a medium bowl, using a hand mixer, beat the egg whites on medium speed until stiff but not dry peaks form.

2. In another bowl, combine the flour, salt, and cumin, then whisk in the beer. In four additions, gently fold the flour mixture into the egg whites, taking care not to deflate the whites.

3. To make the fish tacos: Pour the oil into a 12-inch heavy skillet or casserole to a depth of ½ inch and heat over medium heat for at least 5 minutes. Test the heat by dipping a wooden spoon or the tip of a piece of fish into the oil: It should bubble happily around whatever you dip into it. Set a cooling rack on a baking sheet and cover the rack with paper towels. If you don't have a cooling rack, just cover the baking sheet with paper towels.

4. While the oil is heating, season the fish sticks lightly with salt and pepper. Place the flour on a plate and, one at a time, gently press each fish stick into the flour, flip over, and flour the other side. Tap off excess flour and place on a plate.

5. When the oil is hot, one by one, dip the floured fish sticks into the batter and immediately, but gently, place in the hot oil. Add only as many as you can without crowding the pan. Fry until crisp and light golden brown

continued...

on the first side, 2 to 3 minutes, then flip and repeat on the other side for 2 to 3 minutes, or until crisp and light golden. Remove with tongs (see Cook's Tip) or a slotted spoon and place on the rack. Cover loosely with foil to keep warm while you cook the remaining fish.

6. Serve with the warm tortillas, slaw, and salsa macha.

THE MANY WAYS TO SERVE A TACO

One of the things I love about Mexican food is that there is always more than one way to put a dish together. When I serve these tacos at home, we usually put the fish in the tortillas first, then the slaw, and, finally a drizzle or dollop of salsa. But when I am serving a large crowd, as I recently did at gala for eight hundred people, we slathered the salsa on the tortillas first, then added the fish and then the slaw. Whatever order you choose to layer the components of these tacos, they will be delicious.

MEXICAN COOK'S TIP

When using tongs to handle fried battered food, choose the type with a heatproof silicone protective coating on the tips. Regular metal tongs can tear the delicate coating on the fish sticks. To turn the fish sticks, or anything else you may be frying, you can also use two wooden spoons.

FLUFFY-PUFFY BATTER

I love it when something I have been doing forever in the kitchen without thinking about suddenly turns out to have a good reason behind it. When I gave a friend the recipe for these Cal-Mex Fish Tacos, she questioned the directions, certain that I had made a mistake. The method for the batter calls for adding the dry ingredients to the whipped egg whites, not the other way around, as many recipes do. Gently folding the flour mixture into the whipped egg whites makes an espe-cially puffy batter, resulting in a coating with a lovely golden exterior that is pillowy and tender inside. It is one of the techniques that we use in Mexican kitchens for what we call *poner una capa* or *capear*, a verb meaning "to coat." This longstanding method, which we use with chiles rellenos, croquettes, and many other fried coated foods, produces a very different result than if you simply dipped a piece of food in beaten eggs and then floured it.

FRESH CHEESE AND TOMATO BASKET TACOS (AKA SWEATY TACOS)

TACOS DE CANASTA (SUDADOS) DE REQUESÓN ENTOMATADO

SERVES 6

PREPARATION TIME: 10 minutes

COOKING TIME: 15 minutes

MAKE AHEAD: The filling can be made up to 3 days ahead, covered, and refrigerated.

Canola or safflower oil for frying

1 (½-inch-thick) slice white onion

3 garlic cloves

12 corn tortillas

½ cup thinly sliced scallions or spring onions

1 jalapeño chile, seeded and finely chopped or to taste

1 pound ripe tomatoes, chopped

½ teaspoon kosher or sea salt or to taste

½ cup chopped fresh cilantro leaves and upper part of stems, or epazote

1 pound (about 2½ cups) requesón or farmer's cheese, crumbled

FOR SERVING
(CHOOSE ANY OR ALL)

Salsa, homemade or store-bought

Avocado slices

Store-bought pickled jalapeños

If you are walking the streets in Mexico and see a man riding a bicycle with a gigantic basket attached to it, run as fast as you can to catch him. You will have a terrific taco experience. Known both as *tacos sudados*, "sweaty tacos" because they sweat inside the basket (not because you broke a sweat running), and as *tacos de canasta*, "basket tacos," this is street food at its most comforting. Basket taco vendors have a daily route, so loyal customers know exactly where and when to find them. They usually stop close to a local store like an *abarrotería* that sells soda or water, since that is something the vendors don't carry along on their bikes. They stop, open their baskets, and sell their tacos to workers who stop for a quick lunch break.

The tacos are made every morning, a few hours before the bicycle vendor takes off on his route, so they are fresh. They are packed in the basket inside layers of plastic, kitchen towels, and butcher paper, and because of this, they continue to steam as the vendor cycles along his route, becoming infused with flavor.

They are a great do-ahead dish. Bring them to a potluck, or to your husband or wife at work, or have them waiting (and sweating) when your kids walk in from school.

1. Preheat the oven to 250 degrees. Place a baking dish in the oven.

2. Pour oil to a depth of ½ inch into a 10-inch skillet and heat over medium-low heat. Place a plate or a rack next to the pan and cover it with paper towels. Once the oil is hot, add the onion slice and garlic cloves, reduce the heat to medium-low, and cook for 10 minutes, until completely browned, almost burned. Remove the onion and garlic with a slotted spoon and discard.

3. Raise the heat under the skillet to medium. Using tongs, dip a tortilla into the oil for 3 seconds, flip over, and leave for another 3 seconds (this is what we call "passing the tortillas through oil" in Mexican cooking),

then set on the paper towels. Continue with the remaining tortillas. They should still be soft enough to fold.

4. In a large skillet, heat 3 tablespoons of the seasoned oil over medium heat. Add the scallions and chile and cook for 3 to 4 minutes, until softened. Add the tomatoes and salt and cook, stirring occasionally, for 8 to 10 minutes, until the tomatoes are very soft; they should collapse when you press on them with the back of a spoon. Stir in the cilantro or epazote and cook for 2 minutes more, then remove from the heat.

5. In a large bowl, combine the cheese with the hot tomato mixture, mixing well, and season with more salt to taste if desired.

6. Remove the hot baking dish from the oven. Heat a comal or skillet over medium heat. One by one, top each tortilla with a couple of tablespoons of the filling and fold into a half-moon shape (you could eat them at this point, but they aren't "sweaty" yet!). Place on the hot comal or in the skillet and heat through, a few at a time, about a minute per side, and transfer to the hot baking dish. Continue with the remaining tortillas and filling, arranging the tacos in layers in the baking dish as they come off the comal. Once all the tacos are done, cover the baking dish with plastic wrap, then cover tightly with aluminum foil. (Don't worry about the plastic; it won't melt in the 250-degree oven.) Place the tacos in the low oven to sweat for at least 10 minutes, or up to 2 hours.

7. Serve the tacos with salsa, avocado, and/or pickled jalapeños.

A FLAVORFUL STAND-IN FOR LARD

My sister Sharon, who is a fabulous vegan cook, came up with a method for creating a flavorful oil that can be substituted for lard. She cooks onion and garlic in oil until they are practically charred, giving them plenty of time to release their flavor. Then she discards the onion and garlic and uses the rich-tasting oil. Now I use Sharon's onion- and garlic-scented oil for frying the tortillas for my basket tacos. You can also use coconut oil.

PLANTAIN TACOS WITH WALNUT, PEPITA, AND SUNFLOWER SEED CRUNCH

TACOS DE PLÁTANO MACHO CON CRUJIENTE DE NUEZ DE CASTILLA, PEPITAS, Y SEMILLAS DE GIRASOL

SERVES 5

PREPARATION TIME: 10 minutes

COOKING TIME: 35 minutes

MAKE AHEAD: These tacos taste best if you eat them as soon as the plantains come out of the oven. The pumpkin seed crunch can be made a couple of hours ahead.

2 very ripe plantains (about 1½ pounds)

1 tablespoon olive oil

6 to 8 scallions (white and light green parts only), thinly sliced

1 jalapeño chile, finely chopped (seeded if desired) or to taste

¼ teaspoon kosher or sea salt or to taste

½ cup coarsely chopped walnuts

¼ cup hulled raw pumpkin seeds (pepitas)

¼ cup sunflower seeds

1½ cups refried beans, homemade (page 247) or store-bought

10 corn tortillas warmed (see page 126)

1 recipe Quick Salsa Verde or Julio's Salsa Taquera (page 99 or 102)

These wholesome yet rich-tasting soft vegan tacos filled with chunky, savory refried beans and caramelized ripe plantains will please everybody at your table, including the most fanatic meat taco aficionados. My mom and I came up with the recipe the last time she visited us. We paired the refrieds with the plantains and topped them with a crunchy mix of toasted walnuts and pumpkin and sunflower seeds tossed with seared scallions. Don't hesitate to drizzle a liberal amount of quick salsa verde over the tacos.

1. Preheat the oven to 400 degrees.

2. Roll the unpeeled plantains on your counter for a few seconds to really soften them up. Line a small baking sheet with aluminum foil and place the plantains on it. Bake for 30 to 40 minutes, or until the plantains are completely cooked, have broken through their skin, and are lightly browned on the outside and caramelized.

3. While the plantains bake, heat the oil in a large skillet over medium heat. Add the scallions and jalapeño and cook, stirring occasionally, until softened, 2 to 3 minutes. Add the salt and stir well. Make room in the center of the skillet and add the walnuts and pumpkin and sunflower seeds. Cook for 30 seconds, without stirring, then stir the seeds into the scallions and jalapeño and cook, stirring, for another 2 minutes. The walnuts and seeds should be lightly toasted. Remove from the heat.

4. In a small skillet or saucepan, heat the refried beans over medium heat, stirring often. Remove from the heat. Cover to keep warm.

5. Peel the plantains while they are still hot and slice or chop them.

6. Spoon a couple of tablespoons of refried beans onto the center of each tortilla, add 3 or 4 slices or a couple of tablespoons of chopped plantain, and top with a couple of tablespoons of pumpkin seed walnut crunch. Drizzle salsa on top. Eat while hot!

MEXICAN COOK'S TIP

Make sure that your plantains are very ripe. Their skin should be yellow but almost entirely covered with black spots. Unlike the banana, the plantain, its starchier and sturdier giant cousin, is still unripe when the skin is only yellow. When its skin is green, it is *verde*, completely unripe. If your plantain is yellow but is not covered all over with black spots, it needs time to sit and ripen on your counter in a warm area of your kitchen, like an avocado. If you want to speed its ripening process, wrap it in newspaper or place in a paper bag for a couple of days, just as you would with avocados.

LIME-RUBBED CHICKEN TACOS WITH RUSTIC CORN GUACAMOLE

TACOS DE POLLO AL LIMÓN CON GUACAMOLE CON ELOTE

SERVES 4 TO 6

PREPARATION TIME: 10 minutes

COOKING TIME: 10 minutes

MAKE AHEAD: The chicken can be marinated for up to 12 hours, covered and refrigerated. The guacamole can be made up to 12 hours ahead, covered, and refrigerated.

2 tablespoons freshly squeezed lime juice

2 tablespoons olive oil

½ teaspoon kosher or sea salt or to taste

¼ teaspoon freshly ground black pepper or to taste

1 tablespoon chopped fresh rosemary or ¼ teaspoon dried

1½ pounds boneless skinless chicken breasts or thighs

8 to 12 corn tortillas, warmed (see page 126)

Rustic Corn Guacamole (page 117)

I came up with this dish on a hurried weeknight, and it has become one of our go-tos. The chicken breasts are rubbed with a simple rosemary-scented mix of lime juice and olive oil, marinated briefly (though you could leave them all day in the refrigerator), then quickly cooked and cut into strips. These are accompanied by a rustic guacamole, with cherry tomatoes and corn.

1. Combine the lime juice, 1 tablespoon of the oil, the salt, pepper, and rosemary in a large bowl. Add the chicken, rub with the marinade, and then toss in the bowl.

2. In a large skillet or griddle, heat the remaining 1 tablespoon oil until hot but not smoking. Add the chicken and cook until cooked through and lightly browned, about 4 minutes per side. Transfer to a cutting board and then, when cool enough to handle, slice diagonally against the grain into strips about ½ inch wide. Transfer to a platter or bowl.

3. Serve the warm tortillas with the chicken and guacamole so guests can assemble their own tacos.

"WIRED" FLAT-IRON STEAK TACOS

TACOS DE ALAMBRE DE CARNE

SERVES 5 OR 6

PREPARATION TIME: 15 minutes

COOKING TIME: 10 minutes

MAKE AHEAD: The vegetables and meat can be sliced a day ahead, covered, and refrigerated.

¼ cup canola or safflower oil

2 cups slivered white onions

2 poblano chiles, seeded and cut into thin strips

2 pounds flat-iron steak, cut across the grain into thin strips about ¼ x 2 inches

Kosher or sea salt and freshly ground black pepper

10 to 12 corn tortillas, warmed (see page 126)

Julio's Salsa Taquera (page 102)

The name *alambre* ("wire") for these tacos, which are a standard item in most taquerías in Mexico City, originates from the way they were made many years ago, when meat, onions, and chiles were threaded onto metal skewers shaped like thin swords, as for brochettes. Some taco experts say that this technique came from the Spanish, who borrowed it from the Moors, while others claim that it came from the French, who ruled food trends in Mexico City restaurants from the late 1800s.

Though in the past you might have seen *alambres* in taco stands, there is no time in the fast-paced, bustling Mexico City taquerías to wait around for cubes of meat to be properly cooked on skewers. Taco makers of all stripes long ago figured out that it is less fussy, much faster, and tastier to throw thin-sliced cuts of meat and slivered vegetables directly onto the *plancha*, or flat-iron grill.

1. In a 12-inch heavy skillet or casserole, heat 2 tablespoons of the oil over medium-high heat. Add the onions and chiles and cook, stirring often, for 5 to 6 minutes, until they are cooked through and wilted and the edges have started to brown. Scrape into a bowl.

2. Place the skillet back on the heat and add the remaining 2 tablespoons oil to the pan. Season the meat with salt and pepper to taste. Once the oil is hot but not smoking, add the meat and let it sear, without moving it, until it starts to release juices on top and brown on the bottom, about 2 minutes. Cook, stirring, for another minute, until browned on all sides. Return the onions and chiles to the pan, toss with the meat, and cook until heated through, less than a minute.

3. Serve the filling with the warm tortillas and salsa.

VARIATION: These tacos can also be made with chicken or seafood (shrimp is particularly good). People with a hunger for something more extravagant ask for *con queso fundido* "with melted cheese," and the cheese is melted on top of the filling just before it is tucked into the warm tortillas. If you like that idea, just throw a handful of grated melting cheese, such as Oaxaca, mozzarella, or Monterey Jack, onto the mix a few minutes before serving.

CARNITAS TACOS

TACOS DE CARNITAS

SERVES 6 TO 8

PREPARATION TIME: 5 minutes

COOKING TIME: 2 hours

MAKE AHEAD: The carnitas can be made a couple of hours ahead of time and kept covered, then reheated over medium-low.

½ white onion, coarsely chopped

6 garlic cloves

1 teaspoon dried marjoram

1 teaspoon dried thyme

1 teaspoon freshly ground black pepper

Pinch of ground cumin

4 whole cloves, stems removed

Kosher or sea salt or to taste

1½ cups water

1 tablespoon lard or canola or safflower oil

4 to 5 pounds boneless pork shoulder or butt, cut into approximately 2-inch chunks, fat left on

2 bay leaves

1 cup freshly squeezed orange juice

2 tablespoons sweetened condensed milk

12 to 16 corn tortillas, warmed (see page 126)

Store-bought pickled jalapeños

Fresh Tomatillo-Avocado Salsa Verde (page 101)

I've received countless requests for this iconic Mexican dish—so many that I decided to travel to the Mexican state of Michoacán to visit the town known as the carnitas capital of the world, Quiroga. I came up with this triumphant take, ideal for making at home, that combines some of the secrets from the Quiroga carnitas masters with the flavors of Mexico City's carnitas that I grew up eating, with their hint of citrus and a drizzle of sweetened condensed milk that gives the meat a lightly caramelized coating. When we have new friends over to share a meal, this is the dish my boys request.

Creamy and tangy, with an avocado pureed into the mix, salsa verde cruda makes a soothing, bright drizzle for these complex carnitas. As for the optional pickled jalapeños on the side, they are traditional, introducing a fresh, acidic note.

1. Place the onion, garlic, marjoram, thyme, pepper, cumin, cloves, and 1 tablespoon salt in a blender. Add the water and puree until smooth.

2. In a large Dutch oven or heavy casserole, heat the lard or oil over medium-high heat until melted. Add the pork chunks and sprinkle with ½ teaspoon salt. Brown the meat on all sides, stirring and flipping the pieces, for about 10 minutes.

3. Pour the onion mixture over the meat, bring to a simmer, and cook for 5 to 6 minutes. Add the bay leaves, orange juice, and condensed milk and give it all a good stir. Bring back to a simmer, reduce the heat to low, cover, and simmer, stirring and scraping the bottom of the pot every 15 minutes, until the meat is completely tender and can be pulled apart easily with a fork, 1½ to 2 hours. Remove the lid and simmer for another 4 to 5 minutes.

4. Scoop out the carnitas with a slotted spoon and transfer to a bowl or platter. Before scraping up any remaining sauce to spoon over the carnitas, remove the bay leaves and skim off any fat from the surface and discard. Shred the meat with a fork.

5. Serve the carnitas with the tortillas, pickled jalapeños, if using, and salsa on the side.

TACOS AL PASTOR

TACOS AL PASTOR CASEROS

SERVES 6 OR 7

PREPARATION TIME: 10 minutes, plus at least 20 minutes marinating

COOKING TIME: 15 minutes

MAKE AHEAD: The meat can be marinated for up to 2 days, covered and refrigerated.

3 cups Achiote Adobo (page 112)

3 pounds pork loin, pork sirloin cutlets, or butterflied boneless pork chops, cut into ½-inch-thick slices

½ ripe pineapple, peeled and cut into ½-inch slices

2 to 3 tablespoons canola or safflower oil, as needed

Kosher or sea salt

12 to 14 corn tortillas, warmed (see page 126)

1 cup coarsely chopped fresh cilantro

1 cup coarsely chopped white onion

2 limes, cut into quarters

Quick Salsa Verde (page 99) and/or Julio's Salsa Taquera (page 102)

All over Mexico, at taquerías and stands that offer tacos al pastor, you see long lines of people waiting patiently for their beautifully seasoned pork to be shredded from the hunk of adobo-marinated meat turning slowly and aromatically on a rotisserie grill, then layered with onions, fire-roasted pineapple, and cilantro inside warm tortillas. The tacos are reminiscent of shawarma, which is not surprising, because the roots of this dish are in Mexico's Lebanese communities, which originally used lamb (*tacos al pastor* means "shepherd's tacos"). The dish was adopted in central Mexico, made with pork instead of lamb, and marinated in an adobo sauce made with traditional ingredients like dried chiles, vinegar, and achiote (some versions don't include the achiote, but mine always does).

With my home-style version, you can make tacos al pastor without a rotisserie or a fire-roasting pit and still get all the right flavors. They are great with a tangy salsa verde or a more multilayered salsa taquera.

You can turn al pastor tacos into *gringas* by using flour tortillas instead of corn and throwing some melting cheese on top (they are called *gringas*, because everyone knows how popular flour tortillas and cheese are in the U.S.); see the Variation.

....

1. Reserve ¾ cup of the achiote adobo to brush on the pineapple before cooking and to finish the meat.

2. Toss the meat with the remaining 2¼ cups achiote adobo in a large bowl or baking dish. Cover and marinate for at least 20 minutes, and up to 48 hours, stirring occasionally. If marinating for more than 30 minutes, cover and refrigerate.

3. When ready to make the tacos, remove the meat from the refrigerator if you refrigerated it. Brush the pineapple slices with some of the reserved marinade. Set the rest of the marinade aside.

4. Heat a large heavy skillet over medium-high heat. Once it is hot, add 1 tablespoon of the oil. Place a single layer of pineapple slices in the skillet and sear until juicy and lightly charred on both sides, 2 to 3 minutes per

side. Remove from the heat. Repeat with any remaining slices. Set the pan aside.

5. When they are cool enough to handle, core the pineapple slices and cut into thin strips, 1 to 2 inches long and about ¼ inch thick. Place in a bowl and cover.

6. Add 1 tablespoon oil to the pan and heat over medium-high heat. Lightly sprinkle the meat with salt. Sear as many slices of meat as will fit in the pan without crowding for about 2 minutes per side, until browned on both sides, and transfer to a cutting board. Slice the meat across the grain into thin strips, about ½ inch thick and 1 inch wide. Continue to cook and slice the meat in batches. Once all the meat has been seared and sliced into strips, reduce the heat to medium, return all of the meat strips to the skillet, and pour the reserved marinade on top. Cook, stirring, for another minute. Cover and set aside.

7. Warm the tortillas and bring to the table along with the meat, pine-apple, cilantro, onion, limes, and salsa.

VARIATION: To make *gringas*, use flour tortillas instead of corn tortillas and have ready about 2 cups grated queso asadero, Mexican Oaxaca, Chihuahua, mozzarella, or Monterey Jack (or any other melting cheese of your choice). Heat the tortillas, sprinkle on about 2 tablespoons cheese, fold the tortilla in half, and let the cheese melt as if for a quesadilla. Open the tortilla, add a handful (about 2 tablespoons) of the sliced meat, some pineapple, onion, and cilantro, and fold again to serve.

TRADITIONAL CHICKEN TOSTADAS

TOSTADAS DE POLLO

SERVES 6

PREPARATION TIME: 15 minutes

COOKING TIME: 5 minutes

MAKE AHEAD: You can prepare all the elements up to 24 hours ahead, cover, and refrigerate. Reheat the chicken and beans before serving.

12 corn tostadas, homemade (page 25) or store-bought

2 cups warm refried beans, homemade (page 247) or store-bought

3 cups shredded cooked chicken (see page 40) or from rotisserie chicken

1 cup thinly sliced iceberg or romaine lettuce

1 or 2 ripe Hass avocados, halved, pitted, flesh scooped out and sliced

2 ripe tomatoes, sliced

1 cup crumbled queso fresco, Cotija, or farmer's cheese

½ cup Mexican crema, crème fraîche, or sour cream

1 cup Quick Salsa Verde (page 99) or other salsa

I'm puzzled by the fact that tostadas haven't caught on in the United States in the same way that tacos have. They can be assembled in a matter of minutes, as all the elements can be prepared ahead of time and/or store-bought. They are accommodating: You can decide how much of each topping to add and you can change your mind about what to put on them even if you're halfway through assembly. Moreover, they are the perfect dish for casual entertaining. Set out a basket with the crunchy corn tostadas, along with bowls of refried beans, shredded cooked chicken, and fresh garnishes like avocado, tomatoes, lettuce, onion, cream, and crumbled cheese, invite your friends and family to assemble their own tostadas, and it's a party!

1. Place the tostadas on a large platter and set out all of the toppings and garnishes in separate bowls.

2. To assemble, spread a couple of tablespoons of refried beans on a tostada. Top with a couple of tablespoons of shredded chicken, some lettuce, and 1 or 2 slices each of avocado and tomato. Top it all off with a tablespoon or so of crumbled cheese and drizzle on some cream. Spoon on some salsa.

TUNA TATAKI TOSTADAS

TOSTADAS DE ATÚN TATAKI

**MAKES 8 LARGE TOSTADAS
OR 16 TOSTADITAS**

PREPARATION TIME: 15 minutes

COOKING TIME: 5 minutes

MAKE AHEAD: The sauce can be
made up to 12 hours ahead,
covered, and refrigerated. Whisk
again before using.

2 pounds sushi-grade ahi
   tuna loins or steaks

Kosher or sea salt and freshly
   ground black pepper

1 cup white sesame seeds

1 cup black sesame seeds

¼ cup peanut oil

¾ cup soy sauce

⅓ cup fresh lime juice

3 tablespoons unseasoned
   rice vinegar

⅓ cup olive oil

⅓ cup toasted sesame oil

1 teaspoon packed brown
   sugar

1 tablespoon plus 1 teaspoon
   grated peeled fresh ginger

3 tablespoons finely chopped
   white onion

1 jalapeño chile, finely
   chopped (seeded if desired)
   or to taste

8 (5-inch) tostadas or
   16 (2-inch) tostaditas,
   homemade (page 25) or
   store-bought

1 ripe Hass avocado, halved,
   pitted, flesh scooped out
   and thinly sliced

Sriracha sauce

Asian immigrants have been influencing traditional Mexican cuisine for centuries. Since the Spanish landed in Mexico and sought trade with the West in the 1500s, waves of Asians have flowed into the country. Chinese, Japanese, Koreans, and Filipinos have intermingled their techniques and ingredients with the native ones as they made Mexico their home.

I originally served these Latin-Asian fusion tostaditas as an appetizer at a class on Mexican cooking that I taught at the Mexican Cultural Institute in Washington, DC. They were such a hit that I make them regularly as appetizers.

1. Sprinkle the tuna with salt and pepper to taste. Place the sesame seeds on a plate and mix together. Coat the tuna with the sesame seeds, pressing lightly on all sides; it should be fully covered.

2. Heat a heavy skillet over medium-high heat until very hot but not smoking. Add the peanut oil and let it heat up, then sear the tuna briefly on all sides, 15 to 20 seconds per side. Remove from the heat. Once it has cooled completely, thinly slice the tuna and place in a large bowl or other container.

3. In a medium bowl, whisk together the soy sauce, lime juice, vinegar, olive oil, sesame oil, brown sugar, ginger, onion, and jalapeño. Pour over the tuna slices, turning to coat.

4. Place a couple of slices of tuna tataki on each tostada or one on a tostadita, top with a couple of slices of avocado, and add a dollop of Sriracha sauce. Serve.

ENCHILADAS AND CREPE ENCHILADAS

WHEN YOU MAKE AN ENCHILADA DINNER, you are creating a fiesta of dressed-up tortillas. Of all the different dishes in the Mexican repertoire, none pays homage to the tortilla like enchiladas. The name *enchilada* refers to an adorned tortilla enrobed in a chile sauce. But despite the implication in the name, enchiladas are not necessarily spicy. The sauces vary from region to region. The specific name of the enchilada will often include the ruling local sauce. If you go to central Mexico, you will find enchiladas suizas (page 161), which are crowned with the ruling salsa verde. In Guerrero and the southeast, you will find enchiladas de mole verde. Sometimes the name of the sauce replaces the "chilada" in "enchilada." In Puebla, where mole poblano reigns, you will find *enmoladas*, or enchiladas de mole, and in the north of Mexico, where a fermented milk product called *jocoque* (see the headnote on page 159) is popular, you'll find *enjococadas* or enchiladas de *jocoque*. When the sauce used to bathe the tortillas is a black bean sauce, the enchiladas de frijol are usually called *enfrijoladas*. There are many renditions, including my own overboard version that I call Big Brunch Enchiladas (page 147).

Enchiladas can also be tortillas with no filling at all and an uncomplicated garnish. That is their beauty: They can be simple or complex, and the options are endless.

This chapter is also a natural home for *crepas*. I call them crepe enchiladas, because they're given the same treatment as enchiladas, with sweeter, softer, more delicate crepes—which put down roots in Mexico thanks to the French—standing in for tortillas. Just like tortillas, they are adorned with a luscious sauce, stuffed with a complementary filling, and garnished. In one of the recipes here, the crepes are dressed in a New Mexico–style Hatch chile sauce and balanced with the ultra-Mexican *acelga con papas*, chard with potatoes (page 170). In the other, the crepes are filled with a mild, light, and bright mix of corn, rajas (roasted poblano pepper strips), and zucchini and dressed with an avocado-tomatillo sauce, a welcome summer dish (page 168).

As with so many of the recipes in this book, you can make many of the components of the enchiladas and *crepas* ahead—in particular, the salsas and sauces, and, in the case of the crepe enchiladas, the crepes.

PREPARING CORN TORTILLAS
FOR ENCHILADAS

Invaluable lessons for making corn tortilla enchiladas have been passed down by Mexican cooks through generations and across regions. Follow the guidelines here, and you will have beautiful enchiladas every time. Your tortillas will be malleable, with a toasty layer of flavor, and they won't crack as you roll or fold them, or become soggy once they are sauced. Either of these two simple techniques will work to prepare your tortillas.

. . . .

Heat and Lightly Toast the Tortillas on a Hot Comal or Skillet

This is a great method for people who prefer to use a minimum of oil; it is the one I use at home. Heat a comal or a skillet, preferably nonstick, over medium-low heat until very hot, at least 3 minutes. If the comal or skillet isn't hot enough, the tortillas will stick to it. But if you heat the comal or skillet over very high heat, they will not only stick, but will also burn. This is why I use medium-low heat. Once you lay a tortilla on the hot surface, don't flip or move it until it has heated through and the bottom is beginning to brown or freckle and develop a thin crust, 30 seconds to 1 minute. At this point, you should be able to flip the tortilla easily. Then repeat on the other side.

"Pass" the Tortilla Through Hot Oil

This is the most common technique used in Mexican kitchens. It differs from the way you fry tortillas for tostadas. For enchiladas, you keep the tortilla in the hot oil for a very short time; this is known as *pasar por el aceite*, or "passing it through" to heat it and make it flexible so it won't crack or break and will also have a sturdy cooked surface. The oil must be heated slowly over medium heat until it's hot enough to cook the surface of the tortilla without soaking into it or burning it.

Heat about ½ inch of canola or safflower oil in a medium skillet over medium heat. (You can also use the seasoned oil on page 131 or lard.) Place a platter or cooling rack covered with paper towels next to the pan. After 2 to 3 minutes, the oil should be hot enough. Test the heat by dipping the edge of a tortilla into it; the oil should bubble happily, neither overly aggressively nor too faintly. Using tongs (better if the tongs have those heatproof rubber tips so they won't break the tortillas), one by one, slide each tortilla gently into the hot oil. When you see the tortilla just begin to puff and change color, 10 to 15 seconds, flip it over and leave for another 10 to 15 seconds. Immediately remove from the pan and drain on the paper towels.

Whether you use a comal or hot oil, keep the prepared tortillas warm by covering them with aluminum foil. Once all of them are softened, they are ready to be filled or dipped into a sauce before filling and rolling or folding.

BIG BRUNCH ENCHILADAS WITH EGGS, CHORIZO, AND BLACK BEAN SAUCE

ENCHILADAS DE HUEVO CON SALSA DE FRÍJOL, CHORIZO, QUESO FRESCO, Y AGUACATE

SERVES 6

PREPARATION TIME: 25 minutes

COOKING TIME: 20 minutes

MAKE AHEAD: The black bean sauce can be made up to 3 days ahead, covered, and refrigerated. The enchiladas can be assembled and sauced an hour ahead; cover and keep warm in a 250-degree oven. Add the garnishes just before serving.

3 cups Basic Black Beans (page 244), with 1 cup of their broth, or 2 (14-ounce) cans black beans, drained and rinsed, plus 1 cup chicken or vegetable broth or water

2 tablespoons adobo sauce from canned chipotles in adobo

2 tablespoons brine from pickled jalapeños

1 pound raw Mexican chorizo, casings removed and roughly chopped

3 tablespoons canola or safflower oil

⅓ cup sliced scallions (white and light green parts only)

8 large eggs, beaten until frothy

½ teaspoon kosher or sea salt or to taste

12 corn tortillas

When things go topsy-turvy in our home, I offer to make dinner for breakfast or breakfast for dinner. I learned this trick from my friend Debra, and it has brightened many a gloomy mood. These egg-filled enchiladas fit the bill. The corn tortillas are stuffed with soft, fluffy scrambled eggs, then bathed in a creamy, earthy, richly flavored black bean sauce and garnished with crisp bites of chorizo, crumbled fresh queso, avocado chunks, and store-bought pickled jalapeños. For the black bean sauce, I couldn't decide between adobo sauce from the chipotles and pickling brine from the pickled jalapeños, so I used them both.

When you make these enchiladas, even if there are six of you, you will need nothing else for your meal other than perhaps some fruit and coffee—and a nice big couch to lie down on and take a nap afterward.

1. Place the beans and their liquid in a blender, along with the adobo sauce and pickled jalapeño brine and puree until completely smooth. Transfer to a medium saucepan and bring to a bare simmer over low heat, stirring occasionally. The puree should have the consistency of heavy cream. Reduce the heat to the lowest possible setting, cover, and keep warm.

2. Heat a large skillet over medium heat. Add the chorizo and cook, stirring and breaking it up into tiny bits with a wooden spoon or spatula, until browned and crisped, 5 to 6 minutes. Scrape into a bowl, cover, and set aside.

3. Add the oil to the skillet and heat over medium heat until hot but not smoking. Add the scallions and cook until they are soft and translucent and the edges are beginning to brown lightly, 3 to 4 minutes. Reduce the heat to medium-low, pour in the eggs, add the salt, and cook, stirring

continued...

1 cup crumbled queso fresco, Cotija, farmer's cheese, mild feta, or goat cheese

4 store-bought pickled jalapeños (more or less to taste), stemmed, seeded, and chopped

1 ripe Hass avocado, halved, pitted, flesh scooped out and diced

often and gently, until the eggs are just set (or to taste). I like to stop the cooking when the eggs are still soft and tender, not dry, which takes 4 to 5 minutes. Remove from the heat and cover to keep warm.

4. Prepare the tortillas, using either of the methods described on page 146.

5. One by one, place each tortilla on a plate, spoon about 3 tablespoons of the scrambled eggs down the middle, and roll up, then place on a serving platter, seam side down.

6. Once all the tortillas are stuffed and rolled, pour the warm bean puree over the top. They should be completely covered. Sprinkle on the chorizo, cheese, pickled jalapeños, and avocado. Serve right away.

MINERS' ENCHILADAS WITH QUESO FRESCO, GUAJILLO SAUCE, AND MIXED VEGETABLES

ENCHILADAS MINERAS

SERVES 6

PREPARATION TIME: 20 minutes

COOKING TIME: 25 minutes

MAKE AHEAD: The guajillo sauce can be made up to 5 days ahead, covered, and refrigerated. The enchiladas can be filled and folded an hour ahead; cover and keep warm in a 250-degree oven. When ready to serve, add the vegetables.

12 dried guajillo chiles, stemmed and seeded

1 garlic clove

1 teaspoon dried oregano, preferably Mexican

Kosher or sea salt

¼ cup plus 2 tablespoons canola or safflower oil

1½ cups chicken broth or vegetable broth, home-made (page 40 or 41) or store-bought, or water, or as needed

8 ounces queso fresco, or ranchero, Cotija, or farmer's cheese, crumbled

¼ cup finely chopped white onion

1 pound red potatoes, peeled and cut into small dice

1 pound carrots, peeled and cut into small dice

2 tablespoons distilled white vinegar

Miners' enchiladas come from the city of Guanajuato, in the central Mexican state of Guanajuato, a region that has been an important center of silver and gold mining since the colonial era. These enchiladas are one of the city's signature dishes. Some contend that the enchiladas were made in the mines or for the miners, but it is more likely that the name is a tribute to Guanajuato given to the enchiladas by a local cook who sold enchiladas from her home and is thought to have invented the dish. Soon thereafter, variations spread throughout the state, all on the same theme: corn tortillas moistened with a strong guajillo chile sauce, filled with fresh cheese, and garnished with abundant dressed vegetables and pickled chiles. The slightly sweet cheese filling and the vegetables balance the intense guajillo sauce, and the pickled chiles deliver a lively finish.

1. Heat a comal or skillet over medium-low heat. When it is hot, toast the chiles, flipping them over often, until the inner skin turns opaque and the outer skin darkens and crisps and you can smell the fumes from the chiles, 1 to 2 minutes. Transfer the chiles to a medium saucepan, cover with water, and bring to a boil over medium-high heat. Reduce the heat to medium and simmer for 12 to 15 minutes, until the chiles rehydrate completely and plump up.

2. Transfer the chiles to a blender, along with 1½ cups of their liquid, and add the garlic, oregano, and ½ teaspoon salt. Puree until completely smooth.

3. In a medium saucepan, heat 2 tablespoons of the canola or safflower oil over medium heat until hot but not smoking. Pour in the chile sauce (it should sear when it hits the pan) and partially cover, as the sauce will

continued...

2 tablespoons olive oil

Freshly ground black pepper

Pinch of sugar

4 radishes, trimmed and cut into small dice

4 romaine lettuce leaves, thinly sliced crosswise

12 corn tortillas

Peperoncini, pickled blond peppers, or store-bought pickled jalapeños, for garnish

be jumping all over the place. Cook for 3 to 4 minutes, until the sauce thickens and darkens. Stir in the broth or water and cook until the sauce thickens enough to coat the back of a spoon, a few minutes more. Turn off the heat and cover to keep warm.

4. In a small bowl, stir together the cheese and onion. Taste and add salt if desired (this will depend on the type of cheese you are using). Set aside.

5. Fill a medium saucepan with water, salt generously, and bring to a rolling boil over medium-high heat. Add the potatoes, turn the heat down to medium, and cook at a gentle boil until the potatoes are cooked through but not at all mushy, 4 to 5 minutes. Scoop out with a spider or a slotted spoon and place in a bowl.

6. Bring the water back to a boil and add the carrots. Boil gently until crisp-tender, 2 to 3 minutes. Drain and place in the bowl with the potatoes.

7. In a small bowl, combine the vinegar, the remaining ¼ cup canola or safflower oil, the olive oil, ¼ teaspoon salt, pepper to taste, and the sugar. Whisk well, taste for salt, and add more if desired. Pour over the potatoes and carrots, add the radishes and lettuce, and toss well.

8. Prepare the tortillas using either of the methods described on page 146.

9. If necessary, reheat the salsa. Using tongs, dip a tortilla into the warm salsa, completely drench on both sides, and place on a plate. Spoon 2 to 3 tablespoons of the cheese mixture across the middle of the tortilla and fold it over like a quesadilla, making a half-moon shape. Place on a serving platter. Repeat with the rest of the tortillas, overlapping the enchiladas on the platter.

10. Top the enchilada with the dressed vegetables and garnish with the pickled peppers, or transfer the dressed enchiladas to individual plates and place a couple of chiles on each plate.

CHILES GÜEROS

Banana peppers are known as *chiles güeros* in many regions of Mexico. *Güero* translates as "blond," and the chiles are so called because they are pale yellow. Used as slang, *güero* refers to people with blond or light brown or red hair and a fair complexion. There are different varieties of banana peppers, but they are all pale and light and have waxy skin and a flavor similar to jalapeños. Their heat level is usually mild.

When banana peppers are pickled, they go by *güeros en escabeche* in Mexico. Elsewhere, you can find them as pickled peperoncini peppers. Some are longer and thinner, some are smaller and chubbier.

ASPARAGUS, MUSHROOM, AND GOAT CHEESE ENCHILADAS WITH PINE NUT MOLE SAUCE

ENCHILADAS DE ESPÁRRAGOS, CHAMPIÑONES Y QUESO DE CABRA CON MOLE DE PIÑÓN

SERVES 6

PREPARATION TIME: 25 minutes

COOKING TIME: 30 minutes

MAKE AHEAD: The pine nut mole can be made up to 4 days ahead, covered, and refrigerated. The enchiladas can be assembled and sauced an hour ahead of time; cover and keep warm in a 250-degree oven. Garnish when ready to serve.

FOR THE PINE NUT MOLE

¼ cup olive oil

¼ cup chopped white onion

1 cup raw pine nuts

1 garlic clove, chopped

1 pound ripe tomatoes, coarsely chopped

2 ancho chiles, stemmed, seeded, and coarsely chopped or broken into pieces

½ cup freshly squeezed orange juice

4 cups vegetable or chicken broth, homemade (page 41 or 40) or store-bought

½ teaspoon kosher or sea salt or to taste

¼ teaspoon packed brown sugar or to taste

Although we don't think of pine nuts when we think of Mexican cooking, they are definitely part of the culinary landscape (used most often in sweets). But they are one of my favorite ingredients, and they work very well for thickening moles. (You can use other nuts, such as peanuts, almonds, or walnuts, but give the pine nuts a try first.) The other ingredients that define this mole are ancho chiles, tomatoes, and orange juice, all blended together and cooked down to a thick, rich sauce that marries beautifully with the mushroom and asparagus filling.

The tortillas are dipped into the luscious mole and wrapped around the filling of seared mushrooms and crisp-tender asparagus seasoned with orange zest and thyme, and goat cheese, which melts when the enchiladas are topped with the hot mole sauce. When you have vegetarians coming over for dinner, this dish is a must.

1. To make the mole: Heat 2 tablespoons of the oil in a large casserole or heavy pot over medium heat. Add the onion and cook for 3 to 4 minutes, until completely softened. Stir in the pine nuts and garlic and cook for 2 to 3 minutes, until the garlic becomes fragrant and changes color and the pine nuts are light brown and smell toasty. Raise the heat to medium-high, add another tablespoon of olive oil and the tomatoes, and cook, stirring occasionally, until the tomatoes soften and break down, 7 to 8 minutes. Add the ancho chiles, orange juice, broth, salt, and brown sugar and bring to a simmer. Simmer, stirring occasionally, until the chiles have rehydrated and plumped up and the sauce has thickened, about 8 minutes more.

continued...

1 tablespoon olive oil

1 pound white button or baby
   bella (cremini) mushrooms,
   cleaned and diced

1 tablespoon unsalted butter

1 pound asparagus, tough
   ends removed, peeled from
   just below the tips to the
   bottom, and cut into 1-inch
   pieces

2 teaspoons chopped fresh
   thyme or ½ teaspoon dried

1 tablespoon grated orange
   zest

½ teaspoon kosher or sea salt

Freshly ground black pepper

12 corn tortillas

6 ounces goat cheese, cut
   into chunks (about ¾ cup)

2 tablespoons chopped
   chives, for garnish

2 tablespoons pine nuts,
   toasted, for garnish

2. Transfer the contents of the pot to a blender and let cool for a few minutes, then puree, in batches if necessary, until completely smooth.

3. Rinse out and dry the pot, add the remaining 1 tablespoon oil, and heat over medium heat. Add the pine nut mole, cover partially, and simmer for 5 to 6 minutes, stirring occasionally, until the sauce has darkened and thickened a bit more. Cover and set aside.

4. To make the filling: Heat the oil in a large skillet or casserole over medium-high heat. Add the mushrooms and let them sear and brown, without stirring, for 3 to 4 minutes. Push the mushrooms to the sides of the pan and add the butter to the middle. When the butter begins to foam, add the asparagus, thyme, orange zest, salt, and pepper to taste, stir together with the mushrooms, and cook, stirring occasionally, until the asparagus is crisp-tender, 3 to 4 minutes. Remove from the heat.

5. Prepare the tortillas using either of the methods described on page 146.

6. Dip a tortilla in the mole, place it on a plate, and top with 2 to 3 tablespoons of the mushroom and asparagus mixture and a tablespoon of crumbled goat cheese. Roll up into a chubby enchilada and place seam side down on a serving platter. Continue with the remaining tortillas and filling.

7. Reheat the sauce if necessary. Spoon a generous amount of sauce on top of the enchiladas (use it all if you wish), garnish with the chives and toasted pine nuts, and serve.

SHRIMP ENCHILADAS IN RICH TOMATO SAUCE

ENTOMATADAS CON CAMARONES

SERVES 6

PREPARATION TIME: 15 minutes

COOKING TIME: 30 minutes

MAKE AHEAD: The sauce can be made up to 4 days ahead, covered, and refrigerated. The enchiladas can be assembled up to an hour ahead of time, covered, and kept warm in a 250-degree oven. When ready to serve, add the garnishes.

1½ pounds medium shrimp

5 flat-leaf parsley sprigs

2 garlic cloves

3 or 4 bay leaves

Kosher or sea salt

1½ pounds ripe tomatoes

1 or 2 serrano or jalapeño chiles, stemmed, to taste

4 scallions (white and light green parts only), coarsely chopped

½ teaspoon freshly grated nutmeg

3 tablespoons canola or safflower oil

1 cup Mexican crema or heavy cream, plus a bit more for garnish

12 corn tortillas

2 tablespoons unsalted butter

These are my kids' favorite enchiladas. Quite a few years ago we took a weeklong ride on the Chepe train along the Copper Canyon route, which goes from Chihuahua to Los Mochis, in the northern state of Sinaloa near the Baja, California, Gulf. We stopped in a quaint small town called El Fuerte, where we stayed at a charming hotel called Posada del Hidalgo. It was there that I ate one of the most delicious *entomatadas* I have ever tried. *Entomatadas* are enchiladas in which the tortillas are bathed in a rich tomato base. These *entomatadas* were rich and creamy: I could have eaten the sauce like a soup. With this recipe, I tried to conjure up what the cook told me about this dish, but I also added some elements, including the shrimp filling and nutmeg, a distinctive touch.

1. Remove the shells and tails from the shrimp and reserve. Rinse the shrimp and pat dry. Cut each one into 3 or 4 bite-size pieces.

2. In a medium saucepan, combine the shrimp shells and tails, parsley, 1 of the garlic cloves, the bay leaves, and ½ teaspoon salt. Cover with water and bring to a boil over medium-high heat. Reduce the heat to medium and simmer for 20 minutes. Strain the broth into a large measuring cup or heatproof bowl.

3. Combine the tomatoes, the remaining garlic clove, and chile(s) in a medium saucepan. Cover with water and bring to a simmer over medium-high heat. Reduce the heat to medium and simmer until the tomatoes are thoroughly soft, about 10 minutes. Using a slotted spoon, transfer the tomatoes to a blender. Add the chopped scallions. If you simmered 2 chiles, add only 1 of them to the blender; when you taste the finished puree, you can decide if you want to add the other. Add ½ teaspoon salt, the nutmeg, and 1 cup of the shrimp broth and puree until completely smooth. Taste and add some or all of the other chile if you would like more chile presence and heat.

continued...

FOR GARNISH

4 scallions (white and light green parts only), thinly sliced

1 ripe Hass avocado, halved, pitted, flesh scooped out and sliced

2 ounces queso fresco, farmer's cheese, or mild feta, crumbled (about ½ cup)

4. Rinse out and dry the saucepan. Add 1 tablespoon of the oil to the pan and heat over medium heat until hot but not smoking. Add the tomato sauce, being careful to avoid splatters, cover partially, and simmer, stirring occasionally, until the sauce thickens and deepens in color to a much darker red, about 10 minutes. Uncover, reduce the heat to medium-low, and stir in the cream. Keep at a steady low simmer for 8 to 10 more minutes, until the sauce is thick and creamy and coats the back of a wooden spoon. Taste and adjust the salt. Remove from the heat and cover to keep warm.

5. Prepare the tortillas, using either of the methods described on page 146.

6. To cook the shrimp, work in batches so that they will sear, not steam: Heat 1 tablespoon of the remaining oil and 1 tablespoon of the butter in a large skillet over high heat until the butter is foaming. Add half the shrimp, season with salt, and cook for 2 minutes, stirring and flipping a few times, until just cooked through and lightly browned. With a slotted spoon, transfer to a large plate. Add the remaining tablespoon each of oil and butter to the skillet, and once the butter is foaming, add the remaining shrimp, season with salt, and cook in the same manner; transfer to the bowl.

7. Reheat the sauce if necessary. Glide one of the tortillas through the sauce and place on a plate. Place about 3 of the shrimp across the middle and fold in half, like a quesadilla. Place on a platter and continue with the remaining tortillas and shrimp, overlapping the enchiladas slightly.

8. Once all of the enchiladas are filled, spoon the remaining tomato sauce on top. They should be sauced generously. Garnish with the sliced scallions, avocado, and cheese and serve.

CRABMEAT ENCHILADAS WITH PEAS IN TANGY BUTTERMILK SAUCE

ENJOCOCADAS DE CANGREJO CON CHICHARRITOS

SERVES 6

PREPARATION TIME: 15 minutes

COOKING TIME: 10 minutes

MAKE AHEAD: The enchiladas can be assembled up to an hour ahead of time; cover and keep warm in a 250-degree oven. Garnish when ready to serve.

2 tablespoons unsalted butter

6 scallions (white and light green parts only), sliced

1 jalapeño chile, finely chopped (seeded if desired)

2 garlic cloves, minced or pressed

1 pound jumbo lump crabmeat, picked over to remove cartilage or shells

Kosher or sea salt or to taste

1½ cups fresh or thawed frozen peas

2 tablespoons chopped fresh tarragon or 1½ teaspoons dried

1 tablespoon freshly squeezed lime juice

1½ cups Mexican crema or crème fraîche (see Note)

1½ cups buttermilk

½ teaspoon chipotle chile powder (or a substitute; see page 65)

Pinch of freshly ground black pepper or to taste

12 corn tortillas

In Mexico the sauce that moistens these delicate enchiladas would be made with *jocoque*, a cultured milk product that is similar to cultured buttermilk and is also popular in a strained version called *jocoque seco*, which is much like Greek yogurt or labne. It found its way to Mexico with the large Lebanese population that emigrated there after World War I. Though the Lebanese settled mostly along the Gulf Coast in the early days of their arrival, as the years went by, they made their way to Mexico City and to Puebla. In Puebla you will find the famous and unique *tacos árabes*, which are similar to Tacos al Pastor (page 138) but use pita bread rather than tortillas as wrappers and, along with salsas, are drizzled with Middle Eastern sauces like tahini or *jocoque*.

Jocoque found such a warm welcome in its new country that it quickly spread throughout the central and northern states that have extensive ranchlands, from Querétaro to Sinaloa and Sonora. There it was further Mexicanized and began to be mass-produced. You can now find popular commercial brands in big chain grocery stores, and in rural towns, you can find artisanal *jocoque* made by small producers.

One of the most popular ways to use *jocoque* is to slather it over enchiladas. Here is my take, enchiladas filled with tender crabmeat and lightly cooked sweet peas, seasoned with tarragon and jalapeño, and topped with a tangy chile-spiked *jocoque* sauce. I substitute a mix of buttermilk and cream for the *jocoque*.

Note: If you have access to *jocoque*, omit the buttermilk and cream and use 3 cups *jocoque*.

continued...

Queso fresco or feta cheese, crumbled (optional)

2   scallions (white and light green parts only), sliced

1. Heat the butter in a large skillet over medium heat until it melts and begins to foam. Add the scallions and jalapeño and cook, stirring occasionally, until softened, about 3 minutes. Stir in the garlic and cook until softened and fragrant, 30 seconds to a minute. Stir in the crab, ¼ teaspoon salt, the peas, tarragon, and lime juice and cook for 3 minutes, stirring occasionally, until the mixture is completely heated through and the crab is very lightly colored. Remove from the heat.

2. Place the Mexican cream and buttermilk (or the *jocoque*) in a medium saucepan, along with the chipotle powder, ½ teaspoon salt, and the pepper and whisk together. Place over the lowest possible heat while you prepare the tortillas; heat through, but *do not let it come to a simmer* at all or it will curdle.

3. Prepare the tortillas using either of the methods described on page 146.

4. Dip a tortilla into the sauce, place on a plate, and spoon 3 tablespoons of the crab mixture across the middle. Roll into a chubby enchilada and place seam side down on a serving platter. Continue with the remaining tortillas and crab.

5. Ladle about ½ cup of the sauce over the enchiladas, sprinkle with the cheese, if using, and garnish with the scallions.

SANBORNS' FAMOUS SWISS CHICKEN ENCHILADAS

LAS SUPER-FAMOSAS ENCHILADAS DE POLLO SUIZAS ESTILO SANBORNS

SERVES 6

PREPARATION TIME: 10 minutes

COOKING TIME: 30 minutes

MAKE AHEAD: The salsa verde can be made up to 4 days ahead, covered, and refrigerated. The enchiladas can be assembled a couple of hours ahead of time, then baked when you are ready to eat.

1½ pounds tomatillos, husked, thoroughly rinsed, and quartered

2 garlic cloves

½ cup coarsely chopped white onion

1 to 2 serrano chiles, stemmed (seeded if desired), to taste

1½ cups coarsely chopped fresh cilantro

1 teaspoon kosher or sea salt or to taste

¼ cup water

1 tablespoon canola or safflower oil

1 cup chicken broth or vegetable broth, homemade (page 40 or 41) or store-bought, or water

1 cup Mexican crema or heavy cream

12 corn tortillas

3 cups shredded cooked chicken (see page 40), or use a rotisserie chicken

If you are of my generation, my parents' generation, or my grandparents' generation and you are Mexican, you probably know and love the Swiss enchiladas from Sanborns. Established in Mexico City in 1903 by Walter Sanborn and his brother Frank, both California transplants, Sanborns began as a small general store/drugstore with the first-ever soda fountain in the country. As the years went by, it grew into a national branded institution, a department store with a full-blown cafeteria-style restaurant and locations all over Mexico. (The chain was eventually bought by Carlos Slim, one of the richest men in the world.)

Swiss enchiladas are one of the Sanborns kitchen's earliest creations. They are a variation of salsa verde enchiladas filled with chicken, but with the generous addition of cream and melted cheese (*suizas* is often used to name Mexican dishes that include copious amounts of cream and cheese). These are exactly as I remember them from the days when I would beg my dad to take me to Sanborns. The enchiladas came three to a plate, and I used to cut each roll into six pieces and savor each piece as if it were the last.

1. In a blender, combine the tomatillos, garlic, onion, chiles (start with one and then add all or part of another one, if desired), cilantro, salt, and water and puree until completely smooth.

2. Heat the oil in a medium saucepan over medium heat until hot but not smoking. Add the pureed tomatillo mixture, being careful, as it will sear and splutter, cover partially, and cook, stirring occasionally, until it thickens and darkens, 4 to 5 minutes. Stir in the broth or water, cover partially, and simmer for 5 minutes. Turn off the heat and stir in the cream. Set aside.

continued...

1 cup grated Monterey Jack, Mexican Chihuahua, or white cheddar cheese (about 4 ounces)

3. Preheat the oven to 400 degrees.

4. Prepare the tortillas using either of the methods described on page 146.

5. Pour about 1 cup of the salsa verde into a 9-x-13-inch baking dish. Place a tortilla on a plate or cutting board and arrange about ¼ cup of the chicken across the middle of it. Roll up into a soft, chubby enchilada and place seam down in the baking dish. Continue with the rest of the tortillas and chicken. Pour the rest of the salsa verde over the enchiladas and sprinkle the cheese on top.

6. Bake the enchiladas for 10 to 15 minutes, until the cheese has completely melted and begun to lightly brown. Serve.

MEXICAN COOK'S TIP

Using Jalapeños and Serranos:
When using jalapeño or serrano chiles in salsas or sauces, always begin with just one and then increase the amount if you want more heat. Some of my recipes call for a range, but it's important to begin at the low end, taste, and then add some or all of the second chile if you would like more heat. Chiles that come from the same market, batch, or even plant may have different levels of heat. Generally speaking, though, serranos are spicier than jalapeños. Also, keep in mind that you will often be adding broth or cream to a puree that is the foundation for a sauce, so even if it tastes a little spicy at first, the heat level will reduce considerably as the sauce simmers with the added ingredients.

PORK TENDERLOIN ENCHILADAS WITH MOLE VERDE

ENCHILADAS DE LOMITO DE CERDO CON MOLE VERDE

SERVES 6

PREPARATION TIME: 20 minutes

COOKING TIME: 40 minutes

MAKE AHEAD: The mole verde can be made up to 4 days ahead, covered, and refrigerated. The meat can be seasoned up to 24 hours ahead of time, covered, and refrigerated. The enchiladas can be assembled and sauced an hour ahead of time; cover and keep warm in a 250-degree oven. Garnish when ready to serve.

FOR THE PORK TENDERLOIN

- 2 pounds pork tenderloin (1 large or 2 smaller tenderloins)
- 5 garlic cloves, minced or pressed
- 3 tablespoons finely chopped fresh sage or 1 tablespoon dried
- 1 teaspoon kosher or sea salt
- ¼ teaspoon freshly ground black pepper
- ¼ cup plus 2 tablespoons olive oil
- 3 cups water

FOR THE MOLE VERDE

- 1 pound tomatillos, husked and thoroughly rinsed
- 2 garlic cloves
- 2 serrano or jalapeño chiles or to taste
- ¾ cup hulled raw pumpkin seeds (pepitas)

Mole sauces come in many colors. There seems to be a different one for just about any occasion, each with not only a regional stamp, but a family stamp as well. This is my version of mole verde, green mole.

Mole verde, in any of its interpretations, is not as well known outside of Mexico as mole poblano, the almost-black sauce that boasts chocolate as one of its ingredients. But I am a big fan of mole verde, made with pumpkin seeds, tomatillos, green chiles, green herbs like cilantro, and lettuce; it's much lighter than other moles, amazingly herbal and fresh tasting.

I love using this mole for enchiladas, which I stuff with diced roasted pork tenderloin that has been rubbed with sage and garlic and garnish with pungent red radishes tossed with lime juice and olive oil. You can use the sauce in other ways too, such as for dressing roasted baby potatoes or shredded cooked chicken or for poaching fish (right in the sauce).

....

1. To prepare the meat: Using a sharp knife, make an approximately ¼-inch-deep slit down the length of the tenderloin(s), from one end to the other.

2. In a small bowl, mix the garlic, sage, salt, pepper, and ¼ cup of the olive oil. Spread the seasoning paste all over the meat, including inside the slit. Tie the meat with kitchen twine, or if you have two 1-pound pork tenderloin pieces, tie them together, one on top of the other: Cut a long length of kitchen twine and wrap it around the meat at one end, about 1 inch from the end. Tie a knot, leaving two long ends, and crisscross the remaining string over and around the meat down its length. Wrap the string around one more time at the other end and tie another knot. Although no marinating time is necessary, you can cover the tenderloin and refrigerate for up to 24 hours.

3. Preheat the oven to 375 degrees.

continued...

½ teaspoon kosher or sea salt or to taste

½ cup coarsely chopped white onion

3 romaine lettuce leaves, torn into pieces

1½ cups fresh cilantro leaves and upper part of stems

1 cup fresh flat-leaf parsley leaves and upper part of stems

2 tablespoons canola or safflower oil

1½ cups meat juices from the cooked tenderloin or substitute chicken broth, homemade (page 40) or store-bought, or water

10 to 12 good-size radishes, trimmed and cut into matchsticks (2 cups)

1 tablespoon freshly squeezed lime juice

2 tablespoons olive oil

¾ teaspoon kosher or sea salt or to taste

12 corn tortillas

4. Heat a large ovenproof casserole or a deep 12-inch skillet over medium-high heat. Add the remaining 2 tablespoons olive oil. Add the tenderloin and brown on all sides, about 6 minutes.

5. If you used a skillet to brown the meat, transfer the meat to an oven-proof casserole or baking dish. Add the water to the casserole and roast the pork for 30 minutes. The internal temperature of the meat should be between 150 and 160 degrees. Place the meat on a cutting board, cover with aluminum foil to keep warm, and pour the meat juices into a measuring cup.

6. Meanwhile, to make the mole: Combine the tomatillos, garlic, and chiles in a medium saucepan, cover with water, and bring to a simmer over medium-high heat. Simmer for 10 to 12 minutes, until everything is completely cooked through and soft, and the color of the tomatillos has changed to olive green.

7. Place a small skillet over medium-low heat. Add the pumpkin seeds and toast, stirring often, until you hear popping sounds (like popcorn) and the seeds begin to brown lightly, 3 to 4 minutes; take care not to burn them. Immediately transfer to a bowl or plate and set aside.

8. Drain the tomatillos, garlic, and chiles and place in a blender (add 1 chile at first). Add the salt and puree until smooth. Add the toasted pumpkin seeds, onion, lettuce, cilantro, and parsley and puree until completely smooth. Taste and blend in some or all of the other chile, if desired.

9. Heat the canola or safflower oil in a casserole or heavy pot over medium heat. Add the puree and stir well, being careful, as this sauce *really* likes to jump around; use the lid as a shield. Stir in the 1½ cups reserved meat juices or the broth or water, bring to a simmer, cover partially, and simmer for 15 to 20 minutes, until thickened. Stir the sauce every 4 to 5 minutes to prevent it from sticking to the bottom of the pot; if the sauce appears to be cooking too fast and sticking, reduce the heat to low. The sauce should coat the back of a wooden spoon heavily. Taste and adjust the salt. Turn off the heat and cover to keep warm.

10. In a small bowl, combine the radishes with the lime juice, olive oil, and salt. Mix well. The more time you give them to macerate, the better the radishes will taste.

11. Dice or coarsely chop the cooked pork. If the meat is cold, you can place it back in the casserole after you dice it, along with any remaining meat juices, and heat through over low heat.

12. Prepare the tortillas using either of the methods described on page 146.

13. If necessary, reheat the mole verde. Dip a tortilla into the mole and place on a plate. Place about ¼ cup of the diced meat across the middle and roll into a chubby enchilada. Place seam side down on a serving platter. Continue with the rest of the tortillas and meat.

14. Pour the remaining mole verde on top of the enchiladas, garnish with the marinated radishes, and serve.

BASIC CREPES

CREPAS HECHAS EN CASA

MAKES ABOUT 12 (8-INCH) CREPES

PREPARATION TIME: 5 minutes, plus 30 minutes resting time

COOKING TIME: 15 minutes

MAKE AHEAD: The crepe batter can be made up to 2 days ahead, covered, and refrigerated; whisk well or blend before using. The crepes can be made ahead, cooled, and refrigerated for up to 4 days or frozen for up to 4 months in a sealed plastic bag.

1   cup all-purpose flour

2   large eggs

1   large egg yolk

1   cup whole milk

1   teaspoon sugar

½   teaspoon kosher or sea salt

5⅓ tablespoons (⅓ cup) un-salted butter, melted, plus more butter for cooking the crepes

½   cup water

The use of crepes in Mexican cooking is one of the remnants of the Maximilian Era (1864–1867), when Maximilian I and Carlota were sent by Napoleon III to establish a French monarchy in Mexico. The ruling class became obsessed with anything French, an obsession that continued through the dictatorship of Porfirio Díaz (1876–1911; Díaz dressed like a Frenchman, mustache and all) and right up to the Mexican Revolution. French-style food made with Mexican ingredi-ents was considered civilized and elegant, the fare of fancy restau-rants and state dinners. After the revolution, crepes and French bread (baguettes and the rolls called teleras and bolillos in Mexico) became popular foods that were no longer limited to the upper classes.

Crepas come in many forms, from savory to sweet (the most famous sweet ones being *crepas con cajeta*). When they are wrapped around a savory filling and generously sauced (as they always are), they resemble enchiladas, with the crepes standing in for the tortillas.

Crepes are very easy to make, though I've found that many people find the idea daunting. But any fears you may have will fall by the wayside if you follow these detailed directions. They come from my sister Alisa, a fabulous pastry chef who always shares her best culi-nary tricks with me. Alisa made sure I understood how important it is to allow the batter to rest, crucial for soft, fluffy crepes.

Note: This recipe is for savory crepes, but it will also work for sweet ones. Just add 1 extra tablespoon sugar to the batter.

1. Place the flour, eggs, egg yolk, milk, sugar, salt, and melted butter in a blender or food processor and blend until completely smooth. With the machine running, add the water and blend again until smooth. (Alterna-tively, you can mix the ingredients by hand.) Pour the batter into a con-tainer, cover, and refrigerate for at least 30 minutes. When ready to make the crepes, whisk the batter until smooth.

2. Heat an 8-inch crepe pan or a 10-inch nonstick skillet over medium heat. Once it is hot, add a very thin slice of butter and tilt or brush the pan to coat the surface. The butter should quickly bubble and sizzle; if

it does not, let the pan heat for a little longer. Tilt the pan, ladle a scant ¼ cup batter onto the lower side, and very quickly tilt and turn the pan to spread the batter over the entire surface. Cook until the edges of the crepe are beginning to dry and brown and the bottom is lightly browned, 30 to 40 seconds. With a spatula or your fingers, swiftly lift up one edge of the crepe and quickly turn it over. Cook the second side until lightly browned, which should take only 20 to 30 seconds. Remove the crepe from the pan and place on a plate. Repeat with the rest of the batter, stacking the crepes one on top of another. After making 2 or 3 crepes, you may need to butter the pan again.

MEXICAN COOK'S TIPS

- Make sure you give your pan at least a couple of minutes to heat before adding butter and then batter.
- Add just enough butter to coat the bottom of the pan.
- If the butter browns, wipe the pan clean with a paper towel and add a bit of fresh butter.
- After you ladle in the batter, immediately tilt the pan to cover the bottom of the pan, as the batter cooks and sets quickly. If the batter sets before it has covered the pan, ladle a bit more batter over the empty spots.
- Don't mess with the crepe until the bot-tom has cooked; it should be freckled and browned in spots and the edges should look a bit dry. Then flip the crepe.
- If not using finished crepes right away, stack them between pieces of parchment or wax paper. That way it will be easy to peel them off when you are ready to use them.

LEFTOVER CREPES

Whenever I have extra crepes, I fill them with cheese and poblano rajas or ham and cheese and serve them for breakfast. Any sauce, salsa, or mole that I have in my fridge will do for spooning on top.

Simple Crepe Fillings:
Any guacamole
Scrambled eggs
Refried beans, cheese, and avocado
Poblano rajas and onion (see page 187)
Potato and chorizo (e.g., the filling from the torta on page 73)
Cilantro Baby Potatoes (page 250)
Ham and cheese
Just cheese
Chicken Pibil (page 214), or rotisserie chicken, or shredded chicken from a stew

Simple Crepe Toppings:
Guacamole goes for a topping as well as for a filling
Crumbled queso fresco
Sliced avocado
Red Salsa (page 100)
Quick Salsa Verde (page 99)
Rustic Ranchero Salsa (page 104)
Mexican crema

CREPE ENCHILADAS WITH CORN, RAJAS, AND SQUASH IN AVOCADO-TOMATILLO SAUCE

ENCHILADAS DE CREPAS CON ELOTE, POBLANOS, Y CALABACITAS CON SALSA DE AGUACATE

SERVES 6

PREPARATION TIME: 25 minutes

COOKING TIME: 25 minutes

MAKE AHEAD: The crepes can be assembled (but not sauced) up to 2 hours ahead; cover and keep warm in a 250-degree oven. Top with the sauce when ready to serve. The sauce can be made 2 hours ahead; reheat gently over very low heat.

FOR THE FILLING

- 2 tablespoons canola or safflower oil

- 1 cup chopped white onion

- 1 pound poblano chiles (about 4), roasted, sweated, peeled, seeded, and diced (see page 21)

- ¼ teaspoon ground allspice

- 1 cup fresh or thawed frozen corn kernels

- 1 pound summer squash, preferably a round cala-bacita (see page 195), but regular zucchini will work, diced (about 3¼ cups)

- ¾ teaspoon kosher or sea salt

- Pinch of freshly ground black pepper

The filling for this crepe is one of the signature trios in Mexican cooking: poblano peppers, squash, and corn. Allspice brings out the exuberance of the poblano chiles. Don't let the number of chiles in the recipe worry you; they are tamed in this ménage of sweet corn and subtle squash. The crepes are light, and the sauce is foamy and ethereal, with a tangy-minty flavor.

....

1. To make the filling: Heat the oil in a large skillet over medium heat. Add the onion and cook, stirring occasionally, until softened, translucent, and just beginning to brown, about 6 minutes. Add the poblano rajas and all-spice; stir, cook for about 2 minutes, until the mixture is fragrant with allspice and the rajas have darkened a bit. Add the corn and cook, stirring, for 1 to 2 minutes. Stir in the squash, salt, and the pepper and cook until the squash is barely crisp-tender, about 3 minutes. Turn off the heat.

2. To make the sauce: Place the tomatillos and garlic in a medium saucepan, cover with water, and bring to a boil over medium-high heat. Reduce the heat to medium and simmer until the tomatillos are thoroughly cooked and their color has gone from light green to olive, about 10 minutes.

3. Drain the tomatillos and garlic and transfer to a blender. Add the salt, avocado, and chopped mint and puree until completely smooth.

4. Place a crepe on a plate and spoon ¼ cup of the filling across the middle. Roll up like a chubby enchilada and place seam side down on a serving platter. Continue with the rest of the crepes and filling.

5. Pour the sauce over the crepes, garnish with mint, if desired, and serve.

FOR THE SAUCE

1 pound (7 or 8) tomatillos, husked and thoroughly rinsed

1 garlic clove

½ teaspoon kosher or sea salt

1 large ripe Hass avocado, halved, pitted, and flesh scooped out

¼ cup finely chopped fresh mint plus (optional) whole leaves for garnish

12 crepes, homemade (page 166) or store-bought

CREPE ENCHILADAS WITH SWISS CHARD AND POTATOES IN CREAMY HATCH CHILE SAUCE

ENCHILADAS DE ACELGA CON PAPAS Y SALSA DE CHILE HATCH

SERVES 6

PREPARATION TIME: 25 minutes

COOKING TIME: 35 minutes

MAKE AHEAD: The crepes can be assembled (but not sauced) up to 2 hours ahead, covered, and kept warm in a 250-degree oven. Top with the sauce just before serving. The sauce can be made up to 4 days ahead, covered, and refrigerated; reheat over low heat.

FOR THE FILLING

Kosher or sea salt

1 pound Red Bliss potatoes, peeled and cut into ½-inch dice

3 tablespoons canola or safflower oil

¼ cup chopped white onion

1 jalapeño or serrano chile, minced (seeded if desired)

1 garlic clove, pressed or minced

2 ripe tomatoes (about ½ pound), chopped

1 pound Swiss chard, stemmed and chopped

½ cup water

I have taught at the Mexican Cultural Institute in Washington, DC, for eight years now. I sometimes get ideas for new recipes from requests from my students, and this is one of them. A student asked if I liked New Mexico–style cuisine and if I could make a Mexican dish with New Mexican dried Hatch chiles. I decided to make a creamy chile sauce to top crepe enchiladas. The filling is another popular combo from Mexican kitchens: Swiss chard and potatoes (*acelgas con papas*).

....

1. To make the filling: Fill a medium saucepan with water, add salt, and bring to a boil. Add the potatoes, reduce the heat to medium, and simmer for 4 to 6 minutes, until the potatoes are cooked al dente, or just tender. Drain and set aside.

2. In a large skillet, heat the oil over medium heat. Add the onion and cook until it softens and the edges begin to brown, 5 to 6 minutes. Stir in the jalapeño or serrano and cook for 2 minutes. Add the garlic and cook just until fragrant, 30 seconds to 1 minute. Stir in the tomatoes and cook until they have softened and released their juices, about 5 minutes. Stir in the chard, add the water, cover, and simmer, stirring occasionally, for 8 to 10 minutes, until the chard is very tender.

3. Uncover the pan, stir in the potatoes, season with salt to taste, and cook, uncovered, for another 10 minutes, or until the mixture is tender, fragrant, and moist. Remove from the heat.

4. To make the chile sauce: In a large skillet, heat the oil over medium heat. Add the onion and cook, stirring often, until tender, 4 to 5 minutes. Add the garlic and cook, stirring, just until fragrant, 30 seconds to 1 minute. Add the Hatch chiles, oregano, cumin, salt, and sugar, and cook until the chiles brown slightly and soften, about 2 minutes. Add the vinegar

and water, reduce the heat to low, cover, and simmer for 15 to 20 minutes, or until the chiles are very soft.

5. Open the lid, add the milk, stir, and heat through without boiling.

6. Transfer the contents of the pan to a blender and puree until smooth. Taste and adjust the seasoning.

7. Place a crepe on a plate and spoon ¼ cup of the filling across the middle. Roll up like a chubby enchilada and place seam side down on a serving platter. Continue with the remaining crepes and filling.

8. Top the crepes generously with the sauce and serve, garnished with the cilantro or bacon.

FOR THE CREAMY HATCH CHILE SAUCE

2 tablespoons canola or safflower oil

½ cup chopped yellow onion

3 garlic cloves, chopped

8 dried New Mexico Hatch chiles, stemmed, seeded, and broken into pieces

1 teaspoon dried oregano, preferably Mexican

½ teaspoon ground cumin

½ teaspoon kosher or sea salt or to taste

½ teaspoon packed dark brown sugar

1 teaspoon red wine vinegar

1 cup water

2 cups whole milk

10 to 12 crepes, homemade (page 166) or store-bought

Chopped fresh cilantro or, if you want to go overboard, crumbled fried bacon, for garnish

CASSEROLES, DEEP-DISH PIES, AND SKILLET PIZZAS

WHEN WE WERE FIRST MARRIED AND MOVED TO TEXAS, I wasn't a

good cook. But my husband and I both loved to eat and we missed the food from Mexico, so whenever I had a spare moment, into the kitchen I went. I experimented with absolutely every cooking magazine and cookbook I could find and began to turn out meals that I was proud of.

The problem was, my husband was a workaholic, as he is today (me too), and I never knew exactly when he was going to be home for dinner. Although I tried to time dinner for when he walked in the door, many times he came back from trips very late.

If only I'd known then about casseroles! But now that I have three kids and my own crazy schedule, I am thankful for casseroles, deep-dish pies, and pizzas that can be adapted so easily to our busy lives. They are easy, generous family meals—though there is a celebratory quality to them, too. They also make amazing leftovers that reheat easily, if you are lucky enough to have any, and most of them can also be frozen. Although they are essentially one-dish meals, they are happy in the company of a light green salad.

These are the dishes I turn to when I'm invited to a potluck. You can bake them when you get to the party, or bake them before and just reheat when you arrive. They are also convenient because they stretch. If you're never sure how many friends are coming home with your kids, or whether or not your daughter's boyfriend will be staying for dinner, it's easy to squeeze out another portion or two or three.

Any casserole has a comforting component, but Mexican—or Mexicanized—casseroles are more than just comforting. They go the extra mile when it comes to flavor. Macaroni and cheese will never be the same to you after you taste my poblano-infused version (page 178), and you will be amazed when you taste what happens to macaroni when you fry it in oil, mix it with chipotle-spiked tomato sauce, nestle pieces of chicken in it, and bake it under a blanket of bubbling cheese (page 176).

The tamal casserole on page 183 allows you to have a tamal feast without having to assemble scores of individual tamales. All the elements that I love about tamales are there—the rich, pillowy masa and delectable fillings—but I spread the masa under and over the filling for one big, lasagna-like casserole.

You'll find pizzas in this chapter. That's because I like to bake my Mexican pizzas in a cast-iron pan, deep-dish style, though I give you the option of baking them on a stone as well. As with other recipes in this chapter, all of the elements—the dough, sauce, toppings—can be prepared in advance. If you've never had Mexican pizza, your life is about to change. These toppings—grilled skirt steak with lime-pickled onions (page 196); poblano rajas, corn, and zucchini ribbons with creamy requesón or ricotta (page 199)—are all about flavor.

MACARONI WITH CHIPOTLE CHICKEN

CAZUELA DE POLLO AL CHIPOTLE CON PASTA Y QUESO GRATINADO

SERVES 6 TO 8

PREPARATION TIME: 10 minutes

COOKING TIME: 50 minutes

MAKE AHEAD: The casserole can be assembled up to 12 hours ahead (without adding the grated cheese), covered, and refrigerated.

1½ pounds ripe tomatoes or 1 (28-ounce) can crushed or whole plum (Roma) tomatoes

2 garlic cloves

½ cup coarsely chopped white onion

Kosher or sea salt and freshly ground black pepper

2 tablespoons sauce from canned chipotles in adobo or to taste

1 canned chipotle chile in adobo sauce, seeded, or more to taste (optional)

1½ pounds boneless, skinless chicken thighs

1 teaspoon dried oregano, preferably Mexican

¼ cup plus 2 tablespoons canola or safflower oil

1 pound elbow macaroni or penne

3 cups chicken broth, homemade (page 40) or store-bought

8 ounces Oaxaca, asadero, mozzarella, or Monterey Jack cheese, grated (2 cups)

This layered casserole—pasta toasted and then cooked in a rich chipotle-spiked tomato sauce, crisp chicken thighs browned with oregano nestled in the pasta, with a layer of melted cheese on top—is my kind of comfort food for those nights when we are all hungry and tired from another busy day. Every layer is brimming with flavor. Following Mexican tradition, I fry the pasta in seasoned oil, then finish cooking it in the tomato sauce. The bubbly blanket of cheese on top prevents the pasta and chicken from drying out as the casserole bakes, but even as the pasta and chicken remain soft and moist, the sides and bottom become delightfully browned and crusty. This won't happen if you stir, though, so resist any urge to do so. When you serve this, cut it into wedges, like a savory pie. I top it with Mexican crema and smooth slices of ripe avocado.

1. If using fresh tomatoes, place the tomatoes and garlic in a medium saucepan and cover with water. Bring to a simmer over medium-high heat and simmer until the tomatoes are thoroughly cooked and their skins have started to come off, about 10 minutes. Transfer the tomatoes and garlic, along with ½ cup of the water from the pan, to a blender or food processor and let cool for a couple of minutes (if using canned to-matoes, place with the garlic in the blender or food processor, with their juice). Add the onion, ¾ teaspoon salt, ¼ teaspoon pepper, the adobo sauce, and chipotle chile, if using, to the blender and puree until smooth.

2. Sprinkle the chicken with the oregano, ¼ teaspoon salt, or to taste, and pepper to taste. Heat ¼ cup of the oil in a large deep, casserole or heavy skillet over medium-high heat. Add the chicken thighs and sear until browned, 2 to 3 minutes per side. Transfer to a bowl.

3. Add the remaining 2 tablespoons oil to the casserole and heat until hot. Add the pasta and fry for a few minutes, stirring constantly, until it smells toasty and darkens; take care not to let it burn. Add the toma-to puree, shielding yourself from splatters with the lid (it will splutter dramatically). Stir, cover partially, and cook over medium heat, stirring occasionally, until the sauce darkens and cooks down to a thick puree, about 5 minutes.

4. Stir in the broth and, using tongs or a large spoon, nestle the browned chicken thighs in the pasta. Cover, reduce the heat to low, and cook for 25 minutes.

5. Meanwhile, preheat the oven to 400 degrees.

6. Uncover the casserole and sprinkle the cheese evenly over the top. Bake the casserole, uncovered, for 12 to 14 minutes, until the cheese has completely melted and begun to lightly brown on the edges. Remove from the heat.

7. Garnish the casserole with the avocado slices and serve hot, cut into thick wedges. If desired, drizzle cream over each slice.

VARIATION: Play with your pasta shapes! Longer pastas like angel hair, spaghetti, or fettuccine also work beautifully in this casserole. But to avoid a tangled mess, break the strands of pasta in half before frying them.

FOR GARNISH

1 ripe Hass avocado, halved, pitted, flesh scooped out and sliced

Mexican crema, crème fraîche, or sour cream (optional)

OREGANO

Mexican oregano is different from the Mediterranean oregano used in Italian cooking. It has a stronger yet warmer, mintier flavor and a more pronounced aroma. There are four different recognized varieties in Mexico, though there may be more. The best known is Yucatecan oregano, whose leaves are much larger and browner than the oregano found in central Mexico (though I am more accustomed to the central Mexico variety). My recipes will work with both the Mediterranean variety and Mexican, but if I can get Mexican oregano, it's the type I prefer.

CREAMY MAC 'N' CHEESE MEXICANO

MAC 'N CHEESE ESTILO MEXICANO

SERVES 6 TO 8

PREPARATION TIME: 20 minutes

COOKING TIME: 45 minutes

MAKE AHEAD: The casserole can be assembled up to 12 hours ahead (without adding the grated cheese), covered, and refrigerated.

Kosher or sea salt

1 pound elbow macaroni or penne

1 pound poblano chiles (3 to 4), seeded and cut into chunks

3 cups whole milk

4 tablespoons (½ stick) unsalted butter, plus more for greasing the baking dish

¼ cup plus 2 tablespoons all-purpose flour

Freshly ground black pepper

1 pound Oaxaca, asadero, or mozzarella, or Monterey Jack cheese, grated (about 4 cups)

6 ounces queso añejo, Cotija, or Parmigiano-Reggiano, grated (1½ cups)

6 to 8 thick bacon slices, coarsely chopped (optional)

2 tablespoons olive oil if not using bacon

1 cup chopped white onion

1 cup fresh or thawed frozen corn kernels

8 ounces zucchini, diced (about 1 medium)

Just as Americans love to reinterpret Mexican food, for decades Mexicans have played with American classics. I have not been immune to the impulse. This is one of my favorite spins on classic American mac 'n' cheese, and one of my most prized assets for pleasing a crowd. It is so cheesy inside and out that few can resist it. The cheese is a mild/sharp mixture of a melting cheese—Oaxaca, asadero, mozzarella, or Monterey Jack—and sharp, salty, dry cheese—queso añejo, Cotija, or Parmigiano-Reggiano. There is a lot of it both in the béchamel sauce flavored with poblano chiles that enrobes the pasta and bakes into a fabulous crust on top. Nestled among the creamy noodles are juicy kernels of sweet corn, seasoned onion, and tender bites of zucchini. Though I've made the bacon optional in this recipe, I love the smoky-meaty bite that it adds to the mix.

1. Bring a large pot of water to a boil and salt it generously. Add the pasta and cook until al dente, about 1 minute less than the cooking instructions on the package indicate. Drain and set aside in a large bowl.

2. Preheat the oven to 400 degrees. Butter a 9-x-13-inch baking dish.

3. Combine the poblano chiles and milk in a blender and puree until completely smooth.

4. In a medium saucepan, heat the butter over medium heat. Once it has melted and begun to foam, stir in the flour and cook, stirring constantly, until the mixture is light brown and has a toasty aroma, 1 to 2 minutes. Whisk in the milk, add ¾ teaspoon salt and pepper to taste, and whisk over medium heat until the sauce begins to thicken. Turn the heat down to low and simmer for 8 to 10 minutes, whisking occasionally to prevent lumps from forming.

5. Gradually stir in 3 cups of the grated Monterey Jack, Oaxaca, mozzarella or Manchego cheese, and 1 cup of the Parmigiano-Reggiano, or queso añejo cheese and mix well. Remove from the heat and stir until the cheese has completely melted into the béchamel. Set aside.

continued...

6. If using the bacon, heat a large skillet over medium heat. Add the bacon and cook, stirring frequently, until crisp and lightly browned, 5 to 6 minutes. Remove from the pan with a slotted spoon and place on a plate covered with paper towels, leaving behind as much fat as possible in the skillet. Set the skillet over medium heat. Or, if not using bacon, set a large skillet over medium heat and add the oil. Add the onion and cook, stirring, until soft and translucent, about 5 minutes. Add the corn and cook for 2 minutes. Stir in the zucchini, sprinkle with ¼ teaspoon salt, mix well, and remove from the heat. (You don't want to fully cook the zucchini in the pan, as it will cook further in the oven.) Transfer the contents of the pan to the bowl with the pasta, add the poblano béchamel and the bacon, if using, and gently stir together.

7. Scrape the pasta into the buttered baking dish. Combine the remaining cheeses and sprinkle over the top in an even layer. Bake until the cheese has melted and begun to crisp and brown along the edges, 25 minutes. Serve hot.

BAKED HUEVOS RANCHEROS CASSEROLE

CAZUELA DE HUEVOS RANCHEROS

SERVES 4

PREPARATION TIME: 10 minutes

COOKING TIME: 10 minutes

MAKE AHEAD: The casserole should be assembled just before serving, but you can make the salsa ranchera and refrieds ahead (see recipes).

3   cups refried beans, homemade (page 247) or store-bought

2   teaspoons canola or safflower oil

8   thin slices deli ham or turkey

8   large eggs

Kosher or sea salt

1   recipe Rustic Ranchero Salsa (page 104)

8   ounces Oaxaca, asadero, mozzarella, or Monterey Jack cheese, grated (2 cups)

I wish I could take the credit for this brilliant version of huevos rancheros, but I can't. I learned to make it at a restaurant called Bove in the central Mexican town of San Miguel de Allende. At Bove all the ingredients are from the restaurant's ranch, including the cheese and cream. The dish is served in individual casseroles and called simply Bove, as it is the signature dish. It is a luxury, with the eggs with still-runny yolks, the earthy refried beans, the savory ham, and a thick layer of salsa ranchera and melted cheese, all tucked into your very own individual baking dish. You also get *totopos* (tortilla chips, page 25) for scooping up the delicious mess as you eat.

I too opt for individual casseroles when I make this for guests, but for everyday dining and more casual entertaining, a big casserole makes more sense, especially since my hungry boys (and I) usually can't wait until my husband gets home from work to eat. And no, there is usually nothing left for my husband, so I end up making something else for him.

1. Preheat the oven to 450 degrees.

2. Heat the refried beans in a small saucepan over medium heat, stirring occasionally, until hot, a few minutes. Spread the beans in an even layer in a 9-x-13-inch baking dish.

3. Heat 1 teaspoon of the oil in a large nonstick skillet over medium-high heat. In batches, add the ham or turkey slices and sear for about 15 to 20 seconds per side. Remove from the heat, fold the slices in half, and arrange on top of the beans in a single layer.

4. Reduce the heat to medium-low and add the remaining 1 teaspoon oil. Crack all 8 eggs side by side into the pan, or cook in batches. Sprinkle with salt to taste. Cover and cook for 2 to 3 minutes, just until the eggs are set on the bottom but are not fully done; the yolks should be runny and the top part of the egg whites should not yet be cooked through. Turn off the heat. Alternatively, you can cook the eggs 2 at a time in a small nonstick skillet.

continued...

Alternatively, you can assemble the dish in individual gratin dishes: Spoon ¾ cup refried beans into each ramekin, top with a couple of slices of turkey or ham, and top the meat with a pair of cooked eggs. Ladle a generous amount of the salsa over the eggs—enough to completely cover them—and top with the cheese. Set the ramekins on a baking sheet and bake as directed.

5. With a large spoon or spatula, cut the eggs into 8 portions or arrange them as you cook them in batches and, trying not to break the yolks, place each one on top of a folded slice of meat. Gently ladle the salsa over the eggs so that they are completely covered, and top with the cheese.

6. Bake until the cheese has completely melted, about 3 minutes. Serve immediately.

TAMAL CASSEROLE WITH CHICKEN AND SALSA VERDE

CAZUELA DE TAMAL DE POLLO EN SALSA VERDE

SERVES 10 TO 12

PREPARATION TIME: 15 minutes

COOKING TIME: 1 hour

MAKE AHEAD: The casserole can be assembled up to 12 hours ahead, covered, and refrigerated.

FOR THE TAMAL MASA

1 cup lard, vegetable shortening, or seasoned vegetable oil (see page 131)

½ teaspoon kosher or sea salt or to taste

3½ cups chicken broth, homemade (page 40) or store-bought, plus more if needed

1½ teaspoons baking powder

1 pound (about 3¼ cups) masa harina, preferably for tamales, but masa harina for tortillas will also work (see page 186)

FOR THE FILLING

Vegetable oil, for greasing the baking dish

4 cups (a double recipe) Quick Salsa Verde (page 99)

3 cups shredded cooked chicken (see page 40) or rotisserie chicken

1½ cups Mexican crema, crème fraîche, or sour cream

Anything wrapped and cooked in a husk or leaf is a tamal: ancestral food that lends itself to an infinite universe of possibilities. Usually made with corn masa, tamales come with a variety of fillings and salsas. They have been fiesta food since pre-Hispanic times, when they were considered gifts from the gods, but they are also everyday food, essential pillars of Mexican cuisine. In Mexico you can buy tamales freshly made on just about every corner, like tortillas; they are also sold refrigerated or frozen in grocery stores.

The only catch to making them is that they are quite laborious to prepare. Once you've prepared the filling and the masa, the tamales have to be assembled and wrapped one by one, then steamed for an hour in a big pot. That is why tamal making (and eating) is so often a communal activity, called a *tamaliza*.

If you don't have a big Mexican-American family nearby and you can't find tamales at a nearby corner, a casserole is the perfect solution. The concept is also quite popular in Mexico, especially on New Year's Eve. Many people, including my mother-in-law, buy freshly made tamales, unwrap them, and layer them in a casserole with salsa, cream, and cheese, then bake them as if they were a lasagna.

Even easier is a layered casserole like this one. You use the same elements, but you spread them in layers in the casserole. This one is based on my favorite tamale of all time, with chicken and a generous amount of green salsa sandwiched between two fluffy, moist layers of masa and topped with Mexican crema and cheese.

1. To make the tamal masa: Place the lard or shortening in the bowl of a stand mixer fitted with the paddle attachment and beat on medium speed for 1 minute, or until very light. (If using the seasoned oil, simply substitute it for the lard or shortening and mix it in with the broth, without beating it first by itself.) Add the salt and 1 tablespoon of the broth

continued...

and beat until the mixture is white and fluffy, about 2 minutes. Add the baking powder and beat it in, then take turns adding the masa harina and the remaining broth, in 3 or 4 additions. Add a little more broth if it feels dry. Continue beating for about 10 minutes, until the dough is homogeneous, very fluffy, and aerated. To see if the masa is ready, drop ½ teaspoon of it into a cup of cold water. It should float. If it does not, beat for an additional 4 to 5 minutes and do the test again. (If you do not have a stand mixer, you can use a hand mixer or mix this by hand with a rubber spatula, but it will take more than 10 minutes to achieve the aerated consistency that you need.)

2. Preheat the oven to 400 degrees. Grease a 9-x-13-inch baking dish with oil.

3. To add the filling: Spread half the tamal masa over the baking dish. In a bowl, combine 3 cups of the salsa with the chicken and toss together until the chicken is thoroughly coated. Spread the mixture over the masa. Top with the rest of the masa and spread it evenly, using an offset or rubber spatula.

4. Cover the dish with aluminum foil, making sure that you leave space between the masa and the foil so the masa doesn't stick to the foil as it bakes. Crimp the foil around the edges of the baking dish to seal it well. Bake for 50 minutes, or until the masa is fully cooked yet still moist and lightly browned on top.

5. Remove from the oven and carefully remove the aluminum foil, as the steam will be very hot. Pour the remaining 1 cup salsa over the masa, top with the cream, and sprinkle on the grated cheese. Place in the oven, uncovered, and bake for 10 more minutes, or until the cheese is melted and bubbling. Remove from the oven and let sit for a few minutes.

6. Serve hot, cut into squares or rectangles.

10 ounces melting cheese, such as Oaxaca, asadero, mozzarella, or Monterey Jack, grated (2½ cups)

MEXICAN COOK'S TIP

Oil the foil lightly with vegetable oil to prevent the masa from sticking.

MEXICAN COOK'S TIP

Alternatively, you can assemble the dish in individual gratin dishes or ramekins.

MAKING TAMALES

For tamales, the masa needs to be as fluffy as possible—so airy that if you take a cup of cold water and drop half a teaspoon of the masa into it, it floats. You can achieve this only by beating it for a long time at a good speed. Let the mixer help you out! Do you have 10 minutes to spare? Then you will have fabulous masa for tamales.

Traditionally, tamal masa is made with lard. If top-quality and fresh, lard contributes a delicious flavor and texture (and it doesn't have as much cholesterol as people think).

Some people prefer to use vegetable shortening.

If you don't want to use either, you can use the seasoned oil on page 131. It's great for vegetarians (or you can use coconut oil). In fact, before the Spanish arrived in Mexico and there was no pork, oils extracted from fruits, vegetables, and seeds were used to moisten and season masa for tamales, so feel free to play around—you will be taking the tamales back to their roots.

MASA HARINA

Without a doubt, the most important use of corn in Mexican cuisine has been as *masa*, or dough, for both tortillas and tamales. More than a thousand years ago, indigenous people developed the technique called nixtamalization, which renders dried corn much more digestible and nutritious and transforms it into multipurpose corn masa. The process involves drying the corn, soaking and cooking the kernels in a mix of hot water and mineral lime, then peeling off their outer layer and grinding them. It is very laborious and time-consuming, not something that home cooks have time for today.

Masa harina, or instant corn masa flour, changed all that. The flour is made with corn that has already undergone the nixtamalization process, so that all that is required for making masa for tamales is combining it with lard or another fat and broth or water. (Of course, if there is a tortillería close to you and they make fresh nixtamalized masa, you can opt for that.) In some stores you can get masa harina especially made for tamales; if you can't find it, regular masa will also work for tortillas.

DEEP-DISH CHEESE AND POBLANO PIE WITH AVOCADO CREAM AND PISTACHIOS

CAZUELA DE HOJALDRE DE CHILE POBLANO Y QUESO CON CREMA DE AGUACATE Y PISTACHES

SERVES 6 TO 8

PREPARATION TIME: 15 minutes

COOKING TIME: 20 minutes

MAKE AHEAD: The pie can be assembled up to 1 hour ahead and refrigerated before baking.

- 2 tablespoons unsalted butter, plus more for greasing the baking dish
- 1 tablespoon canola or safflower oil
- 2 cups slivered or thinly sliced white onions
- 1 pound poblano chiles (about 4), roasted, peeled, seeded, and cut into strips (see page 21)

Kosher or sea salt

¼ teaspoon ground allspice

All-purpose flour, for rolling out the puff pastry

- 2 frozen puff pastry sheets (depending on the brand, it may come one or two sheets per package and weigh between 1.2 and 1.6 pounds), thawed
- 8 ounces Oaxaca, asadero, mozzarella, or Monterey Jack cheese, grated (2 cups)
- 8 ounces Oaxaca, asadero, mozzarella, or Monterey Jack cheese, grated (2 cups)

This is like queso fundido, a melted-cheese party, with a roasted poblano topping, all tucked inside puff pastry. It's like a gigantic, crispy, puffy, filling, and exotic quesadilla. To make it even more indulgent, it's topped with avocado cream and sprinkled with crunchy pistachios.

In Mexico we make *hojaldre de queso* in all sorts of forms, from casseroles like this one to empanadas to mini appetizer puffs or triangles. Whatever the presentation, it always flies off the serving dish.

....

1. Heat the butter and canola or safflower oil in a large skillet over medium heat. Once the butter has melted, add the onions and cook, stirring occasionally, until they are tender and the edges have begun to brown, 5 to 6 minutes. Stir in the poblano strips, ¼ teaspoon salt, and the allspice and cook, stirring occasionally, for another 5 minutes. Remove from the heat and set aside.

2. Preheat the oven to 375 degrees. Butter a 9-x-13-inch baking dish.

3. Sprinkle your work surface and rolling pin with flour and roll out one of the puff pastry sheets to an 11-x-15-inch rectangle, sprinkling a little bit of flour on the top as you go to prevent it from sticking to your rolling pin. Carefully roll the pastry loosely around the rolling pin and fit it into the baking dish, easing the pastry up the sides of the dish.

4. Sprinkle the cheeses evenly over the puff pastry (they will melt together during baking). Top with the poblano filling.

5. Roll out the second sheet of puff pastry just a tad bigger than the size of the baking dish, to allow for shrinkage, about 9½ x 13½ inches. Lay it gently on top of the filling and crimp the edges of the pastry sheets together to make a nice rim all the way around. With a fork, gently poke

continued...

1 large egg, beaten with
  1 tablespoon water for egg
  wash

½ cup coarsely chopped
  pistachios

1 large ripe Hass avocado,
  halved, pitted, and flesh
  scooped out

2 tablespoons olive oil

1 tablespoon freshly
  squeezed lime juice

about 15 holes in the pastry to make steam vents, so there will be no pockets formed when the pie bakes. Brush the top with the egg wash.

6. Bake the pie for 30 minutes, or until the top is a deep golden brown, puffed, and crisp.

7. Meanwhile, toast the pistachios: Heat a small skillet over medium-low heat. Add the pistachios and toast, stirring frequently, for 3 to 4 minutes, or until lightly colored and fragrant. Immediately transfer to a small bowl.

8. To make the avocado cream: Mash the avocado with a fork in a bowl. Add the olive oil, lime juice, and ½ teaspoon salt, or to taste, and mash together. Or, if you want a smoother texture, you can process it in a food processor.

9. To serve, cut the pie into approximately 3-inch squares and arrange on a platter. Spoon some avocado cream on top of each square, sprinkle with toasted pistachios, and serve hot. Or pass the avocado cream and pistachios separately and let your guests add as much as they like.

MEXICAN COOK'S TIP

Hojaldre means "puff pastry." Good puff pastry is available in the frozen foods section of just about any supermarket. You have to follow a few rules when you thaw it so that it doesn't become too moist or warm. It should not be outside the refrigerator for no more than 20 to 30 minutes. If you leave it at room temperature for too long, the pastry will become a useless piece of soaked cardboard. It's really best to thaw it in the refrigerator, which will take 2 to 3 hours. Once thawed, it can remain in the refrigerator for up to 3 days. Don't ever put thawed puff pastry back in the freezer, though. Roll the pastry out as soon as you remove it from the refrigerator (or have thawed it briefly at room temperature) and be sure to flour your work surface and rolling pin sufficiently so that it won't stick.

DEEP-DISH TUNA MINILLA PIE

CAZUELA DE HOJALDRE DE MINILLA DE ATÚN

SERVES 6

PREPARATION TIME: 20 minutes

COOKING TIME: 45 minutes

MAKE AHEAD: The filling can be made up to 4 days ahead, covered, and refrigerated.

¼ cup canola or safflower oil

1¼ cups chopped white onions

2 garlic cloves, finely chopped

1½ pounds ripe tomatoes, chopped, or 1 (28-ounce) can crushed tomatoes

½ teaspoon packed brown sugar

1 teaspoon dried oregano, preferably Mexican

½ teaspoon dried thyme

½ teaspoon dried marjoram

¾ teaspoon kosher or sea salt or to taste

3 (7-ounce) cans oil-packed tuna, drained

2 bay leaves

½ cup seeded and chopped pickled jalapeño chiles or to taste

1 tablespoon coarsely chopped capers

2 tablespoons coarsely chopped raisins

⅓ cup coarsely chopped pimiento-stuffed Manzanilla olives

¼ cup chopped fresh flat-leaf parsley

Minilla is a signature fish preparation from the state of Veracruz. It's an economical and delicious way to make a piece of fish, or a can of tuna, go a long way. As with many popular dishes in Mexico, who knows where the name comes from? But, like most of the famous dishes from Veracruz, Mexico's historical port of entry for waves of immigrants, it reflects a happy mingling of Spanish staples and native Mexican ingredients. The main elements are pimiento-stuffed Manzanilla olives, salty capers, and a liberal amount of pickled jalapeños. They are combined with seasoned tomatoes cooked down to a thick, pungent sauce, with shredded tuna added.

Tuna minilla can sit on top of white rice or noodles or be tucked inside a torta or empanada. In Veracruz, you will find it served as a much-loved appetizer inside whole pickled jalapeño chiles. I find that baking minilla inside a big pocket of puff pastry and cutting it into wedges is the perfect way to eat it.

1. In a large skillet or casserole, heat the oil over medium heat. Add the onions and cook, stirring, until soft and translucent, about 5 minutes. Add the garlic and cook, stirring, until fragrant and beginning to color, about 1 minute. Stir in the tomatoes, brown sugar, oregano, thyme, marjoram, and salt and cook, stirring often, until the tomatoes have cooked down and the mixture is thick and fragrant, about 15 minutes.

2. Stir in the tuna, breaking it up with a spatula or fork; there should not be any big chunks. Add the bay leaves, pickled jalapeños, capers, raisins, olives, and parsley and stir well. Reduce the heat to medium-low, cover, and cook for about 10 minutes, stirring occasionally. The mixture should be moist but not watery. Taste for salt and add more if desired. Remove the bay leaves and remove from the heat.

3. Preheat the oven to 375 degrees. Butter a 9- to 10-inch round Pyrex or ceramic baking dish or deep-dish pie plate.

4. Lightly flour your countertop and rolling pin and roll out one of the sheets of puff pastry to a 12-inch square, sprinkling a small amount of

continued...

All-purpose flour, for rolling out the puff pastry

2 frozen puff pastry sheets (depending on the brand, it may come one or two sheets per package and weigh between 1.2 and 1.6 pounds), thawed

1 large egg, beaten with 1 tablespoon water for egg wash

1 teaspoon sesame seeds, for garnish

flour on the top as you go to prevent it from sticking to the rolling pin. Carefully roll the pastry loosely up around the rolling pin and fit it into the baking dish, easing the pastry up the sides of the dish and over the edges. Trim the overhang to about ½ inch. Spoon in the tuna mixture.

5. Roll out the other sheet of pastry to an 11-inch square. With a pastry brush, brush the lip of the bottom pastry with the egg wash. Lay the top pastry sheet over the filling and press the edges against the bottom pastry. Trim away the excess overhang, then pinch the edges together all around the rim of the pie to make an attractive edge. Crimp the edges with a fork all around to decorate and further seal the pastry. With a pastry brush, brush the top of the pastry sheet with egg wash. With a sharp small knife, make four to six 1-inch slits or vents in the top, radiating out from the center, for steam to escape during baking. Sprinkle the sesame seeds over the top.

6. Bake the pie for 25 to 30 minutes, until crisp, puffed up, and golden brown. Cut into wedges and serve.

RICE CASSEROLE WITH POBLANO RAJAS, CORN, AND TOMATOES

CAZUELA DE ARROZ CON RAJAS, ELOTE, Y JITOMATE

SERVES 6 TO 8

PREPARATION TIME: 20 minutes

COOKING TIME: 30 minutes

MAKE AHEAD: The casserole can be assembled a few hours ahead, covered, and refrigerated.

2 tablespoons unsalted butter, plus more for the pan

1 tablespoon canola or safflower oil

1 cup chopped white onion

1 pound ripe tomatoes, chopped

1 teaspoon kosher or sea salt or to taste

Freshly ground black pepper to taste

1 pound poblano chiles (about 4), roasted, peeled, seeded, and cut into 1-x-¼-inch strips (see page 21)

1½ cups fresh or thawed frozen corn kernels

1 cup chicken or vegetable broth, homemade (page 40 or 41) or store-bought, or water

1 cup Mexican crema, crème fraîche, or heavy cream

½ cup requesón or ricotta cheese

4 cups cooked white rice (page 241)

6 ounces Oaxaca, asadero, mozzarella, or Monterey Jack cheese, grated (1½ cups)

This comforting blend of New World and Old World ingredients is very much in the style of the baroque dishes from the old Spanish convents in Mexico. It is a gratinéed mix of rice, which came to Mexico from Spain, and purely Mexican rajas, corn, and tomatoes, enriched with caramelized onion and cheese. It's best served bubbling hot from the oven, but I like to eat the leftovers cold.

1. Preheat the oven to 400 degrees. Butter a 9-x-9-inch or 8-x-11-inch baking dish.

2. Heat the butter and oil in a large skillet over medium heat. Add the onion and cook, stirring occasionally, until translucent and soft and the edges are beginning to brown, 5 to 6 minutes. Increase the heat to high, add the tomatoes, salt, and pepper, and cook for 7 to 8 minutes, stirring occasionally, until the tomatoes have softened and cooked down. Reduce the heat to medium, stir in the poblanos and corn, and cook for about 2 more minutes. Stir in the broth or water, cream, and requesón or ricotta, and cook, stirring, until nicely blended, about 1 minute. The mixture should be very saucy.

3. Spoon the rice into the prepared dish and spread in an even layer. Add the poblano mixture and spread evenly over the rice. Sprinkle on the grated cheese.

4. Bake for 15 minutes, or until the cheese has completely melted. Serve hot.

MEXICAN COOK'S TIP

Typically Mexican rice casseroles use ordinary Mexican white rice, which tends to be long- or extra-long-grain. Jasmine rice works beautifully too. If you want to give the casserole a nuttier flavor, and make it even more wholesome, use brown rice.

ZUCCHINI TORTE

TORTA DE CALABACITAS

SERVES 6

PREPARATION TIME: 15 minutes

COOKING TIME: 35 minutes

MAKE AHEAD: The torte can be baked up to 2 hours ahead and set aside, covered, at room temperature.

1½ pounds zucchini

½ cup rice flour

½ cup all-purpose flour (or substitute additional rice flour for a gluten-free version)

2 teaspoons baking powder

¾ teaspoon kosher or sea salt

8 tablespoons (1 stick) unsalted butter, at room temperature, plus more for the pan

¼ cup sugar

5 large eggs

¼ cup Mexican crema or crème fraîche

¼ cup whole milk

2 ounces melting cheese, such as Oaxaca, asadero, mozzarella, or Monterey Jack, grated (about ½ cup)

2 ounces dry aged cheese, such as queso añejo, ricotta salata, or Parmigiano-Reggiano, grated (about ½ cup)

Mexican tortas (not to be confused with the other tortas—sandwiches made with crusty French-style rolls) are a sort of cross between a fluffy bread, a savory pudding, and a soufflé. They can be a side to both dry and saucy entrées, can be served as a main dish accompanied by a salad, and can travel solo in grand style as a hearty snack. And tortas can help eager parents deceive picky eaters who don't like vegetables. What defines each torta is the vegetable that predominates: The most common are peas, carrots, spinach, zucchini, and corn.

This zucchini torta is the one I make most often. It has a generous layer of cheese on top. As the torta bakes, the salty, dry aged cheese browns nicely on top, while the melting cheese, such as Oaxaca or asadero, is partly absorbed into the upper layer of the zucchini mixture.

1. Preheat the oven to 350 degrees. Butter an 8-x-11-inch baking dish.

2. Trim and grate the zucchini. Place it in a colander and press hard with your hands or the back of a wooden spoon to extract water. Let rest while you prepare the other ingredients, pressing and squeezing the zucchini at intervals to extract the maximum amount of water. You should have about 3½ cups drained zucchini.

3. In a small bowl, stir together the rice flour, all-purpose flour, baking powder, and salt. Set aside.

4. With a hand mixer and a large bowl or in the bowl of a stand mixer fitted with the paddle attachment, beat the butter at medium-high speed for 2 minutes, or until creamy. Add the sugar and beat until well incorporated and fluffy. Beat in the eggs one at a time. Add half the flour mixture and beat in. Scrape down the bowl and paddle. Beat in the cream, the remaining flour mixture, and the milk. Scrape down the sides of the bowl and the paddle.

5. Squeeze the zucchini one more time and add to the bowl. Mix on low speed just until well combined. Scrape the mixture into the buttered

baking dish. Sprinkle on the melting cheese, then sprinkle the dry aged cheese evenly over the top.

6. Bake for 35 minutes, or until the cheese is completely melted and the edges of the torta are a light golden brown. Remove from the oven and serve hot, warm, or cold.

CALABACITAS

In Mexico we call summer squash *calabacitas*. Most of what I find in Mexico is smaller, a lighter green with creamy speckles, and rounder than the green zucchini we find in supermarkets in the United States. It also goes by the name *calabacita italiana*, or *pipián* in Latin stores throughout the U.S., as well as courgette or round zucchini. They are interchangeable in recipes, but the Mexican variety tends to be a bit milder and sweeter. There are countless ways in which calabacita is used in Mexican cooking; it may show up more than any other vegetable. And all of its parts are used: the vegetable, the flower stems (especially in tasty soups), the flowers, and the seeds.

MEXICAN COOK'S TIP

Calabacitas, or zucchini, are very watery. This torta already has a very moist batter, so make sure you drain the squash well, or the mixture will be watery. After you grate it, put the grated squash in a strainer or colander and press hard on it with your hands, then let it sit for a few minutes. Press out the moisture again with the back of a spoon or by taking up handfuls of grated squash and squeezing them. You will be surprised by how much more liquid there is.

MEXICAN PIZZA WITH GRILLED SKIRT STEAK AND SPRING ONIONS

PIZZA CON CARNE ASADA Y CEBOLLITAS

MAKES 1 (10- TO 12-INCH) PIZZA

PREPARATION TIME: 15 minutes, plus 30 minutes resting time

COOKING TIME: 30 minutes

MAKE AHEAD: The meat can be marinated for up to 24 hours, covered, and refrigerated.

FOR THE MARINADE

1 chile de árbol

2 garlic cloves, coarsely chopped

2 tablespoons Worcestershire sauce

½ cup Maggi sauce or soy sauce

½ cup freshly squeezed lime juice

FOR THE PIZZA

8 ounces skirt steak or flank steak

3 spring onions (*cebollitas*) or 1 bunch scallions (white and light green parts only), cut into bite-size pieces

All-purpose flour, for dusting the work surface

½ recipe Foolproof Pizza Dough (page 200)

½ cup Basic Pizza Sauce (page 201)

6 ounces Oaxaca or mozzarella cheese, grated (1½ cups)

Like most people, my family loves pizza. But we like it Mexican style, meaning pizza that is *más sabroso*, supertasty (*sabor* means "flavor"), and enjoyable on an unforgettable level. To *sabrosear* our pizzas, we use marinated toppings like the lime-marinated spring onions on this one, various salsas, and pickled condiments, which add a punch to each bite. Go Mexican-style once, and you will never go back.

1. To make the marinade: Toast the chile in a small dry skillet over medium heat for less than a minute per side, taking care not to burn it. Remove the stem, break the chile into pieces, and transfer to a blender or food processor.

2. Add the garlic, Worcestershire sauce, Maggi sauce or soy sauce, and lime juice to the blender and process until the chile and garlic are finely chopped and the ingredients are well blended. Set aside ¼ cup of this marinade for the spring onions.

3. To prepare the steak and pizza: Place the steak in a shallow baking dish and pour on the remaining marinade. Turn to coat thoroughly. Place the spring onions in a medium bowl and toss with the reserved ¼ cup marinade. Cover both the steak and the onions and refrigerate for at least 30 minutes, or for up to 24 hours, turning the meat and stirring the onions at least once.

4. Preheat the broiler or prepare a medium-hot fire in a grill.

5. Remove the steak from the marinade (discard the marinade). Place in a baking pan and broil for about 4 to 5 minutes per side. Alternatively, grill the steak for the same amount of time. You want to cook the meat to medium. Let rest for 5 to 10 minutes, then slice ¼ to ½ inch thick across the grain and cut the strips into 1- to 2-inch pieces.

6. Preheat the oven to 425 degrees with a pizza stone in it if using. On a lightly floured surface, stretch the pizza dough to a 10- to 12-inch circle.

continued...

½ ripe Hass avocado, pitted, flesh scooped out and sliced

Fresh cilantro leaves

Place on the pizza stone or in a 10- or 12-inch cast-iron pan. Bake for 10 minutes.

7. Remove the crust from the oven and spread the sauce over it, leaving a ½-inch border all the way around. Top the sauce with ¾ cup of the cheese, then arrange the meat and drained onions on top of the cheese; reserve the onion marinade for people to add as an extra sauce for the pizza. Top with the remaining cheese. Bake until the cheese has melted and the crust is crisp, 12 to 14 more minutes. Remove from the stone with a paddle or wide spatula.

8. Transfer the pizza to a cutting board, arrange the avocado slices on top, and sprinkle with the cilantro. Slice and serve with the onion marinade on the side for people to drizzle as they please.

MEXICAN PIZZA with POBLANO RAJAS, CORN, and ZUCCHINI

PIZZA DE CHILE POBLANO, ELOTE, Y CALABACITAS

MAKES 1 (10- TO 12-INCH) PIZZA

PREPARATION TIME: 15 minutes

COOKING TIME: 25 minutes

MAKE AHEAD: The vegetable mix can be made up to 24 hours ahead, covered, and refrigerated.

1 poblano chile, roasted, peeled, seeded, and cut into 1-inch strips (see page 21)

1 small zucchini, trimmed and shaved into ribbons with a mandoline or vegetable peeler (about 1¼ cups)

⅓ cup fresh or thawed frozen corn kernels

¼ cup slivered red onion

2 tablespoons olive oil

2 teaspoons freshly squeezed lime juice

¼ teaspoon chipotle or ancho chile powder (see page 65)

¼ teaspoon kosher or sea salt or to taste

All-purpose flour, for dusting the work surface

½ recipe Foolproof Pizza Dough (page 200)

½ cup Basic Pizza Sauce (page 201)

6 ounces Oaxaca or mozzarella cheese, grated (1½ cups)

¼ cup ricotta or requesón cheese

My vegetarian Mexican pizza is topped with a centuries-old Mexican vegetable trio—squash, corn, and poblanos. The squash is shaved into elegant ribbons, the chile is roasted and cut into rajas, and the corn kernels are cooked only enough to turn them juicy and sweet, so they pop when you bite into them. The three vegetables, as well as red onion, are tossed with a lime-based marinade, then strewn over the lightly sauced crust and blanketed with Oaxaca or mozzarella cheese and dollops of soft ricotta or requesón. They remain crunchy and juicy under the cheese as they bake in the hot oven.

. . . .

1. Preheat the oven to 425 degrees with a pizza stone in it if using.

2. In a medium bowl, toss together the poblano strips, zucchini ribbons, corn, onion, oil, lime juice, chile powder, and salt.

3. On a lightly floured surface, stretch the dough to a 10- to 12-inch circle.

4. Place the dough on a pizza stone or in a 10- or 12-inch cast-iron pan and bake for 10 minutes.

5. Remove the crust from the oven and spread the sauce over it, leaving a ½-inch border all the way around. Top the sauce with ¾ cup of the cheese and then, using a slotted spoon so that the juices will remain behind in the bowl, spoon the vegetable mixture over the cheese. Top with the remaining cheese and spoon on 8 dollops, about a heaping teaspoon each, of ricotta or requesón.

6. Bake the pizza until the cheese has melted and the crust is crisp, 12 to 14 more minutes.

7. Remove from the stone with a paddle or wide spatula. Transfer to a cutting board, slice, and serve.

FOOLPROOF PIZZA DOUGH

MASA FÁCIL PARA PIZZA

**MAKES ENOUGH FOR 2
(10- TO 12-INCH) PIZZAS**

PREPARATION TIME: 25 minutes,
plus 2 hours (or up to 3 days)
resting time

MAKE AHEAD: The dough can be
made up to 3 days ahead, covered,
and refrigerated.

1   teaspoon active dry yeast

1   tablespoon extra-virgin
    olive oil

1   cup lukewarm water
    (110 to 115 degrees)

½   teaspoon sugar

2⅔ cups all-purpose flour,
    plus more for kneading

2   teaspoons kosher or sea salt

My maternal grandmother, one of the best cooks I have ever known, started a pizza-night tradition when she was well into her sixties, making this pizza dough from scratch. All that is required for your own pizza night is a little organization. The dough is easy to make.

1. In a medium bowl, combine the yeast, oil, and water, stirring until well mixed. Add the sugar and stir well.

2. In a large bowl, combine the flour and salt. Make a well in the middle, then add the yeast mixture. Use your hands to incorporate it into the flour and mix until the dough is homogenous, about 2 minutes. It will be sticky and wet. Let the dough rest for 15 to 20 minutes.

3. Flour your counter and your hands generously. Scrape out the dough from the bowl and knead it until it goes from being sticky and gooey to very smooth and malleable; this will take anywhere from 3 to 5 minutes. Add more flour to your counter and hands as necessary, scraping up the dough that sticks.

4. Divide the dough in half, shape into 2 balls, and wrap them in plastic. Refrigerate for at least 2 hours.

5. Bring the dough to room temperature, without removing the plastic wrap, before using.

BASIC PIZZA SAUCE

SALSA DE PIZZA BÁSICA

MAKES ABOUT 2 CUPS

PREPARATION TIME: 5 minutes

COOKING TIME: 12 minutes

MAKE AHEAD: The sauce can be made up to 1 week ahead, covered, and refrigerated or frozen, for up to 3 months.

3 tablespoons olive oil

⅓ cup chopped white onion

2 garlic cloves, minced or pressed

1 (28-ounce) can crushed tomatoes, or 2 pounds ripe tomatoes, quartered and pureed

1 teaspoon dried oregano, preferably Mexican

1¼ teaspoons kosher or sea salt or to taste

This tomato sauce, which I use for all my pizzas, is ridiculously easy. It cooks for a very brief amount of time, just until the tomatoes have broken down a little bit, as it will be subjected to high heat when it's topping the pizza. When you see how much better it tastes than commercial tomato sauces, you'll stick to making your own and won't go back. If you have any left over, toss it with pasta or spread it on panini.

Heat the oil in a medium saucepan over medium heat. Add the onion and cook, stirring occasionally, until tender and beginning to brown around the edges, 4 to 6 minutes. Stir in the garlic and cook until fragrant and beginning to color, about 1 minute. Stir in the tomatoes, oregano, and salt, cover, and simmer for 5 to 6 minutes, until the sauce is thick and dark red. Remove from the heat and let cool.

CHAPTER 8

GUISADOS (STEWS) AND OTHER ONE-DISH MEALS

***GUISADOS* REPRESENT HOME COOKING AT ITS BEST:** aromatic mixtures of meat, fish, or vegetables in a tasty broth or sauce. Some are drier than others, but they are all comforting one-pot meals, happy to be accompanied by rice (if rice isn't an ingredient) or beans or both, and a stack of warm corn tortillas. Dipping into these stews is irresistible, so arm yourself with enough tortillas so you can dip, scoop, or even make little tacos.

In Mexico we know where to go to get the best guisados outside of our mom's kitchen: at *mercados* and in *fondas*, small restaurants known in some Mexican regions as *cenadurías*, where the kitchen and the menu are an extension of the cook's home kitchen. If you want to have a complete shopping and eating experience, walk into any Mexican market. You can get all of your food shopping done, buy a stack of hot freshly made tortillas, and find the most fragrant fresh flowers. Then you'll be ready for lunch. Pick a stand, sit down on a bench at the long communal table (where you can also catch up on the day's gossip), or stand right there at the bar, and choose from the cook's spread of stews bubbling in front of you in gigantic *cazuelas*, open clay pots. They will have all been made that day, and they are beautifully *sazonados* (seasoned), intended to hook you on that particular stand and draw you back every time you come to the market.

This kind of food instills loyalty in both eaters and cooks. In a given city or region of Mexico, you will find more than one market stall, selling the same exact guisados, but customers always go back to their favorite spots. They choose the cooks whose food most reminds them of home.

In this chapter you will find a sampling of traditional regional guisados. There are some that I grew up on in Mexico City, like the Steak and Potatoes in Salsa Verde on page 206. From other regions you'll find one-pot meals like chicken pibil, tradition-ally a slow-cooked marinated chicken dish from the Yucatán (page 214); deviled shrimp stew from the Pacific Coast (page 223); manchamanteles, or tablecloth-stainer mole, from Oaxaca (page 221); and arroz a la tumbada, or Everything-but-the-Kitchen-Sink Seafood and Rice from Veracruz (page 225).

I've also included some of my family's favorites, like the tastiest meatballs you will ever eat (page 208) and my own Tex-Mex chili (page 232). If you're looking for a great main dish for your next dinner party, you've come to the right chapter.

STEAK AND POTATOES IN SALSA VERDE

CARNE CON PAPAS EN SALSA VERDE

SERVES 6

PREPARATION TIME: 10 minutes

COOKING TIME: 1 hour and 15 minutes

MAKE AHEAD: The stew can be made up to 2 days ahead, covered, and refrigerated. Reheat, covered, over low heat.

FOR THE STEAK

2   pounds flank steak, cut into 2-inch chunks

2   bay leaves

½   white onion, plus ⅓ cup coarsely chopped white onion

3   garlic cloves

Kosher or sea salt

10 black peppercorns (optional)

FOR THE STEW

1   pound tomatillos, husks removed and thoroughly rinsed

1   garlic clove

2   jalapeño or serrano chiles or to taste

1   cup fresh cilantro leaves and upper part of stems

2   tablespoons canola or safflower oil

1   pound small red potatoes, any larger ones halved

This shredded meat and potato stew, with its pungent lick-the-plate salsa verde, is on my list of top ten meals. Once when I was with my husband's family, as I wiped up the last of the sauce with a corn tortilla after my second helping, my mother-in-law turned to my husband and said with a smile, *"Tu mujer tiene paladar de campesina* (Your wife has a peasant's palate)."* Indeed I do. The stew makes me so happy that I need nothing else.

. . . .

1.   To prepare the steak: Place the meat in large pot or casserole, along with the bay leaves, ½ onion, the 3 garlic cloves, 1 teaspoon salt, and peppercorns, if using. Add enough water to cover by 2 inches and bring to a simmer over medium-
high heat. Reduce the heat to medium, cover partially, and simmer for 50 minutes to 1 hour, until the meat is tender enough to pull apart with a fork.

2.   Place a strainer or a colander over a bowl and drain the meat. Discard the onion, bay leaves, and (optional) peppercorns and reserve 3 cups of the broth (if you have less, make up the difference with water). Once the meat has cooled enough to handle, pull it apart or shred into small pieces (see Deshebrada/Deshebrado, opposite).

3.   To make the stew: Place the tomatillos, the remaining garlic clove, and the chiles in a saucepan and cover with water. Bring to a simmer and simmer, uncovered, until the tomatillos have gone from bright to pale green and are thoroughly soft, about 10 minutes. Transfer the tomatillos, garlic, and 1 of the chiles to a blender, add the chopped onion, cilantro, and ½ teaspoon salt, and puree until smooth. Taste for heat, and add some or all of the other chile, if desired, until you have the desired amount of heat.

4. Heat the oil in a large casserole over medium heat. When it is hot but not smoking, add the pureed tomatillo mixture, being careful, as it will splutter. Add the potatoes, cover partially, and cook, stirring occasionally, until the sauce thickens slightly, 5 to 6 minutes. Stir in the shredded meat and the reserved broth. Cover partially and simmer for about 25 minutes, stirring occasionally, until the potatoes are tender and the stew has thickened considerably. Taste for salt and add more if desired. Serve hot.

DESHEBRADA/DESHEBRADO

We use *deshebrada*, or *deshebrado*, to refer to any ingredient that is shredded or pulled apart into shreds or threads. *Hebra* is Spanish for "thread"; *deshebrar* means to "unthread," or pull something into shreds. Meat, seafood, and poultry are always shredded along the grain. The delicate, thin threads will soak up all the flavor of any marinade, vinaigrette, seasoning, or sauce that enrobes them.

MEATBALLS IN GUAJILLO SAUCE WITH ZUCCHINI

ALBÓNDIGAS CON SALSA DE TOMATE VERDE Y CHILE GUAJILLO CON CALABACITAS

SERVES 6 TO 8; MAKES ABOUT 24 MEATBALLS

PREPARATION TIME: 15 minutes

COOKING TIME: 55 minutes

MAKE AHEAD: The meatballs and sauce can be made up to 3 days ahead (without the zucchini), covered, and refrigerated. To serve, bring back to a simmer, add the zucchini, and simmer for 5 to 6 minutes, or until the zucchini is tender.

6 dried guajillo chiles, stemmed and seeded

2 pounds tomatillos, husked and thoroughly rinsed

3 garlic cloves

Kosher or sea salt

3 tablespoons canola or safflower oil

1¼ cups finely chopped onions

1 pound ground veal

1 pound ground pork

½ cup unseasoned bread crumbs

1 large egg, lightly beaten

¼ teaspoon freshly ground black pepper

3 cups chicken broth, homemade (page 40) or store-bought, or beef or veal broth

There are two secrets to this dish. The first is that I use two kinds of meat to get more flavor. I prefer a mix of veal and pork, but you could use a mix of veal and beef or beef and pork, or even ground lamb and turkey. The other secret is the tangy, lively, sleek, and glossy tomatillo-guajillo sauce in which the meatballs simmer. As we say in Mexico, "*Pongo mis manos al fuego* (I'll set my hands on fire)," if this combination of guajillo chiles and tomatillos doesn't make it into your monthly repertoire.

I like to serve the meatballs, sauce, and delicate zucchini that completes the dish over generous mounds of white rice in big bowls. The rice soaks up the sauce in the most delicious way, but you can also serve the dish with black beans (page 244), corn tortillas, or bread on the side.

1. Heat a comal or large skillet over medium heat. Add the chiles and toast, turning often, until they are deeply browned and you can smell the chile fumes, about 2 minutes. Transfer to a large pot or casserole, add the tomatillos and garlic, cover with water, and bring to a boil over high heat. Reduce the heat to medium and simmer until the tomatillos are thoroughly cooked, their color has changed from bright green to olive, and the guajillos have plumped up and rehydrated, about 12 minutes. Drain.

2. Transfer the tomatillos, garlic, and chiles to a blender and allow to cool slightly, then add 1 teaspoon salt and puree until completely smooth.

3. Rinse out and dry the casserole, and set over medium heat. Add the oil and heat until hot. Add 1 cup of the onions and cook until they are tender and the edges have just begun to brown, about 5 minutes. Add the tomatillo puree, cover partially, as the thick sauce will sear and splutter, and simmer for 7 to 8 minutes, until the sauce has thickened and darkened.

continued...

2 epazote sprigs (or 4 dried leaves) or cilantro sprigs (optional)

1 pound zucchini, cut into ¼-inch dice

4. Meanwhile, combine the meats, bread crumbs, egg, the remaining ¼ cup onion, ½ teaspoon salt, and the pepper in a bowl and mix together well.

5. When the tomatillo puree has cooked down, stir in the broth, scraping the bottom and sides of the casserole to incorporate any sauce sticking to the surfaces of the pot. Place the meat mixture and a small bowl of water next to the casserole. Wet your hands and start shaping the meat into approximately 1½-inch balls. Gently drop the balls into the sauce as you form them. When all of the meatballs have been added to the sauce, add the epazote or cilantro. Simmer, uncovered, for 30 minutes.

6. Stir in the zucchini and simmer for another 5 minutes, until the zucchini is just tender. Serve hot.

MEXICAN COOK'S TIP
Blending Hot Ingredients

We Mexicans are wild about our blenders; we use them day and night to make smoothies, smooth and chunky salsas, and silky smooth, light soups. When the ingredients you are about to puree are hot, give them a few minutes—or longer if you are uncomfortable working with a hot mixture—to cool after you transfer them to the blender. Do not fill the blender more than halfway, and hold a folded dish towel tightly down over the lid to contain the pressure coming from the heat of the ingredients. If you take out the middle piece from the blender top, you won't get the intense pressure, but remember to cover it with a towel!

DRUNKEN RICE WITH CHICKEN AND CHORIZO

ARROZ BORRACHO CON POLLO Y CHORIZO

SERVES 6

PREPARATION TIME: 15 minutes

COOKING TIME: 40 minutes

MAKE AHEAD: The rice can be made up to 2 hours ahead. Before serving, add 2 tablespoons water and reheat, covered, over low heat.

½ teaspoon saffron threads, crumbled

2 tablespoons boiling water

6 boneless, skinless chicken thighs (about 1½ pounds), each cut into 4 pieces

Kosher or sea salt and freshly ground black pepper

¼ cup plus 2 tablespoons canola or safflower oil

8 ounces raw Mexican chorizo, casings removed and coarsely chopped

2 cups long-grain or extra-long-grain white rice or jasmine rice

½ cup chopped white onion

½ cup chopped green bell pepper

½ cup chopped red bell pepper

1 cup chopped ripe tomato

2 garlic cloves, minced or pressed

¼ teaspoon ground cumin

⅛ teaspoon ground canela (Ceylon cinnamon; see page 264)

3 whole cloves, stems discarded, tops crushed

Every time I am back in the Yucatán, I taste a different version of *arroz borracho*, or drunken rice. These range from simple combinations of vegetables and rice to more complex dishes with chicken, pork, shrimp, or a local chorizo. The underlying flavor and golden color of any *arroz borracho* reflects the presence of either saffron or, more likely, achiote, the "saffron condiment" (see page 213) that is found everywhere in the Yucatán. The dish is called "drunken" because beer or other alcohol is added to the rice early on in the cooking. It really isn't drunk, though, because the alcohol cooks off quickly, leaving behind only its slight acidity to flavor the rice and balance the starchiness of the grain. My kids love this version of *arroz borracho*. They always compete to see who can get the most chorizo, diving in the minute I remove the lid.

1. Place the saffron threads in a small bowl and cover with the boiling water. Soak for 10 to 15 minutes.

2. Season the chicken with ½ teaspoon salt and pepper to taste.

3. Heat 1 tablespoon of the oil in a large casserole over medium heat. Add the chorizo and cook, stirring often, for 4 to 5 minutes, until crisp and lightly browned. Remove with a slotted spoon and place in a bowl, leaving the rendered fat behind in the pot.

4. Add 2 more tablespoons oil to the casserole. Add the chicken and cook for 2 to 3 minutes per side, until lightly browned. Remove with tongs or a slotted spoon and place in the bowl with the chorizo.

5. Add 2 more tablespoons oil to the casserole, stir in the rice, and cook for 3 to 4 minutes, stirring often, until its color begins to change to a deep milky white and the grains feel heavier and begin to crackle in the pot as you stir them.

6. Make some room in the middle of the casserole and add the remaining 1 tablespoon oil, then add the onion, bell peppers, tomato, and garlic. Stir

continued...

the vegetables together, add the cumin, canela, cloves, and 1¼ teaspoons salt, and cook, stirring often, for 3 to 5 minutes. As the vegetables begin to soften, stir them together with the rice. Then add the beer and stir to deglaze, scraping the browned bits from the bottom of the pot into the mix. Let the alcohol evaporate (you will smell it) as the beer is absorbed by the rice, about 2 minutes.

7. Stir in the broth and the saffron, with its soaking liquid, again scraping the bottom of the pot to deglaze, and bring to a simmer. Return the chicken and chorizo to the pot, nestling the chicken in the rice. Cover, lower the heat to the lowest setting, and simmer gently for 20 minutes.

8. Scatter the peas over the top of the rice, cover, and simmer for 4 to 5 minutes, or until most of the liquid has been absorbed. The rice should be soft and thoroughly cooked; if the grains still feel a little hard, add a bit more broth or water and simmer for another 5 minutes or so. Turn off the heat and let sit, covered, for 5 minutes.

9. Fluff the rice with a fork, taste for salt, and serve.

- 1 cup beer, preferably lager
- 3½ cups chicken broth, homemade (page 40) or store-bought, or as needed
- ½ cup fresh or thawed frozen peas

THE YUCATECAN "SAFFRON CONDIMENT"

The Yucatán Peninsula loves saffron. It was brought to Mexico by Spanish settlers, who had learned that an ingredient that was a crucial part of their flavor palate was hard to grow in the new lands but easily transportable. Over the centuries, though, achiote paste, made from the seeds of the annatto tree native to the Yucatán, began to step in for this pricey ingredient. Many dishes from this region of Mexico, especially rice dishes, are yellow, and the color and unique backdrop flavor may come either from true saffron or, more likely, from what the locals call "saffron condiment," made from achiote

(also called annatto seeds). It's a great substitute and is much less expensive than saffron. Also known in Mexico as poor man's saffron, achiote seeds come from the prickly pods of the beautiful pink flowers of the annatto tree. The condiment is sold in large and small markets all over the Yucatán and is found in practically every kitchen in that region. Just like saffron, achiote seeds have a distinctive orange-red brick color that changes to a golden-yellow hue once used in cooking. Saffron and achiote share a similar pungent and slightly metallic taste.

FAST-TRACK CHICKEN PIBIL
(AND DAY-AFTER-THANKSGIVING TURKEY PIBIL)

POLLO PIBIL RÁPIDO

SERVES 4 TO 5

PREPARATION TIME: 15 minutes

COOKING TIME: 30 minutes

MAKE AHEAD: The pilbil can be made up to 4 days ahead, covered, and refrigerated. Reheat, covered, over low heat.

8 ounces ripe tomatoes

¼ red onion

3 garlic cloves, unpeeled

½ teaspoon kosher or sea salt or to taste

2 cups chicken broth, homemade (page 40) or store-bought

2 tablespoons canola or safflower oil

¼ cup freshly squeezed grapefruit juice

¼ cup freshly squeezed orange juice

¼ cup freshly squeezed lime juice

¼ cup distilled white vinegar

½ teaspoon dried oregano, preferably Mexican

¼ teaspoon ground allspice

⅛ teaspoon ground cumin

Freshly ground black pepper

2 tablespoons chopped achiote paste (the one that comes in a bar, not in a jar; see page 113)

The word *pibil* will make any Mexican's mouth water, because it implies the inimitable taste of achiote paste and citrus. This is one of the defining flavors of the cooking of the Yucatán Peninsula, one of Mexico's most important cuisines, known for its pungent, assertive flavors. Pibil traditionally involves a centuries-old way of cooking meats in smoldering underground pits (known as *pib* in the Mayan language, hence the name). Pibil recipes usually dilute the achiote paste with the juice of bitter oranges, a citrus that is not easy to find outside of the Yucatán. Some Asian markets sell bitter oranges, as they are used in certain Asian dishes. But since they are difficult to find, I've developed a great substitute: a mix of equal parts distilled white vinegar and grapefruit, orange, and lime juices. And with achiote paste available in the United States, in markets and online, Yucatecan dishes like pibil are no longer out of reach. Here is a fabulous way to make a fast-track pibil-style chicken or turkey that maintains the soul and essence of the traditional dish and sacrifices none of the distinctive flavors. If anything, we like it even more at home, as the sauce turns out thicker and more concentrated and the chicken moister.

I do recommend that you serve the traditional pickled cabbage and red onions on the side; it can be made ahead of time, ready and waiting for you in the refrigerator.

You can also serve pibil on top of tostadas or use as a filling for sandwiches, quesadillas, tacos, or tortas.

1. Preheat the broiler. Line a small baking sheet or roasting pan with foil. Place the tomatoes, onion, and garlic cloves on the foil, set under the broiler, 3 to 4 inches from the heat, and broil for 4 to 5 minutes, until charred on one side. Flip over and broil for another 4 to 5 minutes, until the skin is blistered and completely charred; the tomatoes should be very soft with the juices beginning to emerge. Remove from the heat.

continued...

6 cups cooked shredded chicken (see page 40) or rotisserie chicken

Pickled Onions and Cabbage (page 119)

2. Once they are cool enough to handle, quarter the tomatoes and place in a blender, along with any juices in the pan. Peel the garlic cloves and add to the blender. Add the onion, salt, and 1 cup of the broth and puree until completely smooth.

3. In a casserole or soup pot, heat the oil over medium heat until hot but not smoking. Pour in the puree, cover partially, as the sauce will sizzle and jump, and cook, stirring occasionally, for 7 to 8 minutes, until the sauce thickens and darkens considerably.

4. Meanwhile, combine the grapefruit juice, orange juice, lime juice, vinegar, oregano, allspice, cumin, pepper to taste, achiote paste, and the remaining 1 cup broth in the blender and puree until completely smooth.

5. Stir the juice mixture into the tomato sauce, bring to a simmer, and simmer for 5 minutes.

6. Add the chicken, stir together well, and cook, uncovered, until the meat has absorbed most of the sauce, about 5 minutes. The dish should be very moist but not soupy.

7. Serve the pibil with pickled onions and cabbage.

DAY-AFTER-THANKSGIVING TURKEY PIBIL

This is an ideal way to use leftover turkey. All you need to do is shred the turkey, make this quick sauce, and let it simmer away. In less than 30 minutes, you will have the most delicious stew, ready to be served over rice or potatoes or tucked into the tastiest and dressiest day-after tortas, sandwiches, or tacos ever. Don't forget to include some of the pickled cabbage and onions as well in the tacos or tortas!

CITRUS CHICKEN with CARROTS and BABY POTATOES

POLLO CON ZANAHORIAS Y PAPITAS AL LIMÓN Y NARANJA

SERVES 6

PREPARATION TIME: 15 minutes

COOKING TIME: 55 minutes

MAKE AHEAD: The chicken can be made up to 2 hours ahead, covered, and refrigerated. Reheat, covered, over medium-low heat.

1 pound ripe tomatoes

¼ cup canola or safflower oil

8 chicken thighs, halved breasts, or drumsticks, or a combination

Kosher or sea salt and freshly ground black pepper

2 cups chopped white onions

4 garlic cloves, minced or pressed

1 teaspoon dried oregano, preferably Mexican

½ teaspoon dried thyme

½ teaspoon dried marjoram

¼ teaspoon ground canela (Ceylon cinnamon; see page 264)

½ teaspoon chipotle chile powder (see page 65) or to taste

1½ teaspoons packed dark brown sugar or grated piloncillo (see page 86)

1 cup freshly squeezed orange juice

2 tablespoons freshly squeezed lime juice

What is in this chicken?—my mom kept asking this question as she took bite after bite the last time she was visiting. I kept on trying to explain the recipe and the ingredients, but I was also making dinner, setting the table, and helping my son Juju with his homework. At one point I had to get her away from the casserole, as she was eating all of the braised carrots and potatoes and the boys hadn't had their dinner yet!

I couldn't blame her, of course, as the sauce is intriguing, with the flavor of roasted tomatoes melding with orange and lime juice, seasoned onion and garlic, chipotle chile powder, and other basic pantry spices that I gravitate to, like oregano, as well as a bit of piloncillo (or dark brown sugar) to help all of the flavors shine.

1. Preheat the broiler. Line a small baking sheet or dish with aluminum foil. Put the tomatoes on the foil, place under the broiler, and broil 2 to 3 inches from the heat for 4 to 5 minutes, until charred on one side. Flip over and broil for another 4 to 5 minutes, until completely charred. Remove from the heat.

2. Once the tomatoes are cool enough to handle, core, chop, and transfer to a bowl, along with their seeds and juices.

3. Heat the oil in a large heavy casserole or skillet over medium-high heat. Season the chicken with ½ teaspoon salt and pepper to taste. Add the chicken pieces skin side down, without crowding the pot (do this in a couple of batches, if necessary). Brown for 4 minutes without moving the pieces so that the surface develops a thin crust; this way the pieces won't stick to the pot when you try to flip them over. Ease a spatula under each piece if necessary, and use tongs to turn the pieces over. Brown on the other side for 3 to 4 more minutes. Remove the chicken pieces and place them in a bowl.

continued...

12 ounces carrots, peeled and sliced about 1 inch thick on the diagonal

1 pound baby red potatoes (if you have larger potatoes, cut into ¾- to 1-inch dice)

MEXICAN COOK'S TIP

I love baby potatoes. Their uniformly small size means their cooking time is predictable and they cook evenly. However, larger potatoes can be substituted; just cut them into ¾- to 1-inch pieces and follow the same cooking directions in the recipe.

4. Reduce the heat to medium, add the onions and garlic to the pot, and cook, stirring occasionally and scraping the bottom of the pot with a wooden spoon to release any browned bits, until the onions are completely soft and the edges are beginning to brown, 5 to 6 minutes. Stir in the oregano, thyme, marjoram, canela, chile powder, brown sugar, and 1 teaspoon salt, then stir in the tomatoes, with their seeds and juices, and the orange and lime juices and mix well. Cover partially and cook, stirring once or twice, for 8 to 10 minutes, until the mixture has cooked down slightly. Stir in the carrots and potatoes, partially cover, and cook for 3 to 4 minutes, until the vegetables begin to soften.

5. Reduce the heat to medium-low, nestle the chicken pieces in the sauce, and gently spoon some of the sauce on top. Cover and cook for 30 minutes, flipping the chicken, moving the vegetables, and scraping the bottom of the pot halfway through. The chicken should be fully cooked, the potatoes and carrots should be completely tender, and the sauce, though still quite soupy, should have thickened at the bottom of the pot.

6. Stir and cook, uncovered, for another 3 to 4 minutes, until the sauce has thickened a bit more. Taste for salt, add more if desired, and serve.

MEXICAN COOK'S TIPS

Searing or Browning Chicken

Many recipes start by searing or browning chicken. Here are some tips:

- Wait until the oil is hot before adding the chicken.
- Season the chicken with salt and pepper before adding it to the oil.
- Don't overcrowd the pot or the chicken pieces will steam rather than sear. If your casserole or pan can't accommodate all of it at once, work in batches.

- If using chicken with skin, brown the skin side first.
- Once you place the chicken in the hot oil, don't move it until it browns a bit and the surface forms a thin crust so you will be able to flip it more easily. Use tongs and, if necessary, a spatula to help you release the skin or meat from the pot before flipping the chicken.
- If the skin comes off, keep on frying it until crisp and eat it as chicharrón (see page 22).

SPICY SWEET-AND-SOUR CHIPOTLE AND TOMATILLO CHICKEN

POLLO CON TOMATE VERDE, CHIPOTLE, Y PILONCILLO

SERVES 6

PREPARATION TIME: 10 minutes

COOKING TIME: 55 minutes

MAKE AHEAD: The chicken can be made up to 3 days ahead, covered, and refrigerated. Reheat over low heat.

8 chicken thighs, legs, or halved breasts, or a combination

1½ teaspoons kosher or sea salt or to taste, and freshly ground black pepper

¼ cup canola or safflower oil

1 large or 2 medium onions, halved lengthwise and sliced very thin (2 cups)

2 garlic cloves, minced or pressed

2 pounds tomatillos, husked, thoroughly rinsed, and quartered

¼ cup grated piloncillo (see page 86), or packed dark brown sugar

2 tablespoons sauce from canned chipotles in adobo or to taste

1 canned chipotle chile in adobo sauce, seeded

1 cup chicken broth, homemade (page 40) or store-bought

My sister Karen, an amazing cook, former caterer, and manager of a French-Mexican restaurant in Mexico City, taught me how to make this chicken early on in my marriage when I needed a dish to serve for a dinner party I was giving for my husband's colleagues. Since then, the dish has never let me down. I like to make it on Passover, as the thick, chunky sauce has all the elements that symbolize the things we remember at the seder: sour, to remember bitter times; sweetness, to appreciate good times; and a spicy kick to add a spark to life.

1. Sprinkle the chicken pieces with ½ teaspoon of the salt and pepper to taste.

2. In a large casserole or heavy skillet, heat the oil over medium-high heat. Add the chicken pieces skin side down in one layer, without crowding, and brown for 4 to 5 minutes. (Do this in batches if necessary.) The skin should be browned and crispy enough to release easily from the pan. Using tongs, flip the chicken pieces over and brown for another 4 to 5 minutes. Remove to a bowl.

3. Reduce the heat to medium, add the onions, and cook, stirring often and scraping the bottom of the pot, for 5 to 6 minutes, until the onions are softened and the edges are beginning to brown. Add the garlic and cook until lightly colored and fragrant, about 1 minute. Stir in the tomatillos, the remaining 1 teaspoon salt, and pepper to taste and cook, stirring occasionally, for 8 to 10 minutes, until the tomatillos have broken down a bit.

4. Add the piloncillo or brown sugar, adobo sauce, and the chipotle chile and stir well. Return the chicken pieces to the pan, add the broth, and bring to a simmer. Reduce the heat to medium-low, cover, and simmer for 15 minutes.

5. Remove the lid and baste the chicken with the sauce, then raise the heat to medium, and cook for another 15 to 20 minutes, until the sauce has thickened to a chunky consistency, the chicken is cooked through, and the mixture is no longer soupy. Serve hot.

TABLECLOTH-STAINER CHICKEN IN RED MOLE SAUCE

MANCHAMANTELES DE POLLO

SERVES 6

PREPARATION TIME: 20 minutes

COOKING TIME: 1 hour 10 minutes

MAKE AHEAD: The mole can be made up to 2 hours ahead. Reheat, covered, over low heat.

4   ancho chiles, stemmed and seeded

¼ cup slivered almonds

¼ cup sesame seeds

1½ pounds ripe tomatoes

½ white onion

1   teaspoon ground canela (Ceylon cinnamon; see page 264)

5   whole cloves, stems removed and tops crushed

1½ teaspoons kosher or sea salt or to taste

Freshly ground black pepper

Canola or safflower oil

1   large plantain, peeled and sliced about ¼ inch thick

2   (1-inch-thick) slices ripe pineapple, cored and cut into ½-inch dice

1   tart apple, peeled, cored, and cut into ½-inch dice

10 to 12 chicken thighs, drumsticks, or halved breasts, or a combination (about 4 pounds)

The "stains" in this mole come from the complex sauce that bathes chicken, sweet potatoes, pineapple, apple, and plantains. The dish is typical of Mexican baroque cooking, with its sweet, tart, spicy, and savory mix of meat, vegetables, and fruits in a richly flavored sauce. Traditionally served at weddings and large celebrations, both in the state of Oaxaca where it originated and in central Mexico, this mole is one of the famous seven Oaxacan moles (though the number of mole sauces in Oaxaca is more likely to run into the dozens).

You need more than one pot to make this dish. I am warning you also that you are bound to stain your clothes while making it, even with a good apron, or while eating it (keep the apron on!). But it is so worth the trouble and extra laundry. Be sure to use paper napkins!

....

1. Place the ancho chiles in a bowl, cover with boiling water, and soak for 10 to 15 minutes, until plump and rehydrated. Drain, reserving the soaking water.

2. Meanwhile, in a medium skillet, lightly toast the almonds over medium-low heat, stirring often, until lightly browned and toasted, 2 to 3 minutes. Immediately transfer to a bowl and set aside. Repeat with the sesame seeds; transfer to the same bowl and set aside.

3. Preheat the broiler and line a small baking sheet or baking pan with foil. Place the tomatoes and onion on the foil, place under the broiler 2 to 3 inches from the heat, and broil for 4 to 5 minutes, until charred on the first side. Flip over and broil for another 4 to 5 minutes. The tomatoes should be charred and very soft, with the juices bursting out, and the onion should be charred and wrinkled. Remove from the heat.

4. When the tomatoes and onion are cool enough to handle, core and coarsely chop the tomatoes, reserving the seeds and juice, and chop the onion.

continued...

2 cups chicken broth, homemade (page 40) or store-bought, or water

1 large sweet potato, peeled and cut into ½-inch dice

⅓ cup raisins

5. Place the soaked chiles, along with ½ cup of their soaking water, in a blender. Add the sesame seeds and almonds, tomatoes, with their seeds and juices, onion, canela, cloves, 1 teaspoon of the salt, and ½ teaspoon pepper. Puree until completely smooth. Set aside.

6. Cover a cooling rack with paper towels. In a large casserole or wide deep skillet, add ½ inch of oil and heat over medium heat. Add the plantain slices and fry for about 2 to 3 minutes per side, until nicely browned and caramelized a bit on the outside. Remove with a spider or slotted spoon, leaving as much of the oil as you can in the pan, and place on the paper towel–covered rack. Repeat with the pineapple and then the apple and drain on the rack.

7. Sprinkle the chicken with the remaining ½ teaspoon salt and pepper to taste. In batches, in the same oil over medium heat, add the chicken to the pot, without crowding, and brown for 4 to 5 minutes per side. Remove the chicken to a sheet pan or bowl as it is browned.

8. Carefully pour off all but a couple tablespoons of the oil from the pot. Add the ancho chile puree to the pot, stir, scraping the bottom of the pot, and cook for 5 to 6 minutes, stirring frequently so that the sauce doesn't stick, until it has thickened and become very fragrant. Return the chicken to the pot, along with any juice that has accumulated, and add the broth or water. Bring to a simmer, reduce the heat to medium-low, cover, and simmer for 10 minutes.

9. Add the sweet potatoes and raisins, stir, cover partially, and simmer for another 20 to 25 minutes, until the sweet potatoes are tender and the sauce has thickened enough to coat the back of a wooden spoon.

10. Gently stir in the pineapple, plantain, and apple and simmer for 3 to 4 minutes. Serve hot.

DEVILED SHRIMP WITH NOPALITOS (OR GREEN BEANS) AND POTATOES

CAMARONES A LA DIABLA CON PAPAS Y EJOTES

SERVES 6 TO 8

PREPARATION TIME: 20 minutes

COOKING TIME: 50 minutes

MAKE AHEAD: The stew can be made up to 2 days ahead, covered, and refrigerated. Reheat, covered, over low heat.

2 pounds medium shrimp

FOR THE SHRIMP SHELL BROTH

Reserved shrimp shells and tails

5 parsley sprigs

2 garlic cloves

3 or 4 bay leaves

1 teaspoon kosher or sea salt or to taste

4 cups water

FOR THE DEVILED SHRIMP

5 dried guajillo chiles, stemmed and seeded

3 cups Shrimp Shell Broth (see above)

1½ pounds ripe tomatoes or 1 (28-ounce) can crushed tomatoes

1 canned chipotle chile in adobo sauce, seeded (optional)

1 tablespoon sauce from chipotle chiles in adobo, or more to taste

A la diabla is a common way to serve seafood along the Pacific Coast of Mexico. In beach-town establishments, diners are typically given a choice of shrimp, fish, or a seafood mix to be served with the sauce. Every cook has his or her own carefully guarded recipe—the devil in the sauce brings out a selfish nature in those who make it. But I don't have to safeguard the recipe for a restaurant, so be as selfless as you want in passing it along. All you need to go with it are some warm corn tortillas or crusty bread to soak up the sauce.

Note: I prefer to make this dish with fresh nopales, but don't hesitate to make the dish if you can't find them or don't want to take the time to prep them. You can use green beans instead and the stew will still be delicious.

....

1. Peel the shrimp and reserve the shells and tails. Refrigerate the shrimp until ready to use.

2. To make the broth: In a medium saucepan, combine the shrimp shells and tails, parsley, garlic cloves, bay leaves, salt, and the water and bring to a boil over medium-high heat. Reduce the heat to medium and simmer for 20 minutes.

3. Strain the broth into a large measuring cup or heatproof bowl and measure out 3 cups.

4. To make the deviled shrimp: Heat a comal or skillet over medium heat and toast the chiles, flipping them a few times, until browned and the chile fumes are evident, about 2 minutes. Transfer to a medium saucepan, cover with water, and bring to a simmer over medium-high heat. Reduce the heat to medium and simmer for 10 to 12 minutes, until the chiles are completely puffed up, rehydrated, and soft. Remove from the heat.

continued...

½ teaspoon dried oregano,
preferably Mexican

1½ teaspoons kosher or sea
salt or to taste

¼ teaspoon freshly ground
black pepper or to taste

3 tablespoons canola or
safflower oil

1 cup finely chopped white
onion

4 garlic cloves, minced or
pressed

1 pound red potatoes, peeled
and cut into ¾- to ½-inch
dice

8 ounces cleaned, diced, and
cooked nopales (cactus
paddles; see page 39) or
green beans, trimmed and
cut into 1-inch pieces

5. Transfer the rehydrated chiles and ½ cup of their cooking water to a
blender. Add 1 cup of the shrimp broth, the tomatoes, chipotle chile in
adobo (if using), adobo sauce, oregano, salt, and pepper and puree until
completely smooth.

6. Heat the oil in a casserole or large heavy pot over medium heat until
hot but not smoking. Add the onion and cook, stirring often, until it is
tender and the edges begin to color lightly, 4 to 5 minutes. Stir in the
garlic and cook, stirring, until fragrant and lightly colored, about 1 minute. Stir in the tomato puree and bring to a simmer. Cover partially and
simmer, stirring occasionally, until the sauce is fragrant, has darkened in
color, and has thickened considerably, about 20 minutes.

7. Raise the heat to medium-high and add the remaining 2 cups shrimp
broth. Bring to a simmer, add the potatoes, and cook until the potatoes
are just tender, about 10 minutes.

8. Stir in the cooked nopales (or raw green beans, if using) and simmer for 3 to 4 minutes, until the nopales are tender or the beans are
crisp-tender. Add the shrimp, stir well, and simmer for 5 minutes, or until
the shrimp are just cooked through, the potatoes are thoroughly tender
and beginning to fall apart; the sauce should be thick.

9. Serve the stew hot.

VARIATION: You can substitute the Anything-Goes Fish or Seafood
Broth on page 228 or store-bought fish, chicken, or vegetable broth for
the shrimp shell broth. If you do use commercial broth, check the salt
and reduce the salt in the recipe accordingly (to about ¾ teaspoon).

EVERYTHING-BUT-THE-KITCHEN-SINK SEAFOOD AND RICE

ARROZ A LA TUMBADA

SERVES 6

PREPARATION TIME: 25 minutes

COOKING TIME: 45 minutes

MAKE AHEAD: The stew should be served immediately.

1½ pounds ripe tomatoes

2 jalapeño or serrano chiles or to taste

8 garlic cloves, 5 minced, 3 left whole

½ cup coarsely chopped white onion

Kosher or sea salt

½ cup plus 2 tablespoons olive oil

1 whole white-fleshed, mild-flavored fish (about 3 pounds), such as red snapper, grouper, or rockfish, filleted and cut into 6 pieces (plus the head, bones, and tail if you are making the fish or seafood broth), or 1½ pounds white-fleshed, mild-flavored fish fillets, cut into 6 pieces

Freshly ground black pepper

1 pound cleaned squid, bodies sliced into ¼-inch rings (tentacles intact)

1 pound medium shrimp, peeled, shells and tails reserved if making the broth

Veracruz, which sits on the Gulf of Mexico, is a seafood port like none other in all of Mexico. Historically the city has been the main port of entry for Mexico's immigrant waves. That may explain the evolution of this soupy kind of rice dish, which resembles dishes from Valencia in Spain but is uncommon in the rest of Mexico. The name of the dish, *tumbada*, from the verb *tumbar*, translates as "throw in" or "fall in." In this case, throw all the seafood you can find into the pot.

The shrimp and squid are quickly sautéed in olive oil with lots of garlic (*al ajillo*) and then the rice is fried in the same garlicky oil before it soaks up a jalapeño-spiked tomato-seafood puree. More seafood broth is added to finish cooking the rice, along with clams, mussels, and fish fillets. Make sure you are ready to eat this as soon as it's off the stove. If it sits, the rice will completely absorb the broth and become stodgy.

Note: If making your own broth, have your fishmonger clean the fish and give you the head, bones, and tail and reserve the shrimp shells and tails.

....

1. Place the tomatoes, chiles, and the 3 whole garlic cloves in a medium saucepan, cover with water, and bring to a simmer over medium-high heat. Simmer until the tomatoes are very soft, about 10 minutes. Transfer to a blender, along with the garlic cloves and one of the chiles. Add the onion and 1 teaspoon salt and puree until completely smooth. Taste for heat and add some or all of the other chile if desired, and puree again.

2. Rinse out and dry the saucepan. Heat 2 tablespoons of the oil over medium heat. Add the tomato puree and cover the pan partially, as the puree will splutter and jump. Cook, stirring occasionally, until the puree is thick, dark, and fragrant, 6 to 7 minutes. Remove from the heat and set aside.

continued...

2 cups long-grain or extra-
   long-grain white rice or
   jasmine rice

5 cups seafood or fish broth,
   homemade (page 228) or
   store-bought

1 large epazote sprig or
   3 cilantro sprigs

12 small to medium clams,
   scrubbed and rinsed

12 small to medium mussels,
   scrubbed, debearded, and
   rinsed

3. Season the fish with ¼ teaspoon salt and pepper to taste. Set aside.

4. In a large wide casserole, heat ¼ cup oil over high heat. Toss in the squid, sprinkle with ½ teaspoon salt, add half the minced garlic, and cook for 2 minutes, stirring halfway through. With a slotted spoon, remove the squid from the oil and place in a heatproof bowl. Add the shrimp to the casserole, along with ½ teaspoon salt and the remaining minced garlic, and cook for 2 minutes, stirring and flipping the shrimp over halfway through. Remove with the slotted spoon and place in the bowl with the squid. Set aside.

5. Reduce the heat to medium, add the remaining ¼ cup oil to the casserole, and heat until hot. Add the rice and cook, stirring often and scraping the bottom of the casserole, for 3 to 4 minutes, until the rice is crackling and coated with oil, feels heavier as you stir it, and has changed from a pale white to a deep milky white. Pour the tomato puree over the rice; it will sizzle and smoke a bit. Cover partially and cook, stirring a couple of times, until the rice absorbs most of the sauce, 2 to 3 minutes.

6. Add the seafood broth and stir the rice, scraping the bottom of the casserole. Add the epazote or cilantro and bring back to a simmer. Reduce the heat to medium-low. Carefully place the shrimp and squid on top of the rice in a single layer, along with the clams, mussels, and fish. Add the juices from the bowl. Cover and simmer for 10 to 12 minutes, until the fish fillets are cooked through and can be easily pulled apart with a fork and the clams and mussels have opened. The rice should be tender and the stew very soupy. Discard any clams and mussels that fail to open. Taste for salt and add more if need be.

7. Serve immediately, in soup plates.

ANYTHING-GOES FISH or SEAFOOD BROTH

CALDO DE PESCADO O MARISCOS

MAKES 5 TO 6 CUPS

PREPARATION TIME: 5 minutes

COOKING TIME: 1 hour

MAKE AHEAD: The broth can be made up to 4 days ahead and stored, tightly sealed, in the refrigerator. It can also be frozen for up to 6 months.

1 to 2 pounds fish heads, bones, and tails, preferably from white-fleshed fish

Shrimp shells and tails (optional)

1   white onion, halved

3   garlic cloves

2 or 3 carrots, peeled and halved

3   celery stalks, halved

1   ripe tomato

5 or 6 parsley or cilantro sprigs

3   bay leaves

½ teaspoon dried thyme

½ teaspoon dried marjoram

5   black peppercorns

2   teaspoons kosher or sea salt or to taste

The best seafood broth for fish soups and stews, seafood pasta, and rice dishes is the broth you make yourself, with fish bones and heads, with shrimp shells, or both. Seek out a fishmonger who sells whole fish, select a beautiful one (preferably white-fleshed), and have him or her fillet it for you. That way, you will have fillets to cook in many ways and the bones and head for a quick broth that you can freeze for months. You could also look for shrimp with the shells, peel them, and use the shells to make a broth. It doesn't take very long to peel them, and shrimp in the shell are likely to be nicer and fresher tasting than shelled shrimp. Stockpile and freeze shells for broth whenever you cook shrimp in other recipes.

1. Place all the ingredients in a large heavy pot and cover by 2 inches with cold water. Bring to a boil over medium-high heat and skim away the foam. Reduce the heat to medium-low, cover partially, and simmer for 45 minutes to 1 hour.

2. Strain the stock through a fine strainer or cheesecloth-lined colander and let cool, then refrigerate or freeze.

CHRISTMAS SALT COD

BACALAO NAVIDEÑO

SERVES 6

PREPARATION TIME: 20 minutes, plus 48 hours soaking time

COOKING TIME: 40 minutes

MAKE AHEAD: Bacalao tastes incredible when reheated. It can be made up to 1 week ahead, covered, and refrigerated, or frozen for up to 6 months. Reheat, covered, over low heat or in a medium oven.

1 pound salt cod (see page 231)

½ cup olive oil

1 white onion, halved lengthwise and thinly sliced

4 garlic cloves, minced or pressed

1½ pounds ripe tomatoes, chopped, or 1 (28-ounce) can crushed tomatoes

1 red bell pepper, roasted, peeled, and diced (see page 21), or ½ cup diced drained jarred fancy pimientos or fire-roasted peppers

1 pound baby potatoes, peeled, halved if larger than 1 inch

Kosher or sea salt

2 teaspoons distilled white vinegar

¼ cup chopped fresh flat-leaf parsley

⅓ cup slivered almonds

¼ cup pimiento-stuffed Manzanilla olives, thinly sliced

Do you want to make something unique and delicious for your holidays, a dish that is happy to be prepared ahead and whose flavors bloom even more when it is reheated? This is the one. The ingredients—shredded salt cod, tomatoes, and roasted bell peppers cooked with onion and garlic, olives, almonds, and buttery baby potatoes—meld and ripen into a delicious whole after they have had a chance to sit and mingle for a while. Which is not to say that the dish isn't fabulous when it's hot off the stove.

Dried salt cod is one of the classic Spanish/Mediterranean ingredients that have become entrenched in Mexican holiday traditions. For many people, Navidad, Christmas, is incomplete without bacalao at the center of the table. I always make extra so there will be *bacalao recalentado* to stuff into crusty bread for tortas or to serve on mini toasts for appetizers.

Note: The salt cod requires 48 hours soaking before beginning the recipe, so plan accordingly.

. . . .

1. Forty-eight hours before you wish to make the dish, place the salt cod in a bowl, cover with water, and refrigerate. The next day, drain the salt cod, rinse, and cover with water again. Refrigerate for another 10 to 12 hours. Drain, rinse, and cover with water again. Refrigerate for another 10 to 12 hours; drain and rinse. Shred the fish, and it is ready to use.

2. Heat the oil in a large casserole over medium heat. Add the onion and cook, stirring often, for 5 minutes, or until softened and beginning to brown around the edges. Stir in the garlic and cook until fragrant, about 1 minute. Stir in the tomatoes and roasted pepper, cover partially, and cook, stirring from time to time, for 10 minutes, or until the mixture has thickened and darkened in color. It should still look somewhat chunky.

3. Meanwhile, in a medium saucepan, boil the potatoes in salted water for about 10 minutes, until just tender; when you insert the tip of a knife, it should go all the way in, but the potatoes should not be falling apart. Drain and set aside.

continued...

4. Stir the shredded cod into the tomato mixture. Stir in the vinegar, parsley, almonds, and olives, partially cover, and cook, stirring occasionally and scraping the bottom of the pot, for 10 to 12 minutes, until the ingredients are well amalgamated and the sauce has thickened even more.

5. Reduce the heat to low, stir in the potatoes and the peperoncini, cover, and simmer for 5 more minutes. The mixture should be very moist and juicy, but not soupy. No need to add salt.

6. Serve with additional pickled peperoncini and, if you'd like, white rice on the side.

VARIATION: For a day-after-Thanksgiving treat, use this same formula, substituting 3 to 4 cups of shredded turkey for the salt cod.

8 to 10 pickled peperoncini peppers (see page 152), plus additional for serving

Cooked white rice (see page 241), for serving (optional)

SALT COD (BACALAO)

Historically, salting fish copiously and drying it was the only method to preserve and transport it. The taste for this ingredient has endured through the centuries.

You can find salt cod in the refrigerated section of Latin grocery stores, Spanish and Italian delis, specialty stores, and some supermarkets.

Wherever you find it, the fish will have a strong fishy-salty smell, will be hard, and will be coated with a film, from the salt it was packed in. It should be very white or grayish, not yellow. If it has a yellow spot here and there it's okay, but if it's yellow all over, it is too old.

In order to use salt cod, you need to de-salt it by soaking it for at least 2 days, changing the water at least three times.

MY VERY MEX TEX-MEX CHILI

TEX-MEX CHILI MEXICANO

SERVES 6 TO 8

PREPARATION TIME: 10 minutes

COOKING TIME: 1 hour and 15 minutes

MAKE AHEAD: The chili can be made up to 4 days ahead, covered, and refrigerated. Reheat, covered, over low heat.

¼ cup canola or safflower oil

1   pound beef stew meat, cut into 1-inch cubes

1   pound ground pork or beef

1   teaspoon kosher or sea salt or to taste

¼ teaspoon freshly ground black pepper or to taste

1   white onion, chopped

1   red bell pepper, cored, seeded, and chopped

1   tablespoon chopped jalapeño (seeded if desired)

4   garlic cloves, minced or pressed

½ teaspoon red pepper flakes

1   teaspoon ancho chile powder (see page 65)

½ teaspoon cayenne pepper

½ teaspoon paprika

1   teaspoon dried oregano, preferably Mexican

½ teaspoon ground cumin

1   tablespoon sauce from canned chipotles in adobo or to taste

1   (28-ounce) can crushed tomatoes

After Daniel and I were married, we moved to Texas. That is where our oldest son, Alan, was born and where he spent his early years. He is our Texican boy and he loves a good chili. So does his grandfather; when my dad shows up from Mexico, he always asks for this Tex-Mex chili, which he devours with a few slices of white sandwich bread.

Over the years I've seen Tex-Mex flourish and evolve into its own well-respected cuisine. It keeps getting better because of the increasing availability of a wider range of Mexican ingredients. Today, generic "chili powder" can be replaced with pure ancho chile powder and/or chipotle chile powder. We also have an array of fresh and pickled chiles to choose from.

I have tried chili made with chunks of meat and made with ground meat. I like to combine the two and sometimes I use two kinds of meat: beef stew meat and ground pork. I brown them before adding vegetables and then simmer them all with beans in a rich tomato sauce seasoned with ancho chile powder, cumin, red pepper flakes, and oregano. Chipotle chiles in adobo, brown sugar, and a bit of vinegar contribute complexity and heat to this hearty stew.

1. Heat 3 tablespoons of the oil in a large wide casserole or Dutch oven over medium-high heat. Add the beef stew meat and begin to brown it on all sides. After 3 to 4 minutes, add the ground meat, sprinkle with the salt and pepper, and brown along with the cubed meat, stirring often, for another 6 to 8 minutes, until the ground meat has released its juices and the juices have cooked off.

2. Push the meats to the sides of the pot and add the remaining 1 tablespoon oil to the center. Add the onion, bell pepper, and jalapeño and cook for 3 to 4 minutes, or until beginning to soften. Add the garlic, red pepper flakes, ancho chile powder, cayenne, paprika, oregano, cumin, and adobo sauce, stir well, and cook for about 1 minute, until fragrant. Add the crushed tomatoes, tomato paste, brown sugar, and vinegar, mix well, and cook, stirring occasionally, for 3 to 4 minutes, until the sauce has thickened a bit.

3. Stir in the broth and bring to a boil. Reduce the heat to medium and stir in the beans. Bring to a simmer, then lower the heat to medium-low and cook, uncovered, at a low, steady simmer, stirring occasionally, for 1 hour. Taste and adjust the seasonings.

4. Serve the chili in bowls and let your guests garnish it with cream, cilantro, cheese, tortilla chips, and scallions as they desire.

TWO KINDS OF MEAT

My mother taught me the value of using two kinds of meat when making stews, meat loaf, and meatballs (page 208). Two different meats will yield both two distinct flavors and two different kinds of fat. For the chili, I like to use two different cuts as well, both cubed and ground meat, so the textures are also different. (Even if I use all beef, some will be ground and some cubed.) That way you can get some nice, big, meaty bites that you can sink your teeth into but you also get the rich taste and consistency of the ground meat.

1 tablespoon tomato paste

1 tablespoon packed dark brown sugar

1 tablespoon distilled white vinegar

4 cups beef broth

2 (15-ounce) cans pinto beans, drained and rinsed (or about 3 cups home-made; see page 244)

FOR GARNISH

Mexican crema or sour cream

Chopped fresh cilantro

Grated cheddar cheese

Tortilla chips, homemade (page 25) or store-bought

6 to 8 scallions (white and light green parts only), thinly sliced

CHILES RELLENOS

SERVES 6; MAKES 6 TO 8 CHILES

PREPARATION TIME: 20 minutes

COOKING TIME: 30 minutes

MAKE AHEAD: The chiles rellenos and the sauce can be made up to 3 days ahead. Cover and store separately in the refrigerator. Reheat the sauce in a large casserole, covered, over low heat. Add the chiles and cook until they are hot and the cheese has melted. Do not add the chiles to the sauce too far ahead, or they will become soggy.

6 large or 8 smaller poblano chiles (about 2 pounds), roasted, peeled, stemmed, slit down one side, and seeded (see page 21)

4 cups grated melting cheese, such as Oaxaca, asadero, mozzarella, or Monterey Jack

½ cup all-purpose flour

4 large eggs, separated

Canola or safflower oil, for deep-frying

1 batch Red Salsa (page 100), prepared *without* the chiles

Chiles rellenos is one of those Mexican dishes that is so well known that its name doesn't need translating. They are one of the most requested dishes by viewers of my PBS show. Meaty poblanos are filled with melted cheese (that oozes out when you cut into them), encased in a tender, fluffy coating, and bathed in a classic cooked tomato salsa. Enjoy them with white rice (page 241) or black beans (page 244) on the side, or do as many chile relleno aficionados do—use them as a filling for amazing tacos or tortas.

1. Stuff each roasted chile with about ½ cup cheese, or as much as will fit inside without preventing the chiles from closing with a little bit of overlap. Close the chiles, overlapping the edges, and if desired, seal each one with a toothpick inserted horizontally, as if you were sewing up the chiles.

2. Place the flour on a plate, roll the stuffed chiles in the flour to coat entirely, and set aside. (The flour coating will help the batter adhere to the chiles.)

3. To prepare the batter (or *capeado*): With a hand mixer in a large bowl or in the bowl of a stand mixer fitted with the whisk attachment, beat the egg whites on medium speed to stiff but not dry peaks. In a small bowl, beat the egg yolks with a whisk or fork. Using a rubber spatula, carefully fold the egg yolks into the egg whites.

4. Add 1 inch of oil to a large casserole or wide deep skillet and heat over medium-high heat (see page 237). Cover a cooling rack or platter with paper towels and set it next to your stove. Test the heat of the oil with a thermometer (it should be at 350 degrees) or by dropping in a teaspoon of the batter to see if active and happy bubbles immediately form all around it.

5. When the oil is ready, working in batches, dip the stuffed and floured chiles into the egg batter to coat thoroughly, then gently place in the hot oil, slit side up, without crowding. Using a large spoon, gently spoon some of the hot oil on top to seal the chiles. Fry for about 2 minutes per side, until golden brown; flip them gently with a slotted spoon or two

continued...

(I find that it's too easy to tear them if I use tongs). Once they are cooked, place on the paper towel–covered rack or platter.

6. Meanwhile, heat the salsa in a saucepan.

7. Serve the chiles hot (before the cheese begins to cool!), spooning a generous amount of salsa on top. Alternatively, you can heat the salsa roja and chiles rellenos together in a large casserole or soup pot; heat the salsa, then add the fried chiles rellenos and spoon some of the hot salsa on top. Serve right away from the casserole. Don't wait, or the batter will become soggy.

Note: If not serving them right away, transfer the fried chiles to a casserole or baking dish. Heat the chiles, uncovered, in a 300-degree oven for 8 to 10 minutes, until the cheese melts. Warm the salsa and serve.

VARIATIONS: Simmered Chiles Rellenos without Batter

- If you do not want to batter and fry the chiles rellenos, simply fill the peeled roasted peppers as directed and omit the batter. Bring the salsa roja to a simmer over medium heat in a casserole and place the filled peppers in the sauce. Simmer until the cheese is hot and soft, 8 to 10 minutes.

- You can also stuff the peppers with other fillings, like soft scrambled eggs and refried beans (page 247), a favorite combination at home, or a seasoned rice like the Green Herbed Rice with Spinach on page 242.

DANCING WITH YOUR BURNER

When you deep-fry, you must continue to regulate the heat so that the temperature of the oil, for most recipes, remains between 350 and 375 degrees. I call this dancing with the burner. Once your oil reaches the proper temperature and you begin to add food to the pan, the temperature will start to drop. If you notice that the bubbling is slowing down, raise the heat a bit. If the bubbles are becoming a bit hyperactive, lower the heat a bit. It should waver between medium-low at the lowest and medium-high at the highest.

SIDES

IN MEXICO, SIDE DISHES ARE AS TASTY AS THE MAINS. We don't

just steam a pot of plain white rice to serve under our saucy stews and alongside our tasty enchiladas. First we sear the rice in oil, along with onions and aromatics to add flavor, before adding another layer of flavor with the rich-tasting broth we simmer it in. In my recipe (opposite), I brighten up the grains with one more surprise, a squeeze of fresh lime. The rice is good enough to serve as the main event, topped with a fried egg or a few slices of creamy avocado.

This chapter contains recipes for basic dishes that are universal throughout Mexico: an incredibly herbal green rice (with four different herbs, plus greens; page 242) and black beans, both simmered and refried (pages 244-247).

These basics can be put to many different uses. Simmered black beans are great as they are, but if you need a heartier side dish, add bacon, chipotle, and adobo sauce (page 246). Serve your potatoes roasted, a little bit smashed and crusty, topped with queso añejo or its cousin Parmesan, or pan-fried in a zingy cilantro lime sauce. My boys and I are particularly fond of *esquites*, simmered corn with chiles and epazote (page 251). This is one of my favorite Mexican street foods—you can buy cups of the brothy shaved corn from carts in cities and towns all over Mexico—and the wonderfully seasoned vegetables can be put to many uses: Wrap them in tortillas for the best tacos or quesadillas ever, stir them into scrambled eggs, or add the leftovers to a salad.

NO-NONSENSE MEXICAN-STYLE WHITE RICE

ARROZ BLANCO

SERVES 6

PREPARATION TIME: 5 minutes

COOKING TIME: 25 minutes

MAKE AHEAD: The rice can be made up to 2 days ahead, covered, and refrigerated. To reheat, add 2 tablespoons water to the rice in a saucepan, cover, and heat over low heat.

3 tablespoons canola or safflower oil

2 cups long-grain or extra-long-grain white rice or jasmine rice, soaked if desired

½ cup finely chopped white onion

4 cups chicken broth, homemade (page 40) or store-bought

2 teaspoons freshly squeezed lime juice

1 teaspoon kosher or sea salt or to taste

1 celery stalk, cut in half

2 flat-leaf parsley sprigs

1 jalapeño or serrano chile (optional)

Mexican white rice is the most basic of all our country's rice variations: one that can accompany almost any dish without overshadowing it. Yet with its hint of lime juice, as well as onion, and a few aromatics, it is unexpectedly flavorful. It's a master at soaking up sauces and it can also be used as a base for soups and casseroles (see page 193).

1. Heat the oil in a medium saucepan over medium-high heat until hot but not smoking. Add the rice and cook, stirring often, until it becomes milky white, crackles, and feels heavier as you stir it, 3 to 4 minutes. Make room in the center of the pan, add the onion and cook, stirring, for 2 to 3 minutes, until the onion begins to soften.

2. Add the chicken broth, lime juice, and salt and stir once. Place the celery, parsley sprigs, and chile, if using, on top of the rice, raise the heat to high, and bring to a rolling boil, then cover and reduce the heat to the lowest setting. Simmer for 12 to 15 minutes, until most of the liquid has been absorbed but there is still some moisture in the pan. The rice should be tender; if it is not but all the liquid has been absorbed, add 2 table-spoons water, cover, and cook for a couple more minutes. Remove from the heat and let the rice rest, covered, for 5 minutes.

3. Remove the celery and parsley sprigs, fluff the rice with a fork, and serve. At my table we all fight for the chile, which has absorbed all the fla-vors from the pan. It's pretty tame by the time it has cooked with the rice.

MEXICAN COOK'S TIP
Freshly Squeezed Lime Juice

Some Mexican cooks add a splash of freshly squeezed lime juice to their white rice, and some don't. Like me, many con-sider it of the utmost importance: It gives the rice a kind of shine, enhancing both its appearance and flavor. The rice will not taste citrusy, but the lime juice brightens the flavors of all of the ingredients.

GREEN HERBED RICE WITH SPINACH

ARROZ CON HOJAS VERDES

SERVES 6

PREPARATION TIME: 10 minutes

COOKING TIME: 25 minutes

MAKE AHEAD: The rice can be made up to 2 days ahead, covered, and refrigerated. To reheat, add 2 tablespoons water to the rice in a saucepan, cover, and heat over low heat.

2 cups tightly packed coarsely chopped spinach

1 cup tightly packed coarsely chopped fresh flat-leaf parsley leaves and upper part of stems

1 cup tightly packed coarsely chopped fresh cilantro leaves and upper part of stems

1 cup tightly packed coarsely chopped fresh basil

½ cup tightly packed coarsely chopped fresh mint

1 jalapeño or serrano chile, coarsely chopped

4 cups chicken broth, homemade (page 40) or store-bought

3 tablespoons canola or safflower oil

2 cups long-grain or extra-long-grain white rice or jasmine rice

½ cup chopped white onion

1 garlic clove, minced or pressed

This striking green, deeply herbal rice has so much flavor that you could serve it on its own. It boasts four different herbs—parsley, cilantro, basil, and mint—plus spinach and jalapeño, all blended together into a healthful and delicious puree that flavors and colors the rice. First the rice gets the Mexican treatment of a quick sear in oil, then it's cooked risotto-style with the puree, and finally it simmers in broth with a splash of lime juice and zest. When you remove the lid 15 minutes later, you will see a creamy green film on top, which gets redistributed when you fluff the rice, filling your kitchen with its fabulous herbal aroma.

1. In a blender or food processor, combine the spinach, parsley, cilantro, basil, mint, chile, and 1 cup of the chicken broth and puree until smooth. Pass the puree through a strainer into a large liquid measuring cup, pressing through as much of the puree as you can.

2. Heat the oil in a medium saucepan over medium-high heat until hot but not smoking. Add the rice and cook, stirring often, until it becomes milky white, crackles, and feels heavier as you stir it, 3 to 4 minutes. Clear a space in the center of the pan, add the onion and garlic, and cook, stirring, for 2 to 3 minutes, until the onion begins to soften, then mix with the rice.

3. Stir in the green puree and cook, stirring often, until the puree darkens, thickens, and is absorbed by the rice, 1 to 2 minutes. Stir in 3 cups chicken broth, along with the lime zest, lime juice, and salt, raise the heat to high, and bring to a boil, then cover and reduce the heat to the lowest setting. Cook until the rice is tender and most of the liquid has been absorbed but there is still some moisture in the pan, 14 to 15 minutes. When you open the lid, there will be a thick film of creamy green sauce on top of the rice, but if you insert a spatula or fork to check, there should be no liquid in the bottom of the pan. Remove from the heat and let the rice rest, covered, for 5 minutes.

4. Fluff the rice with a fork, stirring the green sauce into it, and serve.

Grated zest of 1 lime

1 tablespoon freshly squeezed lime juice

1¼ teaspoons kosher or sea salt or to taste

BASIC BLACK BEANS

FRIJOLES NEGROS

MAKES 5 GENEROUS CUPS COOKED BEANS AND ABOUT 2 CUPS BROTH

PREPARATION TIME: 5 minutes

COOKING TIME: 1½ hours, more or less, depending on age of beans

MAKE AHEAD: The beans can be made up to 4 days ahead of time, covered, and refrigerated.

1 pound dried black beans (about 2¼ cups)

½ large white onion

3 quarts water

1 tablespoon kosher or sea salt or to taste

A couple of cilantro or epazote sprigs (optional)

I'm almost embarrassed to tell you just how many black beans we eat at home. As my youngest son, Juju, replied when asked recently what his favorite food was and how many times a week he eats it: black beans, six days a week. If we don't eat them on the seventh, it is probably only because I haven't kept up with the speed at which we go through our supply.

I can make a meal out of a bowlful of these beans, with a spoonful of sauce from chipotles in adobo spooned in and a couple of tortillas and slices of ripe avocado on the side, but they also make a great side for many a main dish. Use them as a base for a soup (page 36) or a sauce for enchiladas (page 147). Or turn them into refried beans (page 247) and spread them inside a torta (page 70); the possibilities are endless.

Note: Other beans, such as pintos or white beans, can be cooked in the same way.

....

1. Pick over the beans, rinse in cold water, and drain. Place them in a large pot or casserole, add the onion and water, and bring to a rolling boil over high heat. Reduce the heat to medium-low and cook at a happy simmer, partially covered, until the beans are cooked through and soft, 1¼ to 1½ hours, depending on the age of the beans.

2. Add the salt and cilantro or epazote, stir, and cook for 15 minutes more, or until the beans are so soft that they fall apart if you press one or two between your fingers and the broth has thickened to a soupy consistency. If the beans are not quite there and the pot is drying out, add hot water (make sure it is really hot) and cook a few minutes longer.

3. Remove the onion and herbs with a slotted spoon before serving or using the beans.

BLACK BEANS, NO SOAKING REQUIRED

Let's cut to the chase: Black beans (or pinto, or white) do not need to be soaked before cooking. Not even for a minute. Yes, it is lovely to have kitchen rituals that have been passed down from your grandmother and your mom, but some rituals prevent you from making delicious dishes on a regular basis. If the thought of having to remember to soak beans discourages you, don't worry. Soaking reduces the cooking time by very little, a fourth at most. And it won't make the beans taste better or make them less gaseous. In fact, what will help as far as digestion is concerned is to eat more beans, so your body gets used to them—which you will be able to do if you don't soak them.

EPAZOTE

Epazote has a distinctive, unusual taste, strong but deeply clean and aromatic. It makes a perfect, earthy pairing with black beans, mushrooms, corn, and squash blossoms. If you can't find fresh epazote, you can use it dried, reducing the amount called for by about two thirds. If you can't find epazote in any form, choose a different herb with another flavor profile altogether, such as cilantro.

BACON AND CHIPOTLE BLACK BEANS

FRIJOLES CON TOCINO Y CHIPOTLE

SERVES 4 TO 6

PREPARATION TIME: 5 minutes

COOKING TIME: 20 minutes

MAKE AHEAD: The beans can be made up to 4 days ahead, covered, and refrigerated.

8   ounces thick-sliced bacon, coarsely chopped

¾ cup chopped white onion

1   recipe Basic Black Beans (page 244), with 2 cups of their broth, or 5 cups canned beans, rinsed and drained, plus 2 cups water or broth

2   tablespoons sauce from canned chipotles in adobo or to taste

Kosher or sea salt

Of the many ways you can dress the basic black beans on page 244, this is one of the simplest and tastiest. All you need is good thick-sliced bacon and some of the addictively spicy, wanna-be sweet adobo sauce of chipotles in adobo. Add the sauce to the beans, and heat them with crispy bacon and onion that has been softened in the rendered bacon fat.

1. Set a large skillet or casserole over medium-high heat. Once it is hot, add the bacon and cook, stirring occasionally, until lightly browned and starting to crisp, 3 to 4 minutes. Stir in the onion and cook, stirring a couple of times, until the onion softens a bit and the bacon browns and crisps further, 2 to 3 minutes.

2. Add the beans, the broth or water, and the adobo sauce to the mix, stir well, and reduce the heat to medium. Cook, stirring occasionally, until the beans are still saucy but not soupy, about 10 more minutes. Taste and add salt if necessary. Serve hot.

MEXICAN COOK'S TIP

You can use any kind of bacon, even turkey bacon, but if you decide to leave out the pork, add a couple of tablespoons of canola or safflower oil to the skillet before adding the onion. If you do go for pork, get thick slices—they make nice hearty bites.

REFRIEDS

FRIJOLES REFRITOS

MAKES ABOUT 4 CUPS

PREPARATION TIME: 5 minutes

COOKING TIME: 25 minutes

MAKE AHEAD: The beans can be made up to 4 days ahead, covered, and refrigerated (or frozen, but it's unlikely that you will have any leftovers to freeze).

1   recipe Basic Black Beans (page 244), drained, reserving 1 cup of their broth, or 5 cups canned beans, plus 1 cup water

3   tablespoons canola or safflower oil

½   cup chopped white onion

1   jalapeño chile, finely chopped (seeded if desired)

½   teaspoon kosher or sea salt or to taste

Whenever I make beans, I make a double batch so that I can use half of them for *refritos*. Contrary to what their name may imply, refried beans are not double fried. The word *refrito* actually translates as "well fried." When Mexicans want to emphasize an action or an attribute, we add the prefix *re*—so if something is expensive, we would use the word *caro*, but if it is *really* expensive, we would say *recaro*.

We use these beans not only as a side dish but also as a thick and nutritious spread for tortas like the *Pepitos* on page 75 and as a base in casseroles like the huevos rancheros on page 181.

There are many options when it comes to seasoning refried beans. I like onion cooked in lard or oil, and I add a jalapeño, which doesn't contribute much heat but does add a lot of flavor. As for method, traditionally *refritos* are smashed in the pan with the likes of a potato masher as they cook. However, pureeing them in a blender before cooking renders the task much easier and the refried beans smoother and creamier. If you want a more rustic texture, you can puree them partially, leaving them a bit chunky, with some of the skins intact. These are incredibly easy to make.

1. Place the beans and the broth or water in a blender and puree until they reach the desired consistency: For very smooth refried beans, puree completely. For more rustic refried beans with more texture, leave them a bit chunky.

2. Heat the oil in a large skillet over medium heat until hot but not smoking. Add the onion and cook, stirring occasionally, until softened, about 4 minutes. Add the jalapeño and cook until the onion and jalapeño are tender and the onion has begun to brown around the edges, 2 to 3 more minutes.

3. Add the beans and cook, stirring frequently, until they have the consistency of a thick puree, 12 to 15 minutes. Season with the salt. Serve.

SAMI'S SMASHED POTATOES

PAPAS APLASTADAS DE SAMI

SERVES 4 OR 5

PREPARATION TIME: 10 minutes

COOKING TIME: 35 minutes

MAKE AHEAD: You can make these to the point when they are ready to be baked up to 2 hours ahead and leave them on the baking sheet.

1½ pounds baby potatoes, rinsed

½ cup olive oil, plus more for the baking sheet

10 garlic cloves, minced or pressed

1 tablespoon chopped fresh rosemary or 1 teaspoon crumbled dried

½ teaspoon ancho (mild) or chipotle (spicy) chile powder (see page 65) or to taste

½ teaspoon kosher or sea salt or to taste

4 ounces Parmigiano-Reggiano or queso añejo, grated (1 cup)

My middle son, Sami, likes potatoes cooked every which way, but this recipe is his favorite. In fact, we developed it together. First we smashed the cooked potatoes, just enough to flatten them a little in their skins, and tossed them in olive oil with plenty of garlic. Then we added more flavor with rosemary and decided to take advantage of the many varieties of ground dried Mexican chiles that are now readily available, spiking them up with a bit more flavor and heat. Finally we decided to top them with grated Parmigiano-Reggiano right before putting them in the oven. The resulting robust, crisp, thick-skinned version became our ultimate smashed potato.

1. Bring a large pot of salted water to a boil over medium-high heat. Drop in the potatoes and cook until tender all the way through when pierced with the tip of a sharp knife, about 20 minutes. Drain.

2. Place a rack in the upper third of the oven and preheat the oven to 400 degrees.

3. Brush a baking sheet or large baking dish with olive oil. Place a hot potato on the baking sheet and, holding onto the potato with one hand, flatten the top (unevenly) by smashing it lightly but firmly with the back of a soup spoon. Take care not to break the potato apart. Continue with the remaining potatoes. (Don't let them cool too much, or it won't be as easy to smash and lightly flatten them.)

4. In a small bowl, mix the olive oil with the garlic, rosemary, chile powder, and salt. Spoon some of the garlic mixture on top of each smashed potato. Cover with the grated cheese.

5. Bake the potatoes for 25 to 30 minutes, until they are golden and crisp on top and their bottoms have crisped a bit. Serve hot.

CILANTRO BABY POTATOES

PAPITAS AL CILANTRO

SERVES 5 OR 6

PREPARATION TIME: 5 minutes

COOKING TIME: 35 minutes

MAKE AHEAD: These are best served right away.

3 tablespoons canola or safflower oil

2 pounds red baby potatoes, rinsed and dried

Kosher or sea salt and freshly ground black pepper

½ cup freshly squeezed lime juice

½ cup chicken or vegetable broth, homemade (page 40 or 41) or store-bought

2½ cups tightly packed coarsely chopped fresh cilantro leaves and upper part of stems

1 jalapeño or serrano chile, sliced (seeded if desired)

These baby potatoes are seared in oil, then slowly cooked in a bright, citrusy cilantro sauce that penetrates the flesh of the potatoes just enough to flavor them through and through. Creamy on the inside and insanely flavorful, they are not to be missed.

1. Heat the oil over medium heat in a large skillet that can accommodate all of the potatoes in a single layer. Make sure the potatoes are dry, then add to the hot oil and season with ½ teaspoon salt and pepper to taste. Let the potatoes cook and brown gently, stirring occasionally, for 20 minutes, or until their skins have begun to wrinkle and change in color from pink to light brown; they should remain intact.

2. Meanwhile, combine the lime juice, broth, cilantro, jalapeño, and ½ teaspoon salt in a blender and puree until completely smooth.

3. Pour the puree over the potatoes, reduce the heat to medium-low, and simmer for 2 to 3 minutes. Cover the pan and cook for 10 to 12 minutes, stirring halfway through, until the potatoes are completely cooked and very soft and the sauce has thickened into a puree. Serve hot.

MEXICAN COOK'S TIP

Dry Your Potatoes

After you scrub the potatoes, drain and dry them well. If they are not completely dry when you add them to the hot oil to sear them, the oil will splutter all over the place.

SIMMERED SHAVED CORN WITH CHILES AND EPAZOTE

ESQUITES

SERVES 5 OR 6

PREPARATION TIME: 10 minutes

COOKING TIME: 35 minutes

MAKE AHEAD: The *esquites* can be made a couple of hours ahead and kept in the covered saucepan at room temperature.

2   tablespoons unsalted butter

1   tablespoon canola or safflower oil

1   serrano or jalapeño chile, chopped (seeded if desired) or to taste

6   cups fresh corn kernels (from about 10 ears corn)

2   cups water

2   tablespoons fresh epazote leaves, chopped, or 1 teaspoon dried (or substitute fresh cilantro, which has a different flavor but also works)

1   teaspoon kosher or sea salt, or more to taste

GARNISHES
(CHOOSE ONE OR MORE)

2   limes, quartered

½ cup mayonnaise and/or Mexican crema

½ cup crumbled queso fresco, Cotija, or mild feta

Chile piquín powder

In Mexican cooking, corn is eaten (and drunk, see the Chocolate Atole on page 307) in just about every possible way. *Esquites,* freshly shaved corn cooked in a buttery broth with epazote and serrano chile and served in a cup, is one of the most popular renditions. So much so that my boys counted eight *esquite* street carts in the somewhat small downtown square of Chihuahua, the capital city of the northern state of Mexico of the same name.

Esquites is a versatile dish. Depending on your mood and your taste, you can dress it with some or all of the traditional garnishes—mayonnaise or Mexican crema, crumbled salty Cotija or queso fresco, a healthy squeeze of lime juice (enough to make you wince), salt, and/or ground dried chile piquín.

. . . .

1. Combine the butter and oil in a large saucepan or medium casserole and heat over medium-high heat. When the butter has melted, add the chile and cook, stirring, until softened, 1 to 2 minutes. Stir in the corn and cook, stirring, for 2 minutes. Add the water, epazote (or cilantro), and salt, stir, and bring to a simmer. Cover, reduce the heat to medium-low, and cook for 10 minutes, or until the corn is tender and the broth tasty and nicely seasoned.

2. Serve in small cups or bowls. Pass the garnishes for your guests to add as desired.

SKILLET CORN BREAD WITH POBLANOS, CORN, BACON, AND CHEDDAR

PAN DE ELOTE CON POBLANOS, ELOTE, TOCINO, Y QUESO CHEDDAR

SERVES 8 TO 10

PREPARATION TIME: 15 minutes

COOKING TIME: 35 minutes

MAKE AHEAD: The corn bread can be made a day ahead, cooled, and covered. You can reheat it, covered, in a 250-degree oven before serving.

6 to 8 slices thick bacon, preferably center-cut

1¼ cups all-purpose flour

½ cup yellow cornmeal

⅓ cup packed packed dark brown sugar

1 teaspoon baking powder

1 teaspoon baking soda

½ teaspoon kosher or sea salt

½ teaspoon freshly ground black pepper

4 large eggs

1 cup whole milk

½ cup heavy cream

8 ounces cheddar cheese, grated (2 cups)

3 poblano chiles, roasted, peeled, seeded, and diced (see page 21)

2 cups fresh or thawed frozen corn kernels

I grew to love skillet corn bread when I lived in Dallas. It was one of the first solid foods my oldest son, Alan, who was born there, ate. He started with plain corn bread when he was a toddler, and as he grew older, we kept adding ingredients he liked. It wasn't until we moved to DC that we added the poblanos, which was where we stopped with our now thoroughly Tex-Mex skillet corn bread.

The other bonus ingredients are cheddar cheese, fresh corn kernels, crisp bacon, and bacon fat, which add depth of flavor, sweetness, crunch, and moistness to the bread.

1. Preheat the oven to 375 degrees.

2. Heat a 9- or 10-inch cast-iron skillet over medium-high heat. Add the bacon and cook until crispy, about 3 minutes per side. Remove the bacon from the pan, leaving the fat in the skillet, and drain on a paper towel–lined plate. Set the pan aside.

3. In a large bowl, stir together the flour, cornmeal, brown sugar, baking powder, baking soda, salt, and pepper. Beat the eggs in a small bowl, then whisk in the milk and cream.

4. Whisk the wet ingredients into the dry. Fold in the cheddar cheese, poblano chiles, and corn. Crumble the bacon and fold it in. Pour in most of the bacon fat from the cast-iron pan, leaving about 1 tablespoon in the pan, and combine well.

5. Reheat the skillet and the remaining bacon drippings over medium heat, and when the pan is hot, pour in the batter, scraping in every last bit with a rubber spatula. Transfer to the oven and bake for 30 minutes, or until the corn bread is golden brown and a tester inserted in the center comes out clean.

6. Cut into wedges and serve hot or warm.

STIR-FRIED GREEN BEANS WITH PEANUTS AND CHILE DE ÁRBOL

EJOTES CON CACAHUATES Y CHILE DE ÁRBOL

SERVES 4

PREPARATION TIME: 15 minutes

COOKING TIME: 10 minutes

MAKE AHEAD: This should be served right away.

Kosher or sea salt

1 pound green beans or Chinese long beans, sliced on the diagonal into 2-inch pieces

1 tablespoon soy sauce

¼ cup chicken or vegetable broth, homemade (page 40 or 41) or store-bought

½ teaspoon packed brown sugar

2 tablespoons peanut oil

½ cup roasted peanuts

4 garlic cloves, minced or pressed

3 or 4 dried chiles de árbol, stemmed and thinly sliced (seeded if desired)

4 to 6 scallions (light green and white parts only), thinly sliced

Mexicans are crazy about Chinese food. We love to visit the Chinese restaurants and cafés that have proliferated in Mexico City's Barrio Chino (Chinatown) and in the state of Baja California, where there has been a great deal of Chinese immigration. My maternal grandmother, Lali, often cooked Chinese food and was very good at it. What she liked most were stir-fry dishes, so she bought herself an electric wok. After she passed away, that wok found its way into my kitchen, and I've cherished it, but I haven't used it! I've dragged that wok through so many house moves that I managed to lose its electrical cord—but I'm too devoted to my grandmother's wok to buy a new one.

Still, I've managed to make many a successful Chinese-Mexican dish using a frying pan or a casserole, and so can you, as long as they are wide and heavy enough to withstand high heat. Tender, crunchy, and fresh, with its double dose of peanuts (oil and nuts) and a healthy amount of garlic and chile de árbol, this is one of our staple dishes at home.

1. Fill a large pot with water, salt generously, and bring to a boil. Add the green beans and boil for 2 to 3 minutes, until al dente and still very crisp. Drain and set aside.

2. Combine the soy sauce, chicken broth, sugar, and ½ teaspoon salt in a small bowl and mix well.

3. Heat the peanut oil in a large heavy skillet or wok over high heat until hot but not smoking. Add the peanuts and stir-fry for about 20 seconds. Beware, peanuts burn more quickly than you would think, so don't wait until they look browned. Add the garlic and chiles and stir-fry for about 10 seconds, then add the scallions and stir-fry for another 10 to 15 seconds. Add the green beans and stir to combine all the ingredients. Add the soy sauce mixture and stir-fry for 3 to 4 minutes, until the green beans are crisp-tender. Serve at once.

WARM NOPALITOS WITH GUAJILLO CHILES AND CORN

NOPALITOS SALTADOS CON GUAJILLOS Y ELOTES

SERVES 6

PREPARATION TIME: 20 minutes

COOKING TIME: 30 minutes

MAKE AHEAD: The nopalitos can be made a couple of hours ahead and set aside, covered, at room temperature. Reheat gently before serving.

- 3 tablespoons canola or safflower oil

- 2 pounds nopales (cactus paddles), cleaned and diced (see headnote and page 39)

- 1 teaspoon kosher or sea salt or to taste

- ½ cup finely chopped white onion

- 2 garlic cloves, finely chopped

- 5 dried guajillo chiles, stemmed, seeded, and finely chopped

- 1½ cups fresh or thawed frozen corn kernels

- 1 teaspoon freshly squeezed lime juice

Nopales are one of the most beloved vegetables in Mexico. If you have never tried them before, this is a good dish to begin with. After you taste them you will see why our nickname for the cactus paddles contains the loving suffix *ito*. Tart, lemony, meaty, with a touch of sweet crunch and mild heat, this dish makes a great accompaniment—or enjoy it on its own with rice and/or black beans. I love them so much that if a month has passed and I haven't had my nopalito fix, I get my nopalito blues.

1. Heat 2 tablespoons of the oil in a large skillet or casserole over medium-high heat. Add the nopales to the skillet, along with the salt, and cook, stirring occasionally, for 2 minutes. Cover, reduce the heat to medium, and let the nopales cook and sweat for 15 to 20 minutes, stirring halfway through. They will have exuded a gelatinous liquid that will cook off.

2. Uncover, stir, and check to see that the gelatinous liquid has evaporated. If it has not, cook uncovered for a few more minutes. Make room in the center of the pan and add the remaining 1 tablespoon oil, along with the chopped onion, garlic, chiles, and corn. Cook these for about a minute in the middle of the pan, then stir together with the nopales and cook for another 3 to 4 minutes, stirring occasionally. Add the lime juice, stir, cover, and cook for another 3 to 4 minutes. Taste for salt and add more if desired.

3. Serve hot or warm.

DESSERTS

DESSERTS HAVE BEEN A CONSTANT THEME running through the many chapters of my life. My mom's side of the family is descended from a long line of accomplished Austrian cooks. My Austrian-born Great-Aunt Annie, who barely survived the Second World War, was famous for the desserts she made in Mexico City, where she and my grandmother settled after the war. Later, when she moved to Acapulco, she opened a pastry shop called Pastelería Viena on the main coast road. She grew to love Mexican ingredients, which worked their way into her tarts and cakes. And every time I visited my father's mother, my *bobe*, another survivor of European pogroms and wars, she delighted me with her cookies and pound cakes, which were a mix of Eastern European tradition and the flavors of her new home.

Throughout my life sweets have always been a pleasurable backdrop to help me along through all my starts and stops. There was the disastrous first time I tried my hand at making scrambled eggs and added so many ingredients from the cupboard that the eggs came out gray (too much enthusiasm, my mom said). Thank goodness my dad had stopped to get a big bag of sweet rolls at the local panadería! When I wanted to be a ballet dancer, sweets were there in the form of the most delicious chocolate cake that my dad would treat me to at a nearby coffee shop whenever he picked me up after my arduous daily classes. During my years of studying to be a flutist, I treated myself every Friday to cookies from the panadería.

You will see as you cook in this chapter what a weakness I have for the sweets of my Mexican childhood—Mexico's most well-known tres leches cake (page 281), custardy *jericallas* (page 262) and my aunt's favorite cookies. You'll also see that I can never resist putting my own spin on these treats: My tres leches cake is marbled with chocolate, and my rich chocolate jericalla custards are topped with a wonderful blackberry sauce. Cook your way through this chapter and I think you'll also understand why I adore mangoes: How can you not if you're from Mexico, where the ripe fruits are always dropping from their trees, ready to be folded into cakes and mousses or lavished on tarts, leaving you the wonderful task of eating the last of the juicy ripe flesh that clings to the pit?

When I was putting together this chapter the researcher/historian in me loved uncovering desserts from the past in the collection of centuries-old cookbooks that my dad has helped me put together over the years, and recreating them in new ways, using contemporary measures and instructions without sacrificing their soul. I tested and retested my rediscovered favorites, such as the sublimely simple Mango Poundcake (page 278), so you can make them at home without having to find an eighteenth-century bucket or guess the size of a seventeenth-century Aguascalientes cook's hand to measure flour.

CHOCOLATE CUSTARDS WITH BLACKBERRY, MINT, AND LIME COULIS

JERICALLA DE CHOCOLATE CON SALSA DE ZARZAMORA Y MENTA

SERVES 10

PREPARATION TIME: 10 minutes, plus chilling time

COOKING TIME: 50 minutes

MAKE AHEAD: The *jericallas* can be made up to 5 days ahead, cooled, wrapped tightly in plastic wrap, and refrigerated.

5 cups whole milk

1 tablespoon vanilla extract

1 (2-inch) stick canela (Ceylon cinnamon; see page 264)

8 ounces semisweet chocolate, cut into small (¼-inch) pieces

9 large egg yolks

1 cup sugar

Pinch of fine sea salt

1 recipe Blackberry, Mint, and Lime Coulis (page 264)

Jericalla is a creamy, custard-like dessert popular in Jalisco, a state in central Mexico that is home to some of the country's most treasured traditions, such as mariachis and tequila. *Jericalla* is like a crème brûlée (no kitchen torch necessary, although you can use one if you like; see the Variation) or pot de crème. Its origins are in Spain and, like many beloved Mexican sweets, it came to Mexico via Spanish nuns. The dessert became a popular street food, but it is still not well known outside of Mexico.

Despite being rich and creamy, *jericalla* seems light. I have tasted many different versions, but my favorite is this ultra-chocolaty one. To make it shine even brighter, I spoon a blackberry coulis on top.

1. Place the milk, vanilla extract, and canela stick in a medium saucepan and bring just to a bare simmer over medium heat. Reduce the heat to the lowest possible setting and simmer for 5 minutes. Remove from the heat and set aside to cool, then remove the canela stick.

2. Preheat the oven to 350 degrees.

3. Place the chocolate in the top of a double boiler or in a metal bowl set over a saucepan filled with 1 inch of water; make sure that the bottom of the bowl is not touching the water. Bring the water to a simmer and melt the chocolate, stirring occasionally with a heatproof spatula to make sure all of the chocolate is evenly melted. Remove from the heat.

4. In a medium bowl, using a whisk, combine the egg yolks, sugar, and salt and whisk until thickened and the color has gone from bright to pale yellow, about 1 minute (or count 60 Mississippis). Slowly whisk in the melted chocolate until thoroughly combined. A ladleful at a time, whisk in the cooled milk.

5. Fill a baking dish or roasting pan large enough to accommodate ten 6-ounce ramekins or flan or custard molds with ½ inch of hot water.

Place the molds in the water bath. Using a ladle, carefully fill the molds with the custard, up to about ¼ inch below the rims. Place the baking dish in the oven and bake for 40 minutes, or until the custard has begun to set. The top layer should be thick and resemble the top of a brownie; it should not be browned, but there may be a few small spots here and there. The *jericalla* should jiggle and will look a bit runny under the thickened tops, like a thin pudding.

6. Remove the pan from the oven and the ramekins from the water bath. The *jericalla* will thicken and set as it cools.

7. Serve at room temperature or, once cool, chill in the refrigerator and serve cold, with the coulis and garnished with the mint leaves.

VARIATION: Some Mexican cooks brown or caramelize the top of their *jericallas* by briefly running them under a broiler. If you want a darker caramelized topping, place the custards under the broiler for 30 seconds after they have cooled.

MEXICAN COOK'S TIP

Baking Time: Sometimes Less Is More

The key to making a good *jericalla* is to not leave it in the oven for too long. You must remove it before it looks set; it should look creamy, even a bit runny under the surface. It will set and thicken as it cools. If it bakes for too long, it won't be creamy; it will be like a bad rendition of a set flan. Here, less time is more.

WHAT TO DO WITH ALL THOSE EGG WHITES?

Egg whites were once used in Mexican convents as a shiny varnish and protective cover for painted ornaments and gold-painted wood. The nuns who cooked in those convents used a lot of egg yolks for their creations. *Jericalla* is just one example; another one is *rompope*, Mexican-Style Eggnog (page 305). They had to use the egg whites for something! You may not want to varnish your wood or ornate decorations with egg whites, but do hold onto them in the refrigerator. You can use them when you whip up omelets or scrambled eggs in the morning, make floating islands (page 267), or make the meringue, mascarpone, and strawberry cake on page 283.

BLACKBERRY, MINT, AND LIME COULIS

SALSITA DE ZARZAMORA CON MENTA Y LIMÓN

MAKES ABOUT 1¼ CUPS

PREPARATION TIME: 5 minutes

MAKE AHEAD: The sauce can be made 5 days ahead, covered, and refrigerated.

2 cups blackberries, rinsed and drained

2 tablespoons sugar or to taste

2 tablespoons coarsely chopped fresh mint

1 teaspoon freshly squeezed lime juice or to taste

We whip up this quick sauce whenever we visit my mother-in-law in Valle de Bravo, a small town about two hours from Mexico City, where fresh blackberries almost the size of limes abound and mint grows wild. We bring baskets full of blackberries home from the market, give them a quick rinse, and throw them into my mother-in-law's old blender, along with mint that grows in her backyard. Then we strain the sauce and add a bit of freshly squeezed lime juice.

The sauce is completely *multiusos*, as we say in Spanish—"multipurpose." It goes beautifully with ice cream and can be spooned over pound cake, cheesecake, and, my favorite, chocolate custards (page 262). My mother-in-law has been known to polish it off on its own if there is any left behind.

Place the blackberries, sugar, and mint in a blender and puree until smooth. Pass the sauce through a fine strainer set over a bowl. Stir in the lime juice. Cover and refrigerate until ready to use.

CANELA (CEYLON CINNAMON)

Most of the cinnamon used in Mexican cuisine is called *canela*, also known as Ceylon cinnamon, or true cinnamon. Canela is quite different in appearance, taste, and aroma from cassia cinnamon, which is the type that most American supermarkets sell (though we are beginning to find more Ceylon cinnamon/canela here).

Ceylon cinnamon has a milder, warmer, and sweeter taste and a more pronounced fragrance, with none of the astringent qualities of cassia. The layered stick of canela is softer, with a papery texture that makes it much easier to crumble, which is great for the many Mexican dishes that call for grinding it—canela is much gentler on the blades of your blender or spice grinder. Cassia cinnamon sticks are hard and much more uniform, which may be one reason why they appeal to spice purveyors, as they are easier to package.

MANGO MOUSSE

GELATINA ESPUMOSA DE MANGO

SERVES 12

PREPARATION TIME: 10 minutes

COOKING TIME: 10 minutes, plus at least 1 hour chilling time

MAKE AHEAD: The mousse can be made up to 5 days ahead and kept in the refrigerator.

1 cup lukewarm water

2 envelopes (about 2 table-spoons) unflavored gelatin

1 (14-ounce) can sweetened condensed milk

4 cups cubed fresh or thawed frozen mango

1 tablespoon freshly squeezed lime juice

2 cups heavy cream

1 cup diced fresh mango or berries, for garnish (optional)

If you've never been a fan of sweet gelatin desserts, you haven't tried those in the Mexican repertoire. Forget about the 1950s-style Jell-O salads and the dreary Jell-O in hospitals. Mexican *gelatinas* are something to boast about. They come in red, green, orange, blue, or any color you can dream up, flavored with vanilla, cajeta, *jamaica*, chocolate, coffee, fruits, nuts, or just about any embellishment you crave. Some are smooth, others chunky; they can be creamy or foamy, heavy or light. We haven't even mentioned shapes. Did you say your son likes Spiderman or your mom likes flowers?

In Mexico *gelatinas* also come in individual servings made in molds, sold by street vendors and very frequently at bus stops and at gas stations, where drivers waiting for their turn can't resist them. Now you know why I always tagged along with my dad to fill up the tank! It's hard to show up at a kids' party in Mexico and not see *gelatina*, but you will encounter more sophisticated versions at grown-up parties, with generous splashes of rum, tequila, or rompope (Mexican eggnog, page 305) in the mix.

The *gelatina* creations that I crave are the creamy, foamy *gelatinas espumosas*. They are like a cross between a mousse and Jell-O. The texture is easy to achieve—unflavored gelatin, sweetened condensed milk, and whipped cream being the key elements—no matter what flavor and/or seasonal ingredient you choose. Since we are big on mango at my house, this is the one we opt for most often.

1. Pour the lukewarm water into a medium heatproof bowl and add the gelatin. Stir and let stand until the gelatin blooms (softens), about 3 minutes. The mixture will increase slightly in volume.

2. Meanwhile, fill a medium saucepan with 2 to 3 inches of water and bring to a simmer over medium-low heat. Set the bowl with the gelatin mixture over the saucepan and heat, stirring occasionally, until the gelatin completely dissolves, 2 to 3 minutes. Remove from the heat.

continued...

3. Combine the sweetened condensed milk, mango chunks, and lime juice in a blender and puree until completely smooth. Add the dissolved gelatin and blend on low speed for a few seconds to combine. Pour into a large bowl.

4. With a hand mixer in a large bowl or in a stand mixer fitted with the whisk attachment, beat the heavy cream at medium speed just until it holds soft peaks and you can see a trail in it as the whisk is beating through it, 3 to 4 minutes; be careful not to overbeat it.

5. Fold the whipped cream into the mango gelatin, which should have started to set a bit, until thoroughly combined. Pour the mousse into individual molds or ramekins. Cover tightly with plastic wrap and refrigerate until completely chilled and set, at least 1 hour. Alternatively, you can chill the mousse in a large bowl.

6. When ready to serve, remove the mousse from the refrigerator and decorate the individual molds with diced mango or berries, if desired. Or, if you chilled it in a large bowl, spoon into individual bowls and garnish with fruit, if desired.

MEXICAN COOK'S TIP

Working with Gelatin

Many cooks complain about clumping when they use gelatin in desserts. The secret is to let the gelatin "bloom," or swell, first in a small amount of liquid. Then, to dissolve the gelatin so that it can be dispersed evenly throughout the dessert, heat the mixture in a double boiler. You can devise a makeshift double boiler by setting the bowl over a saucepan above a couple of inches of simmering water. Heat the mixture for 2 to 3 minutes, stirring occasionally. Remove from the heat when the gelatin has completely dissolved into a barely amber and almost clear liquid. Now it's ready to add to your fruit puree or any mousse or combination you've dreamed up.

LALI'S FLOATING ISLANDS
WITH MEXICAN-STYLE EGGNOG

ISLAS FLOTANTES CON ROMPOPE DE MI LALI

SERVES 12

PREPARATION TIME: 15 minutes

COOKING TIME: 35 minutes, plus cooling and chilling time

MAKE AHEAD: The floating islands can be made up to 3 days ahead, left in the molds, cooled, covered loosely with plastic wrap, and refrigerated. Bring to room temperature before serving and dip the bottoms of the molds in boiling water for 5 to 10 seconds to loosen before unmolding. Rompope sauce will keep for 2 weeks in the refrigerator.

FOR THE CARAMEL

1½ cups sugar

1 tablespoon water

FOR THE FLOATING ISLANDS

12 large egg whites, at room temperature

½ teaspoon cream of tartar

⅛ teaspoon fine sea salt

1 teaspoon vanilla extract

½ teaspoon almond extract

¾ cup sugar

3 cups Mexican-Style Eggnog (page 305)

12 strawberries, sliced, or other fruit of your choice (optional)

This is my Grandmother Lali's version of the beloved French classic floating islands (*îles flottantes*)—delicate, fluffy mounds of caramelized meringues floating in a sea of vanilla custard sauce; a legacy of the Maximilian era. She added a Mexican twist by floating the islands in rompope, Mexican eggnog, instead of in the traditional vanilla custard. The delicate meringues, with their caramel topping, are unmolded like flans. They are delicious freshly made, but they can also be made ahead, along with the rompope.

. . . .

1. To make the caramel: Set twelve 6-ounce custard cups or flan molds on a sheet of parchment on your work surface. Place the sugar and water in a saucepan set over medium heat and swirl the pan occasionally as the sugar melts so that it will dissolve evenly. *Do not stir*, but tilt the pan as the sugar starts to melt. Once all of the sugar has melted, simmer over the lowest possible heat until the caramel is golden brown. Don't let it foam; if it does, immediately remove it from the heat—it is ready. Immediately pour a thin layer of the caramel into the bottom of each mold. The caramel will quickly cool and set.

2. To make the floating islands: Position a rack in the middle of the oven and preheat the oven to 250 degrees.

3. With a hand mixer in a large bowl or in the bowl of a stand mixer fitted with the whisk attachment, combine the egg whites, cream of tartar, and salt and beat on medium speed until soft peaks begin to form, 3 to 4 minutes. Add the vanilla and almond extracts and then slowly add the sugar, a tablespoon at a time. Increase the speed to high and continue beating until the meringue is glossy and holds stiff peaks, 6 to 8 minutes.

4. Spoon the meringue very generously into the caramel-lined molds. The lovely waves of meringue should rise at least an inch or so above the top of the molds.

continued...

5. Place the molds in a large baking pan. Pour ½ inch of boiling water into the pan and bake for 22 to 25 minutes. The top of the islands should be very lightly browned and the islands should look foamy and spongy. Turn the oven off, prop open the oven door (use the handle of a wooden spoon if necessary), and let the islands cool slowly in the oven for 10 minutes. Remove from the oven and allow to cool slightly.

6. Once the molds have cooled enough for you to handle them, unmold the meringues: You can briefly dip the bottom of the molds into boiling water for 5 to 10 seconds to help loosen and liquefy the caramel on the bottom. Then run a knife around the edges of the molds and carefully turn the meringues out onto serving plates. Drizzle the caramel from the bottom of the molds over the islands.

7. Pour about ¼ cup eggnog on top of each meringue, and garnish with the strawberries or other fruit, if desired. Serve.

TITA CHELO'S FROSTED FLAKES COOKIES

GALLETAS DE ZUCARITAS DE LA TITA CHELO

MAKES ABOUT 40 COOKIES

PREPARATION TIME: 15 minutes

COOKING TIME: 40 minutes

MAKE AHEAD: The cookies will remain crisp in a tin or jar for up to a week.

2 sticks plus 5⅓ tablespoons (1⅓ cups) unsalted butter, at room temperature

1¼ cups sugar

3 large eggs, at room temperature

1 tablespoon vanilla extract

⅛ teaspoon fine sea salt

3 cups all-purpose flour, plus an additional ¼ cup for shaping the dough

4 cups Frosted Flakes

The cookies that my husband loved the most when he was a child were his Grandmother Consuelo's. A beautiful, elegant woman, Tita Chelo was a great storyteller and a very generous hostess. Her food was so spectacular that after she passed away, the family compiled a cookbook with her recipes. It has so many cookie recipes in it, almost sixty. These, the simplest and most unsophisticated of the bunch, are the ones everyone remembers most fondly.

1. With a hand mixer in a large bowl or in the bowl of a stand mixer fitted with the paddle attachment, whip the butter until soft and fluffy, about 2 minutes. Add the sugar ¼ cup at a time, beating well after each addition. Scrape down the sides of the bowl and the paddle. Add the eggs and beat until well mixed, about 1 minute. Beat in the vanilla and salt. Add the 3 cups flour ¼ cup at a time, beating for a few seconds after each addition, and continue to beat until the flour is completely incorporated. The dough should be very smooth, homogenous, and soft. Remove the bowl from the mixer.

2. Position the racks in the middle and bottom third of the oven and preheat the oven to 325 degrees. Line two large baking sheets with parchment paper.

3. Place the frosted flakes on a baking sheet and, using your hands, squeeze and crumble the flakes to make them smaller, taking care not to pulverize them completely. Place the remaining ¼ cup flour on another plate and set it next to the plate with the frosted flakes. Flour your hands with the flour on the plate, pick up a tablespoon of dough, roll it into a ball, flatten the ball slightly in your hands, and then press it into the crumbled frosted flakes to "bread" the cookie. Gently press the dough into the flakes as you add about a teaspoon of crushed flakes to the top, then press the dough into a ¼-inch-thick 2½- to 3-inch disk. Transfer to one of the baking sheets. Continue with the rest of thecookies, placing them 2 inches apart.

4. Bake for 18 to 20 minutes, switching the pans from top to bottom and front to back halfway through, until the cookies are light golden brown around the edges. Remove from the oven and allow to cool on the pans or on racks. Store in a tin or a jar.

EVERYTHING-IN-THE-PANTRY COOKIES

GALLETAS DE LA ALACENA

MAKES ABOUT 34 COOKIES

PREPARATION TIME: 15 minutes

COOKING TIME: 12 minutes

MAKE AHEAD: The cookies will keep in a tin or jar for up to a week.

2¾ cups all-purpose flour

1 teaspoon baking powder

1 teaspoon baking soda

½ teaspoon fine sea salt

14 ounces (3½ sticks) unsalted butter, cut into pieces, at room temperature

1 (14-ounce) can sweetened condensed milk

1 cup dark chocolate chips

½ cup peanut butter chips

1 cup broken pretzels (½-inch pieces)

Store-bought cajeta or dulce de leche, for drizzling (optional)

These cookies have accompanied my boys on sleepovers, first days of school, lots of rides in the car and school bus, and even to a school dance. We mix all the things my boys like to snack on right into the dough. Sometimes I vary the mix and throw in dried cherries, coconut flakes, pumpkin seeds, and/or one kind of nut or another. What holds the treats together is a soft, fluffy, light dough made with a sweetened condensed milk base but no eggs.

1. Position the racks in the middle and bottom third of the oven and preheat the oven to 350 degrees. Line two baking sheets with parchment paper.

2. In a medium bowl, whisk together the flour, baking powder, baking soda, and salt. Set aside.

3. With a hand mixer in a large bowl or in a stand mixer fitted with the paddle attachment, beat the butter on medium speed until fluffy. Add the sweetened condensed milk and beat until it is incorporated and the mixture is fluffy. Reduce the mixer speed to low and add the flour mixture ½ cup at a time, stopping to scrape down the sides of the bowl after each addition. Continue to mix until the dough is smooth, about 1 minute. Remove the bowl from the mixer and fold in the chocolate chips, peanut butter chips, and pretzel pieces with a rubber spatula.

4. Using a small scoop or tablespoon, scoop up the dough by the tablespoon and place 1 inch apart on the baking sheets. The cookies will not look uniform, but that's what you want.

5. Bake for 10 to 12 minutes, switching the pans from top to bottom and front to back halfway through, until the bottoms of the cookies are lightly browned. Remove from the oven and let cool on the pans or on racks.

6. For an extra treat, drizzle cajeta or dulce de leche on top of the cookies right before eating.

CHOCOLATE AND JAMAICA (HIBISCUS FLOWER) COOKIES

GALLETAS DE CHOCOLATE CON JAMAICA

MAKES 18 TO 20 COOKIES

PREPARATION TIME: 15 minutes

COOKING TIME: 20 minutes

MAKE AHEAD: The cookies will keep in a tin or jar for up to a week.

FOR THE REHYDRATED HIBISCUS

6 cups water

½ cup honey

2 ounces dried hibiscus flowers (about ⅔ cup)

FOR THE COOKIES

½ cup all-purpose flour

1 tablespoon unsweetened cocoa powder

½ teaspoon baking powder

¼ teaspoon baking soda

½ teaspoon fine sea salt

12 ounces semisweet chocolate, coarsely chopped, or chocolate chips

4 tablespoons (½ stick) unsalted butter

3 large eggs

1 large egg white

1¼ cups sugar

2 teaspoons vanilla extract

The rehydrated hibiscus flowers, finely chopped

I had been dreaming of this pairing—*jamaica* (hibiscus flowers) and dark chocolate—for some time. I'd thought about using hibiscus syrup in brownies or a chocolate cake. But I also wanted to use the gorgeous flowers, *flores de jamaica*, as I've always had a weakness for them. Hibiscus infusions, both iced and hot, have been around for centuries, but the flowers are usually discarded once simmered. This is unfortunate, because they have a delightful tart, acidic flavor that is reminiscent of cranberry and a deliciously chewy consistency. I decided to incorporate them into a dark chocolate cookie and found that they make a great chewy, tangy addition. The cookies are thin, crunchy on the outside, and a bit fudgy and gooey in the middle. The bonus you get when you make these cookies is the wonderful hibiscus concentrate for tea or an agua fresca that you are left with after rehydrating the flowers.

1. To rehydrate the hibiscus: In a medium saucepan, bring the water and honey to a boil. Stir in the dried flowers, reduce the heat, and simmer for 15 minutes, or until the flowers are completely rehydrated and soft.

2. Place a strainer over a bowl and drain the flowers, pressing them against the strainer to extract as much liquid as possible. Finely chop the flowers. Reserve the liquid to enjoy as tea or agua fresca.

3. To make the cookies: In a medium bowl, whisk together the flour, cocoa powder, baking powder, baking soda, and salt.

4. Bring 1 inch of water to a simmer in a saucepan. Place the chocolate and butter in a heatproof bowl and set over the saucepan; the bottom of the bowl should not touch the water. Melt the chocolate and butter, stirring occasionally with a heatproof spatula. As soon as the chocolate and butter have melted, turn off the heat.

continued...

5. With a hand mixer in a large bowl or in the bowl of a stand mixer fitted with the whisk attachment, combine the eggs, egg white, and sugar and beat on medium-high speed until very frothy, 2 to 3 minutes. Scrape in the melted chocolate and butter and the vanilla extract and beat on medium-low until completely combined.

6. Remove the bowl from the stand, add the flour mixture, and use a rubber spatula to stir and fold it in until completely combined. Fold in the chopped hibiscus flowers. Cover the bowl with plastic wrap and chill in the refrigerator for 30 minutes.

7. Position the racks in the middle and lower third of the oven and pre-heat the oven to 350 degrees. Line two baking sheets with parchment paper.

8. Using a tablespoon or a 1½-inch scoop, spoon the batter in heaping tablespoons onto the prepared baking sheets, about 2 inches apart; the cookies will spread quite a bit as they bake. Bake for 12 to 14 minutes, switching the pans from top to bottom and front to back halfway through, until the top is slightly crusty and beginning to crack. Allow the cookies to cool on the pans for about 5 minutes, until you are able to lift them without breaking them, and then transfer to cooling racks to cool completely.

TRIPLE LIME POUND CAKE

PANQUÉ TRIPLE DE LIMÓN

SERVES 10

PREPARATION TIME: 20 minutes

COOKING TIME: 50 minutes

MAKE AHEAD: The cake can be made up to 4 days ahead. Cover tightly to prevent it from drying out.

FOR THE CAKE

16 tablespoons (2 sticks) unsalted butter, at room temperature, plus additional for buttering the pan

1¾ cups all-purpose flour, plus additional for dusting the pan

1½ teaspoons baking powder

Pinch of fine sea salt

1 cup sugar

7 large eggs, separated, at room temperature

Finely grated zest of 1 lime

FOR THE SYRUP

½ cup freshly squeezed lime juice

⅓ cup sugar

FOR THE GLAZE

2 tablespoons freshly squeezed lime juice

½ teaspoon vanilla extract

⅔ cup confectioners' sugar

This moist, homey cake is a new favorite in my pound cake repertoire. It is triple-powered by lime: I add zest to the batter, lime juice to the syrup that saturates the cake, and more lime juice to the glaze that tops it. The cake tastes even better if you cover it and let it sit for a day, so I like to make it the night or the morning before I want to serve it. It's great for entertaining.

1. To make the cake: Preheat the oven to 350 degrees. Position the rack in the middle. Butter a loaf pan and lightly dust with flour.

2. In a medium bowl, whisk together the flour, baking powder, and salt.

3. With a hand mixer in a large bowl or in the bowl of a stand mixer fitted with the paddle attachment, beat the butter on medium speed until soft and creamy, about 2 minutes. Add the sugar and beat until fluffy, about 5 minutes. One at a time, beat in the egg yolks, beating well after each addition. Scrape down the paddle and the sides of the bowl, then add the lime zest and beat until fully incorporated, another minute or so. Reduce the speed to low and add the flour mixture in three additions, then beat for another 2 minutes. The batter should be completely homogenous. Transfer the batter to a large bowl.

4. Wash the mixer bowl and dry thoroughly. Switch to the whisk attachment and beat the egg whites on medium-high speed until they hold stiff peaks, 4 to 5 minutes. Gently stir a bit of the whites into the batter to lighten it, then gently fold in the remaining whites until the batter is completely homogenous but still light and fluffy. Don't overmix or you will deflate the egg whites.

5. Pour the batter into the prepared pan. Bake for 50 minutes, or until the cake is golden brown on top and has risen nicely and a toothpick inserted in the center comes out clean. Let cool for 15 minutes in the pan.

6. Meanwhile, make the lime syrup: In a small saucepan, combine the lime juice and the sugar and heat over medium heat, stirring, until the sugar has dissolved. Remove from the heat.

7. Run the tip of a knife around the edges of the pound cake. Invert onto a platter or board, then invert again onto a serving platter. With a toothpick, poke holes all over the top of the cake, going as deep as the toothpick will go. Slowly and gradually pour the lime syrup over the pound cake. Let sit for 10 minutes.

8. To make the lime glaze: In a small bowl, combine the lime juice, vanilla, and confectioners' sugar and stir until smooth. Using a tablespoon, spoon the glaze over the pound cake, spreading it gently over the top with the back of the spoon and letting some of the glaze drizzle down the sides. Let the cake cool and the glaze set.

9. Serve or cover and let stand for a day before serving.

MANGO POUND CAKE

PANQUÉ DE MANGO

SERVES 9 OR 10

PREPARATION TIME: 20 minutes

COOKING TIME: 30 minutes

MAKE AHEAD: The cake will keep for 5 days, covered.

8 tablespoons (1 stick) unsalted butter, at room temperature, plus more for the baking pan

2½ cups all-purpose flour, plus more for the baking pan

1 teaspoon baking powder

1 teaspoon baking soda

¼ teaspoon kosher or sea salt

1¾ cups diced fresh or thawed frozen mango

¼ cup buttermilk

1 teaspoon almond extract

1 teaspoon vanilla extract

1⅓ cups granulated sugar

2 large eggs

Confectioners' sugar, for dusting (optional)

Berries, for garnish (optional)

My father knows the depth of my obsession for trying old recipes, and for those manuscripts and old cookbooks that hold them and their stories. So each time he visits, he brings a "find." "*Mira lo que me encontré, Pato*" ("Look what I happened to find!"), he says with a big smile, knowing that I know that he didn't just "find" that "find" but has been searching high and low for it. He has friends in the most hidden bookstores in the *centro histórico*, Mexico City's historic downtown, who help him hunt for old cookbooks. You can find in the collection that he has amassed for me everything from the more than fifty traditional ways to cook iguana in the state of Colima to recipes for milk soup from Sor Juana Inés de la Cruz, the most famous nun in the history of Mexico.

One of my most treasured cookbook finds is the seminal 1831 cookbook *El Cocinero Mexicano*, a three-volume compendium of the foods of Mexico. Its dessert section includes hundreds of ways to make pound cakes, cakes, and tortas. As I tried to make these recipes from another era, I gained a deeper understanding of the foundations of my country's cuisine and of how Mexican cooking has evolved. They require quite a lot of testing and retesting, because the old recipes have no measurements as we know them today, and the idea of a detailed instruction can be "use enough flour and mix it with the sufficient amount of water to coat 5 mangoes the size of your fist." My goal was to re-create the recipes with contemporary measures and instructions while not sacrificing their soul. Here is one of them, a comforting but dazzling mango pound cake.

1. Preheat the oven to 350 degrees. Position the rack in the middle. Butter a 9-x-13-inch baking pan and dust with flour.

2. In a medium bowl, whisk together the flour, baking powder, baking soda, and salt. Set aside.

3. Combine the mango, buttermilk, and almond and vanilla extracts in a blender and puree until completely smooth.

4. Using a hand mixer in a large bowl or in the bowl of a stand mixer fitted with the paddle attachment, beat the butter on medium speed until soft and fluffy, about 2 minutes. Add the granulated sugar and beat until well mixed and fluffy, about 5 minutes. One at a time, add the eggs, beating well after each addition.

5. In two additions, gradually add the mango puree and dry ingredients to the butter mixture, alternating the wet and dry ingredients and mixing until completely combined.

6. Scrape the batter into the prepared baking pan. Bake for 30 minutes, or until the cake is golden brown on top and springy to the touch and a wooden toothpick inserted in the center comes out clean. Remove from the oven and let cool on a rack.

7. Invert the cake onto a board and then flip right side up onto a platter. Dust liberally with confectioners' sugar before serving, garnished with berries if desired.

MARBLED TRES LECHES CAKE

PASTEL DE TRES LECHES MARMOLEADO

SERVES 10 TO 12

PREPARATION TIME: 25 minutes, plus chilling time

COOKING TIME: 25 minutes

MAKE AHEAD: The cake can be assembled up to 3 days ahead and refrigerated, covered loosely.

FOR THE CAKE

Softened unsalted butter, for the pan

9 large eggs, separated, at room temperature

1 cup sugar

2 cups all-purpose flour

1 teaspoon baking powder

Pinch of salt

1 tablespoon vanilla extract

½ cup hot water

⅓ cup unsweetened cocoa powder

FOR THE TRES LECHES SAUCE

1 (14-ounce) can sweetened condensed milk

1 (12-ounce) can evaporated milk

1 cup whole milk

1 tablespoon vanilla extract

FOR THE WHIPPED CREAM TOPPING

2 cups heavy cream

3 tablespoons confectioners' sugar

It would seem that every Latin American country claims the tres leches cake as its very own. Of course we Mexicans think ours is tops. The traditional version is vanilla, but there are plenty of other renditions—strawberries and cream, chocolate, coconut, pineapple, coffee, or cajeta or dulce de leche. This marbled version is the result of my motherly mediation when my boys couldn't agree on whether we should make a chocolate or vanilla tres leches cake to bring to a friend's high school graduation party so I suggested we mix them. As we put together the batter, we started indulging, making the chocolate part more fudgy and chocolaty. We added grated grainy Mexican chocolate as a garnish and sprinkled it with a bit of cinnamon. At the party, it was devoured before we had a chance to try it.

1. To make the cake: Position a rack in the middle of the oven and preheat the oven to 350 degrees. Butter a 9-x-13-inch cake pan.

2. With a hand mixer in a large bowl or in the bowl of a stand mixer fitted with the whisk attachment, beat the egg whites on medium-high speed until they hold soft peaks, 4 to 5 minutes. Reduce the speed to medium and gradually add the sugar, then continue to beat until the whites hold stiff, shiny peaks. Transfer to a large bowl and set aside.

3. In a medium bowl, stir together the flour, baking powder, and salt.

4. In another large bowl, whisk the egg yolks until thick and pale yellow. Whisk in the vanilla. Gently fold the egg yolk mixture into the egg white mixture with a rubber spatula, taking care not to deflate the whites. Gently fold in the flour ¼ cup at a time; the batter should look a bit streaky.

5. In a medium bowl, combine the hot water with the cocoa powder and whisk until smooth. Add half the cake batter and gently fold in with a rubber spatula until thoroughly mixed.

6. Spread the vanilla batter in the prepared pan. Pour the chocolate batter in a straight line down the center of the vanilla batter. With a knife or spoon, make a swirling design from one side of the pan to the other.

continued...

1 disk/tablet Mexican-style chocolate, such as Abuelita (approximately 3 ounces)

Ground canela (optional; Ceylon cinnamon; see page 264)

7. Bake for 22 to 25 minutes, until the top of the cake is light brown and springs back when lightly pressed. Remove from the oven and let cool completely on a rack. Then, using a fork or toothpicks, poke plenty of holes all over the top of the cake so that it will absorb the sauce.

8. To make the sauce: In a large bowl, combine the three milks and vanilla and stir to blend well. Gradually pour about two thirds of the sauce over the cake. Don't worry if it looks like there is too much sauce—the cake will absorb it. Cover and refrigerate for at least 2 hours, or overnight. Refrigerate the remaining sauce.

9. When you are ready to finish the cake, remove it from the refrigerator and spoon the remaining sauce over the top.

10. To make the topping: In the bowl of a stand mixer fitted with the whisk attachment, or in a large bowl using a hand mixer, whip the cream with the confectioners' sugar on medium speed until it forms stiff peaks, 3 to 4 minutes, taking care not to overbeat and curdle the cream. Spread the whipped cream over the top of the cake. Garnish with the grated chocolate and canela, if using.

VARIATION: If you want to make this even more indulgent, right before you pour on the sauce, spread a thick layer of store-bought cajeta or dulce de leche over the cake. Then poke holes in it again.

MERINGUE CAKE WITH MASCARPONE AND STRAWBERRIES

PASTEL DE MERENGUE CON CREMA Y FRESAS

SERVES 10 TO 12

PREPARATION TIME: 20 minutes

COOKING TIME: 1 hour, plus 4 hours drying time

MAKE AHEAD: The meringues can be made a day ahead, cooled, and covered. The assembled cake will hold for 4 to 6 hours.

FOR THE MERINGUES

7 large egg whites

1 teaspoon freshly squeezed lime juice

1¼ cups sugar

2 tablespoons cornstarch

FOR THE WHIPPED CREAM FILLING

1½ cups heavy cream

8 ounces (1 cup) mascarpone or requesón cheese (see page 285), chilled

1 teaspoon Mexican vanilla extract

2 cups sliced strawberries

Sliced strawberries, for garnish

This is the dessert of my dreams, the one I could eat every single day for the rest of my life. It's a cake version of a childhood treat that we used to eat on special Sundays, when we would buy gigantic individual meringues at a bakery called Elizondo. We would bring the meringues home, my mom would whip up some heavy cream to spoon on top, and we would add sliced strawberries or a mix of berries and sprinkle them with confectioners' sugar.

In this rendition, the cake layers are four large pale white meringues, also known as pavlovas—sweet, crisp, and airy, with whimsical waves on the surface. Two of the layers are filled with a whipped cream and mascarpone mix that is just sturdy enough to hold its shape, the middle with a creamy layer of juicy strawberries, and a plain meringue finishes it off. Once the cake is assembled, the meringue layers begin to moisten ever so slowly so that they become slightly chewy. In my house, the cake doesn't last a day—but I must confess that I have only myself to blame for that.

Note: The meringues require 4 hours in the oven to dry out completely, so plan accordingly.

1. To make the meringues: Position the racks in the upper and lower thirds of the oven and preheat the oven to 200 degrees.

2. Line two large baking sheets with parchment paper and trace two 8-inch rounds on each sheet of paper. Turn the parchment over so that the pencil is not on the exposed sides.

3. With a hand mixer in a large bowl or in the bowl of a stand mixer fitted with the whisk attachment, whip the egg whites and lime juice on medium speed until frothy, 3 to 4 minutes. Gradually add the sugar, 1 to 2 tablespoons at a time. Then increase the speed to high and beat until the mixture holds very stiff, glossy peaks, about 8 minutes.

continued...

4. Remove the bowl from the stand. Sift the cornstarch over the meringue through a strainer and, using a spatula, gently fold it in until completely incorporated. Transfer the meringue to the prepared baking sheets, dividing it evenly among the four 8-inch measured circles. Using a rubber or offset spatula, spread the meringue to fill the circles. They don't have to be even or perfect at all; a few waves across the tops are lovely.

5. Bake for 1 hour, switching the pans from top to bottom and front to back halfway through. Reduce the temperature to 175 degrees or the lowest setting and let the meringues dry in the oven for another 4 hours. The outside should be crisp and the meringues should detach easily from the parchment.

6. To make the filling: Using a hand mixer and large bowl or, in the bowl of a stand mixer fitted with the whisk attachment, combine the heavy cream, mascarpone or requesón and vanilla and whip on medium speed until soft peaks form, 3 to 4 minutes. Then continue to beat to stiff peaks, another 2 minutes or so. Watch carefully; do not overbeat or you will turn your cream into butter.

7. In a medium bowl, combine the sliced strawberries with 1¼ cups of the whipped cream mixture.

8. To assemble the cake: Place one meringue on a platter and spoon on half of the remaining whipped mascarpone cream; spread to cover evenly. Cover with a second meringue and top with the strawberries and cream mixture; spread to cover evenly. Top with another meringue and spoon on the remaining whipped mascarpone cream; spread to cover evenly. Top with the final meringue.

9. Slice and serve, garnished with more strawberries.

VARIATION: Want to take this cake to an even more decadent level? Drizzle some melted bittersweet chocolate over the top.

MEXICAN COOK'S TIP

I was always told not to bake meringues if it's raining. Humidity can prevent meringues from drying and crisping properly. To ensure that your meringues are dry and crisp, be there sunshine or rain, sift cornstarch over the egg white mixture and fold in, as in the recipe. The cornstarch absorbs excess moisture.

MEXICAN COOK'S TIP

Use the egg yolks left over from making the meringues to make the chocolate custards on page 262 or, if you are in the mood for a sweet and creamy drink, rompope (page 305).

REQUESÓN AND MASCARPONE

When I make this in Mexico, I use requesón (see page 28) instead of mascarpone. Until recently, requesón has not been available in the United States, so I developed the recipe using mascarpone, which is the closest relative that I can find here. Although mascarpone is denser and not tangy like requesón, it does a phenomenal job in this cake.

CAJETA AND PECAN CINNAMON ROLLS

ROLLOS DE CANELA CON CAJETA Y NUEZ

MAKES 12 LARGE ROLLS

PREPARATION TIME: 20 minutes

COOKING TIME: 30 minutes, plus 2½ hours resting time

MAKE AHEAD: The rolls can be made a couple of days ahead, though they are best eaten the day you bake them. Cover them so they don't dry out. You may want to reheat them slightly before eating. You can also make the dough and shape the rolls, place them in the baking dish, and refrigerate for up to 24 hours. Remove from the refrigerator about an hour before baking.

FOR THE DOUGH

¾ cup lukewarm milk

½ cup lukewarm water

2¼ teaspoons (¼-ounce) active dry yeast (1 packet)

1 tablespoon sugar

4 cups all-purpose flour, plus additional for kneading

2 large eggs, lightly beaten

½ cup sugar

Pinch of fine sea salt

8 tablespoons (1 stick) unsalted butter, melted, plus more butter for the bowl

FOR THE FILLING

¾ cup store-bought cajeta or dulce de leche

¾ cup coarsely chopped pecans

These big puffed-up American cinnamon rolls with a Mexican twist ooze with deliciously gooey cajeta. They are a true spectacle when brought to the table, still hot from the oven. We have made them a morning-after tradition for our Thanksgiving holiday. After all that meal planning (and eating!) for the Thanksgiving dinner, we like our houseguests to have something delicious to enjoy the next morning. I make the dough and shape the rolls the day before, then leave them to rise overnight in the refrigerator. In the morning, before everybody is up, I slip downstairs and take them out of the fridge for their final rise, then pop them into the oven. My family wakes up to the amazing sweet aroma of the baking cinnamon rolls, which are on the table by the time they come down for breakfast. Everybody waits impatiently for them to cool just enough so we can dig in.

. . . .

1. To make the dough: Combine the lukewarm milk and water in a small bowl. Make sure that the mixture is neither too hot nor too cold—too hot, and it will kill the yeast; too cold, and the yeast won't properly activate. Sprinkle the yeast over the liquid, add the sugar, and whisk together. Set aside until foamy, about 10 minutes.

2. Place the flour in a large bowl. Make a well in the middle and pour in the beaten eggs, yeast mixture, sugar, and salt. Begin mixing the ingredients with a rubber spatula or wooden spoon. After a few strokes, add the melted butter and stir vigorously until fully combined. The dough will be very sticky and gooey. (You can also mix the ingredients in a stand mixer fitted with the paddle attachment. Change to the dough hook to knead it. Knead for 5 minutes).

3. Sprinkle your counter or work surface very generously with flour. Turn out the sticky dough onto the surface and knead until soft and elastic, about 5 minutes. Add a bit more flour to the counter as necessary, and use a bench scraper, a plastic dough scraper, or a wide metal spatula to lift the sticky dough from the counter and fold it over as you knead. Shape the dough into a ball.

continued...

CAJETA

Cajeta is a caramel-like confection made with milk and dark brown sugar. It has a deep, almost nutty flavor and is much more milky and satiny than sugar caramel. Although it's Mexico's version of dulce de leche, we pride ourselves on the fact that cajeta came into being long before dulce de leche (which originated in Argentina). We tend to make ours with goat's milk, or a combination of goat and cow's milk, rather than only cow's milk, and we think ours has a much richer and more complex flavor.

Cajeta is ideal with . . . *everything*: crepes, flans, pound cake, and more. You can dip fruit into it (try strawberries, apples, or bananas); make sandwich cookies with it using butter cookies, graham crackers, or vanilla wafers; or add it to smoothies and milk shakes, ice creams, pastry fillings, and glazes. But in my opinion, the best way of all to enjoy cajeta is to dip a big tablespoon into it and eat this decadent and luxurious treat right from the jar.

4. Butter a large bowl, place the dough in it, cover the bowl with a kitchen towel or with plastic wrap, and set in a warm, draft-free spot in your kitchen to rise for 1 to 1¼ hours, or until doubled in size.

5. To shape the rolls: Butter a 9-x-13-inch baking pan.

6. Sprinkle your counter or work surface generously with flour. Place the dough on the floured counter and knead a couple of times, then begin to gently press into a rectangle, with a long side closest to you. Sprinkle a rolling pin with flour and use it to roll the dough into a rectangle about 10 inches wide and 24 inches long.

7. To assemble the filling: Leaving a 2-inch border on the top and bottom of the rectangle, spread the cajeta over the dough in a fairly even layer. Sprinkle the chopped pecans, canela, and butter chunks evenly over the cajeta. Brush the top border with water. Starting from the long side near you, roll up the rectangle into a tight cylinder. Press the moistened top edge of the dough against the roll to seal and turn the roll seam side down.

8. Cut into 12 rolls: I cut the log in half first, then each half in half, and each of these quarters into 3 rolls. Place in the buttered baking pan, cut side down. Cover the baking pan with a kitchen towel and let rise in a warm, draft-free spot in your kitchen, until the rolls double in size, about 1 hour.

9. Meanwhile, preheat the oven to 350 degrees. Position a rack in the middle.

10. Bake the rolls for 27 to 30 minutes, until they are fully cooked and golden brown on top. Remove from the oven.

11. Immediately, make the glaze: In a medium bowl, beat together the melted butter, vanilla, lime juice, and condensed milk. Add the confectioners' sugar and beat until smooth.

12. Drizzle the glaze over the rolls while they are still hot. Let the glaze set, then serve.

1 teaspoon ground canela (Ceylon cinnamon; see page 264)

4 tablespoons (½ stick) cold unsalted butter, cut into ¼-inch pieces

FOR THE GLAZE

2 tablespoons unsalted butter, melted

2 teaspoons vanilla extract

2 teaspoons freshly squeezed lime juice

⅓ cup sweetened condensed milk

⅓ cup confectioners' sugar

CHARDONNAY MANGO PECAN TART

TARTA DE NUEZ CON MANGO Y CHARDONNAY

SERVES 10

PREPARATION TIME: 25 minutes, plus a couple hours resting time

COOKING TIME: 25 minutes

MAKE AHEAD: The crust, pastry cream, and glaze can be made 2 days ahead of time. Cover the baked crust so it does not dry out. Cover and refrigerate the pastry cream and glaze. When ready to use, reheat the glaze over low heat until it liquefies. The tart can be assembled up to 2 days ahead, covered, and refrigerated.

FOR THE CRUST

4 tablespoons (½ stick) cold unsalted butter, cut into small pieces, plus more for the pan

1½ cups pecans

1 cup all-purpose flour

¼ cup packed dark brown sugar

Pinch of kosher or sea salt

1 large egg

FOR THE PASTRY CREAM

1 cup whole milk

1 tablespoon vanilla extract

3 large egg yolks

¼ cup sugar

2 tablespoons cornstarch

My mom's side of the family comes from a long line of accomplished Austrian cooks, but the pastry queen was my Great-Aunt Annie. Annie barely survived the Second World War, but she moved to Mexico and not only regained her health, but went on to bake desserts with such success that she eventually opened a soon-to-be famous bakery, where she and her desserts thrived for decades.

In this tart I use Annie's pastry cream, but otherwise I've broken with tradition. Yes, a classic tart crust is nice, but wait until you taste one that is almost entirely made with pecans, called *nueces pecaneras* in Mexico. And why brush the mangoes just with the usual apricot jam glaze when you can add a little tang by spiking the glaze with Chardonnay?

1. To make the crust: Preheat the oven to 375 degrees. Position a rack in the middle. Very lightly butter a 9-inch tart pan with a removable bottom (you should not be able to see the butter on the pan).

2. Place the pecans in a food processor and pulse a few times, until finely ground. Add the flour, brown sugar, and salt and pulse a few times, until combined. Add the egg and butter and pulse until thoroughly mixed and the butter has broken into the smallest of pieces; the mix should resemble coarse meal. Don't expect to get a homogeneous dough that can be gathered into a ball—this one has a crumbly consistency.

3. Scrape the mixture into the tart pan and press it evenly over the bottom and up the sides. Then press on the sides so they extend about ¼ inch above the rim of the pan. As you press, the mix will start feeling and looking more like dough.

4. Place the tart pan on a baking sheet and bake for 15 to 17 minutes, until the crust is cooked through and light golden brown. Remove from the oven and set aside to cool completely.

5. To make the pastry cream: Combine the milk and vanilla in a medium saucepan and bring just to a simmer over medium heat. Watch carefully, and as soon as it begins to bubble around the edges of the saucepan, turn off the heat.

continued...

¼ cup apricot jam

¼ cup Chardonnay
(see tip below)

3 large ripe Champagne or
   Kent mangoes

MEXICAN COOK'S TIP

Choose Your *Piquete*

Piquete translates as "little pinch" or "shot." In culinary terms it refers to a splash of any spirit, liquor, or other alcoholic beverage added to a dish or drink. I used Chardonnay for this tart because I felt the tart called for a semi-dry, fruity wine. Other light dry or semi-dry wine and even a bubbly wine such as Champagne or Prosecco would also work. My general rule of thumb is to use whatever you may want to drink with the dish, or already have open. Did I hear you say tequila? By all means, give it a go!

6. In a medium bowl, beat together the egg yolks, sugar, and cornstarch until thoroughly mixed. Slowly stream the milk into the beaten eggs, whisking constantly. Transfer the mixture back to the saucepan and stir with a heatproof spatula over medium heat until the mixture comes to a simmer. Simmer, taking care to scrape the bottom and get into the corners of the pan with the spatula so that the custard doesn't stick, for 1 to 2 minutes, until the mixture is thick and creamy and coats the back of the spatula; it should leave a channel when you run your finger down the middle of the spatula. Scrape into a bowl and place a piece of plastic wrap directly on the surface. Cover the bowl with plastic wrap and refrigerate until thoroughly chilled.

7. To make the glaze: Combine the jam and wine in a small saucepan and heat, stirring, over medium heat until the jam liquefies and blends with the wine. Bring to a simmer, reduce the heat to low, and simmer for 1 to 2 minutes. Remove from the heat and set aside.

8. When ready to assemble the tart, slice vertically down each side of the flat seed of each mango to remove the cheeks—*cachetes*—of the mangoes. Run a small sharp knife around the edges of each cheek, between the flesh and the skin, to make it easy to remove the flesh, and then scoop it out with a spoon. Slice the cheeks on the diagonal into ¼-inch-thick slices.

9. Spread the cold pastry cream in an even layer in the tart crust. Place the mango slices on top: You can arrange them overlapping in concentric circles or in lines radiating from the outside to the center of the tart. Reheat the glaze if necessary and brush the mangoes generously with the glaze.

10. Refrigerate the tart for a minimum of 2 hours before serving so that it sets nicely and chills.

FIVE-SPICE PLUM AND APRICOT EMPANADAS

EMPANADAS DE CIRUELA Y CHABACANO CON CINCO ESPECIAS

MAKES 10 EMPANADAS

PREPARATION TIME: 30 minutes, plus chilling time

COOKING TIME: 20 minutes

MAKE AHEAD: The empanadas can be made up to 2 days ahead and kept covered at room temperature. You may want to slightly reheat them in a low oven before serving.

FOR THE PASTRY

2   cups all-purpose flour

½ cup sugar

Pinch of fine sea salt

1   large egg

3   tablespoons sour cream

12 tablespoons (1½ sticks) cold unsalted butter, diced

FOR THE FILLING

8   ounces plums, halved, pitted, and diced (about 1½ cups)

4   ounces apricots, halved, pitted, and diced (about ¾ cup)

½ cup pecans, finely chopped

¼ cup packed dark brown sugar or grated piloncillo (see page 86)

1½ teaspoons cornstarch

⅛ teaspoon five-spice powder

1½ teaspoons freshly squeezed lime juice

1   egg, beaten, for egg wash

Sugar, for sprinkling

One day, while I was shopping at a Chinese grocery store in Virginia with my friend Janet Yu, a phenomenal Chinese chef, we talked a lot about five-spice and how good it is with fruits and sweets. Inspired, I came home and got to work on these Mexican empanadas, which are like little hand pies, filled with fruit, with a dash of Chinese five-spice powder.

1. To make the pastry: In a large bowl or the bowl of a stand mixer fitted with the paddle attachment, mix together the flour, sugar, and salt. In a small bowl, beat together the egg and sour cream.

2. With your fingers or at low speed, mix or rub the butter into the dry ingredients until the mixture resembles coarse meal; it should be crumbly. Add the egg and sour cream and mix into a smooth, malleable dough. Press the dough into a disk, wrap in plastic wrap, and refrigerate for at least 1 hour.

3. To make the filling: In a medium bowl, combine the plums, apricots, pecans, brown sugar, cornstarch, five-spice powder, and lime juice and mix well.

4. To assemble and bake the empanadas: Preheat the oven to 350 degrees. Position the rack in the middle. Line two baking sheets with parchment paper. Generously flour your kitchen counter. Flour your rolling pin. Roll out the dough to a thickness of ⅛ to ¼ inch. Cut out as many 4-inch circles as you can, using a cookie cutter, saucer, or a lid as a guide. Gather together the dough scraps, and roll out again and cut out more circles to get a total of 10 circles). Place a heaping tablespoon of filling in the middle of each circle, brush the edges with the beaten egg, and fold over to make a half-moon, pressing with your fingers to seal the edges. Then gently press all along the edges with the back of a fork to get a good seal.

5. Arrange the empanadas on the prepared baking sheets. Brush with the beaten egg and sprinkle with sugar. Bake the empanadas for about 20 minutes, until golden brown. Serve hot or warm.

CHAPTER 11

DRINKS

DRINKS HAVE NEVER BEEN JUST AN ASIDE IN MEXICO. They refresh

and quench thirst, nourish and restore, and also, of course, make a party. My father, a handsome, charming lady's man, thought that he should teach his beloved four daughters how to hold our liquor so that no man would ever be able to get us drunk and take advantage of us. His efforts had poor results—because it turned out that none of us has much of a tolerance for alcohol (and nobody ever tried to get us drunk).

This doesn't mean that I don't love concocting drinks. I like cocktails to be a complete experience that can be slowly sipped as if they were a meal. Over the years, I have taken more and more pleasure in combining ingredients to create new profiles. I love the way one new ingredient will transform a familiar cocktail into something completely different, like the silky-smooth Coco Lime Margarita on page 298, a classic tangy lime margarita is transformed into something much more tropical when coconut cream and a sweet, munchable garnish of lightly toasted coconut dusted with grated lime zest are added.

I enjoy nonalcoholic drinks as well and have as much fun with them as with cocktails. I blend two of our favorite treats in my luxurious Chocolate and Cajeta Milkshake (page 309), and I love hibiscus flower and honey tea, hot or cold.

Some of the recipes in this chapter are for traditional Mexican drinks that speak of history and legend. Chocolate Atole (page 307), a robust version of Mexican chocolate, is a variation of a masa-based drink, or *atole,* that has been feeding our people since pre-Hispanic times. (It is yet another example of how versatile corn masa can be.) Rompope (page 305) is a type of eggnog that has been dearly loved in Mexico since the Spanish nuns created it in the convent kitchens of Santa Clara during the colonial era. When it comes to the juices and blended drinks or the current cocktail craze, we Mexicans have been in the vanguard for centuries.

GRAPEFRUIT AND GUAVA SPRITZER

BEBIDA DE TORONJA Y GUAYABA

SERVES 8

PREPARATION TIME: 15 minutes

MAKE AHEAD: The drink can be made up to a couple of hours ahead, covered, and refrigerated.

2 cups freshly squeezed grapefruit juice, chilled

4 cups guava nectar, chilled

¼ cup light agave syrup, or more to taste

16 ounces tequila blanco (optional)

Chilled citrus-flavored sparkling mineral water, as needed

Ice cubes

FOR GARNISH

8 grapefruit or lime wedges

8 jalapeño slices, seeded (optional)

Instead of gin, I reach for tequila blanco—that's the Mexican in me—to combine with citrusy sparkling water and grapefruit juice. A heavy pour of guava nectar, which you can get in any Latin and many international stores, tastes great—and it also does a good job of masking the alcohol, so be careful!

The bubbly pink drink is pretty on its own, but I like to dress it up with a jalapeño slice and a grapefruit or lime wedge garnish. It makes an elegant drink for a dinner party, or make a pitcher. If you want to include the kids, just omit the tequila.

In a large pitcher, combine the grapefruit juice, guava nectar, and agave syrup and stir well. Taste for sweetness and add more agave if necessary. Pour into ice-filled glasses and add 2 ounces of tequila and a splash of mineral water to each one. Garnish with grapefruit or lime wedges and jalapeño slices, if desired, and serve.

VARIATION: If you can't find guava nectar or don't feel like using it, you can use any other kind of Latin-style nectar. Mango, peach, pear, and passion fruit all work well.

COCO LIME MARGARITA

MARGARITA DE COCO CON LIMÓN

SERVES 4

PREPARATION TIME: 15 minutes

COOKING TIME: 6 to 7 minutes

MAKE AHEAD: The margarita mix (without the ice) can be made up to a day ahead, covered, and refrigerated.

½ cup sweetened shredded coconut or Coconut Angel Flakes

Grated zest of 1 lime

Pinch of kosher or sea salt, plus more for the glasses

1 lime, quartered, for the glasses

1½ cups cream of coconut

1 cup white or silver tequila

⅔ cup Triple Sec, Cointreau, or other orange liqueur

⅓ cup freshly squeezed lime juice

2 cups ice cubes, for making slushy style or serving on the rocks

If you've made margaritas, you're probably familiar with the 3-2-1 ratio for a classic margarita. The ratio applies as well to my coco lime version: 3 parts tequila, 2 parts Triple Sec, and 1 part lime juice. However, since sometimes more is more, I add a generous amount of silky coconut cream for a tropical and lavish finish, then I pump it up even more with a garnish of very lightly toasted sweetened coconut seasoned with lime zest and a sprinkle of salt.

I like my coco lime margarita on the rocks, but if you are getting ready for your Cinco de Mayo fiesta, I bet your guests will appreciate it if you serve it slushy style. In that case, pour everything except for the coconut garnish into the blender along with a couple of cups of ice and buzz it all together. Serve it in cold glasses with toasted coconut flakes on top.

1. Preheat the oven to 325 degrees.

2. Spread the coconut on a small baking sheet, sprinkle with the lime zest and pinch of salt, mix well, and spread out again. Bake for 5 to 6 minutes, until the coconut is just barely beginning to color; it should not brown. Transfer to a small bowl; set aside.

3. Pour some salt onto a small plate. Rub the rims of the glasses with the quartered lime, squeezing a little of the juice over them, then gently dip in the salt, coating the rims all around. Set aside.

4. Combine the cream of coconut, tequila, orange liqueur, and lime juice in a blender and puree until completely smooth. If making slushy-style margaritas, add the ice and blend until almost smooth. Pour into glasses and serve with the toasted flakes on top. Or, if serving on the rocks, fill each glass with about ½ cup ice cubes, pour in the margarita mixture, and top with the coconut flakes.

SIMPLE SYRUP

Simple syrup is a mix of water and sugar simmered together until the sugar dissolves. You can use sugar and water in equal proportions, but if you use slightly more sugar, as here, the syrup will keep better if you are not using it all right away.

⅓ cup sugar
¼ cup water

Combine the sugar and water in a small saucepan and stir together with a rubber spatula. Bring to a boil over medium heat, then reduce the heat and simmer briskly until all of the sugar has dissolved. Remove from the heat and allow to cool. Store in a jar in the refrigerator if not using right away. It keeps for months.

GRILLED PINEAPPLE MARGARITA

MARGARITA DE PIÑA ASADA

SERVES 6

PREPARATION TIME: 15 minutes

COOKING TIME: 5 minutes

MAKE AHEAD: The mix can be made up to 12 hours ahead, covered, and refrigerated.

Safflower or canola oil, for greasing the grill

1 pineapple, peeled, cored, and cut into ½-inch-thick rings

1 jalapeño, chopped (seeded if desired) or to taste

¼ cup chopped fresh cilantro leaves and upper part of stems

⅓ cup grated piloncillo (see page 86) or packed dark brown sugar

3 cups pineapple juice

1 cup white or silver tequila

¾ cup freshly squeezed lime juice

½ cup agave syrup or Simple Syrup (page 300)

2 tablespoons kosher or sea salt

2 tablespoons piquín chile powder or other Mexican chile powder (see page 65)

1 lime, quartered for the glasses (optional)

My pineapple margarita hits a range of flavor notes—with gusto. The grilled pineapple chunks, juice, and piloncillo (or dark brown sugar) make it the fruity drink every good fiesta requires, while the jalapeños and a salty rim with ground dried chile throw a sweet and spicy punch it is happy to accept. I toss in some chopped cilantro to cool everything off and some lime juice to brighten up all of the flavors as they mingle together.

I like to have my pitcher of pineapple margaritas ready to go in the refrigerator ahead of time, but you can impress your guests by tossing the pineapple on the grill during the party. Serve the mix chunky, making sure everyone gets some pineapple, jalapeño, and cilantro in their glass for the full experience.

1. Prepare a medium-hot fire in a grill.

2. Brush the grill with oil, place the pineapple rings on it, and cook, flipping once, until charred on both sides, 3 to 4 minutes total. Set aside to cool.

3. In a large pitcher, combine the jalapeño, cilantro, and 2 tablespoons of the piloncillo or brown sugar. Using a muddler or the handle of a wooden spoon, muddle or grind the ingredients together. Chop all but 2 of the pineapple slices (set these aside for garnish) into 1-inch pieces and muddle with the jalapeño mixture. Add the pineapple juice, tequila, lime juice, and agave or simple syrup and stir well to combine. Let sit for at least 10 minutes, or refrigerate until ready to serve.

4. Cut the reserved pineapple slices into small wedges for garnishing the glasses. Combine the remaining 3⅓ tablespoons sugar, the salt, and chile powder on a small plate. Fill a saucer with water. Dip the rims of the margarita glasses into the water to moisten—alternatively, rub the rims with the quartered lime—then dip into the chile mixture. Fill each glass with margarita mix, making sure to include some muddled pineapple, chile, and cilantro, and garnish each one with a wedge of pineapple.

SPIKED POMEGRANATE COCKTAIL WITH MEXICAN CHOCOLATE AND STAR ANISE

CÓCTEL DE GRANADA CON ANÍS ESTRELLA Y CHOCOLATE

SERVES 4

PREPARATION TIME: 15 minutes

COOKING TIME: 5 minutes

MAKE AHEAD: The cocktail can be made up to a day ahead, covered, and refrigerated.

2 star anise pods

1½ cups pomegranate juice

1 cup freshly squeezed orange juice

1½ cups vodka

½ cup triple sec, Cointreau, or other orange liqueur

¼ cup grated Mexican chocolate, such as Abuelita

1 orange, quartered, for the glasses

Like my mother, I sometimes have surprising cravings. Tart flavors combined with chocolate is one of them. I delight in doing that in this unusual drink. The tart pomegranate juice and the sweet orange juice create a base for the crisp vodka. Triple sec provides a sweet balance, and it all gets spiked with the strong, spicy toasted star anise. When you taste the sugary Mexican chocolate on the rim, you'll want to sip the drink as slowly as you can.

1. Heat a comal or small skillet over medium heat. When it is hot, gently toast the anise pods, flipping them occasionally, until fragrant, about 2 minutes. Immediately transfer to a pitcher. Add the pomegranate and orange juices, vodka, and orange liqueur, stir, and refrigerate for at least 30 minutes, or until ready to serve. Remove the star anise before serving.

2. Place the grated Mexican chocolate on a small plate. Rub each glass, preferably tumblers, with an orange quarter and dip into the grated chocolate. Place a couple of ice cubes (or more) in each glass and top with the pomegranate cocktail.

HONEY AND HIBISCUS FLOWER TEA OR AGUA FRESCA

TÉ O AGUA FRESCA CON MIEL

PREPARATION TIME: 2 minutes

COOKING TIME: 20 minutes

MAKE AHEAD: The tea, or agua fresca, can be made up to a week ahead, covered, and refrigerated.

6　cups water

½　cup honey

2　ounces dried hibiscus flowers (about ⅔ cup)

Whether you make this drink as a warming hot tea or a refreshing chilled agua fresca, you will get a bonus—the simmered, rehydrated, tart, and deliciously chewy hibiscus (jamaica) flowers, which are a crucial ingredient in my Chocolate and Jamaica Cookies (page 273).

1. Combine the water and honey in a medium saucepan and bring to a boil. Stir in the hibiscus flowers, reduce the heat to low, and simmer for 15 minutes, or until the flowers are completely rehydrated and soft and the water is bright red. Strain the tea, and reserve the flowers for the Chocolate and Jamaica Cookies (page 273) if desired.

2. Serve the tea hot, or chill and serve as an agua fresca. Taste for sweetness as well as intensity before drinking, and add more honey and/or water to taste, if desired.

MEXICAN-STYLE EGGNOG

ROMPOPE DE LAS MONJAS DE SANTA CLARA

SERVES 10 TO 12

PREPARATION TIME: 5 minutes

COOKING TIME: 35 minutes

MAKE AHEAD: The rompope will keep in the refrigerator for up to 7 days.

6   cups milk

3   whole cloves

1   (3- to 4-inch) stick canela (Ceylon cinnamon; see page 264)

½   teaspoon freshly grated nutmeg

1   teaspoon vanilla extract

¼   teaspoon baking soda

1⅓ cups sugar

12 large egg yolks

¾   cup pure sugarcane alcohol, rum, cachaça, or brandy or to taste

Rompope is a custardy mixture of eggs, milk, sugar, and alcohol (usually sugarcane alcohol or rum). The most famous rompope in Mexico comes from the Santa Clara Convent in the state of Puebla.

In addition to evangelizing the local population during the colonial era, nuns in convents all over Mexico specialized in making sweets. They brought their recipes, techniques, and indomitable love of desserts from Spain, and proceeded to intermingle them with Mexican ingredients and techniques. Convent kitchens were ground zero for much of mestizo cuisine, which is essentially what defines Mexican cooking. In the aristocracy and upper hierarchy of the church, the nuns competed with one another for culinary prestige. Later they used the sweets as a valuable source of income when resources from Spain had become scarce and a newly independent Mexico broke ties with the church.

Rompope usually contains alcohol, but there are also versions that are alcohol-free. In addition to serving the drink cold over ice, there are many ways to use it in desserts: instead of traditional vanilla sauce for floating islands (page 267), and as a sauce for cold berries, sliced ripe mango, pound cake, baked apples, crepes, or ice cream. It can also be used instead of milk in a tres leches cake (page 281) or drizzled into coffee.

1. Combine the milk, cloves, cinnamon, nutmeg, vanilla extract, and baking soda in a large saucepan and bring just to a simmer over medium heat. Reduce the heat to low and simmer gently for 15 to 20 minutes. Remove from the heat and add the sugar, but don't stir. Allow the mixture to cool for a few minutes.

2. Meanwhile, make an ice bath by filling a large bowl with ice or ice and water.

3. Whisk the egg yolks in a large bowl until they have thickened considerably and are pale yellow, 1 to 2 minutes.

continued...

4. With a whisk or heatproof spatula, stir the sugar into the milk; it will dissolve easily now. Slowly whisk in the egg yolks.

5. Rinse out and dry the egg yolk bowl and place in the ice bath. Set a fine sieve or a strainer lined with cheesecloth over the bowl.

6. Return the saucepan to low heat and cook, stirring with a heatproof spatula, until thickened and creamy; do not allow the mixture to boil. It is ready when it leaves a channel when you run your finger down the middle of the spatula. Remove from the heat and whisk in the alcohol. Pour through the strainer into the medium bowl and cool completely in the ice bath, stirring occasionally. Once cool, transfer to a jar or container and refrigerate until ready to use. Serve chilled.

VARIATION: Coconut Rompope

For a tropical version, substitute coconut milk (not canned) for the milk and coconut rum or coconut tequila for the sugarcane alcohol, rum, cachaça, or brandy.

CHOCOLATE ATOLE

CHAMPURRADO

SERVES 8

PREPARATION TIME: 10 minutes

COOKING TIME: 12 minutes

MAKE AHEAD: The drink can be made a day ahead, cooled, covered, and refrigerated. Whisk over medium heat until hot before serving.

4 cups warm water

1 cup corn masa flour (masa harina)

4 cups milk

8 ounces Mexican chocolate for drinking, such as Abuelita, grated or cut into small chunks (1 cup)

¼ cup grated piloncillo (see page 86), or packed dark brown sugar

1 (3-inch) canela stick (Ceylon cinnamon; see page 264)

This masa-thickened hot chocolate drink makes a comforting ending to any Mexican meal. It's also a hearty morning starter, sold before sunrise in metro and bus stations along with tortas and tamales.

Drinks made with corn masa may have a water or milk base, and fruit or a flavoring ingredient (like chocolate) can be added. There are other atoles, but chocolate atole is so beloved that it has its own name, *champurrado*.

. . . .

1. Place the warm water in a bowl and stir or whisk in the corn masa flour, mixing well. Let sit for a couple of minutes, then strain into a large saucepan.

2. Stir in the milk, bring to a simmer over medium heat, and simmer for 4 to 5 minutes, until the mixture begins to thicken. Stir in the chocolate, piloncillo or brown sugar, and cinnamon stick and simmer for about 5 minutes, stirring occasionally, until the chocolate melts and the sugar dissolves. Serve hot.

CHOCOLATE AND CAJETA MILKSHAKE

MALTEADA DE CHOCOLATE CON DULCE DE LECHE

SERVES 4

PREPARATION TIME: 10 minutes

COOKING TIME: 10 minutes

MAKE AHEAD: The cream can be whipped up to an hour ahead, covered, and refrigerated.

½ cup heavy cream

1¼ cups whole milk

¾ cup cajeta or dulce de leche

3 cups chocolate ice cream

2 ounces semisweet chocolate or Mexican chocolate, shaved or grated

On those occasions when I give my kids ice cream, I say, *¡Vamos con todo!* ("Let's go all the way")! Our favorite flavor is chocolate, and one of my most cherished indulgences is cajeta, so we pair the two, whiz them together into an unforgettable milkshake, and top it with whipped cream and shaved chocolate.

1. In a medium bowl, whisk the heavy cream until stiff peaks form. Refrigerate until ready to use.

2. In a small saucepan, combine the milk and cajeta or dulce de leche and whisk over medium-low heat until the cajeta has completely dissolved. Set aside to cool.

3. In a blender, combine the ice cream and cajeta or dulce de leche mixture and blend until completely smooth. Transfer to glasses and top each with a dollop of whipped cream and some chocolate shavings.

INDEX

Page numbers in *italics* indicate illustrations